ANTHROPOCENE GEOPOLITICS

ANTHROPOCENE GEOPOLITICS: Globalization, Security, Sustainability

Simon Dalby

University of Ottawa Press
2020

The University of Ottawa Press (UOP) is proud to be the oldest of the francophone university presses in Canada and the oldest bilingual university publisher in North America. Since 1936, UOP has been "enriching intellectual and cultural discourse" by producing peer-reviewed and award-winning books in the humanities and social sciences, in French or in English.

Library and Archives Canada Cataloguing in Publication

Title: Anthropocene geopolitics : globalization, security, sustainability / Simon Dalby, Balsillie School of International Affairs, Wilfrid Laurier University.
Names: Dalby, Simon, author.
Series: Politics and public policy (University of Ottawa Press)
Description: Series statement: Politics and public policy | Includes bibliographical references and index.
Identifiers: Canadiana (print) 20190238933 | Canadiana (ebook) 2019023895X | ISBN 9780776628899 (softcover) | ISBN 9780776628882 (hardcover) | ISBN 9780776631172 (PDF) | ISBN 9780776631189 (EPUB) | ISBN 9780776631196 (Kindle)
Subjects: LCSH: Geopolitics. | LCSH: Boundaries. | LCSH: Globalization. | LCSH: Sustainability.
Classification: LCC JC319 .D35 2020 | DDC 320.1/2–dc23

Legal Deposit: First Quarter 2020
Library and Archives Canada

Copy editing Robert Ferguson
Proofreading Heather Lang
Typesetting Counterpunch Inc.
Cover design Steve Kress
Cover image *Oil Fields #1, Belridge, California, USA 2002*. photo(s)
© Edward Burtynsky, courtesy Nicholas Metivier Gallery, Toronto.

The University of Ottawa Press gratefully acknowledges the support extended to its publishing list by the Government of Canada, the Canada Council for the Arts, the Ontario Arts Council, and the Federation for the Humanities and Social Sciences through the Awards to Scholarly Publications Program, and by the University of Ottawa.

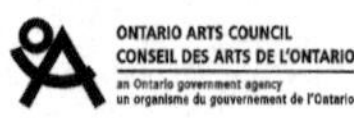

In memory of Neil Smith,
geographer, activist, scholar, friend, and inspiration

CONTENTS

ACKNOWLEDGEMENTS

The dedication for this book is to the memory of Neil Smith, a geographer, activist, and scholar whose critiques of the ideology of nature in the 1980s first peaked my intellectual curiosity on the themes that, three decades later, appear throughout this volume. I wish he had lived so that we could have had further discussions of all these themes, but nonetheless here, very belatedly, is acknowledgement of my intellectual debt.

In working out the arguments in this book I have benefited greatly from the Borders in Globalization partnership grant funded by the Canadian Social Sciences and Humanities Research Council (grant number 895-2012-1022). My thanks to Emmanuel Brunet-Jailly, the director of the program; Victor Konrad, the associate director; and Nicole Bates-Eamer, the ever efficient administrator who coordinated our various diverse investigations of contemporary bordering practices.

The Research Council has provided support to fund graduate student assistants who have helped in assembling the material that has gone into this volume. Thanks in particular to Alex Szaflarska, Derek Orocz, Masaya Llavaneras-Blanco, Clay DaSilva, Rupinder Mangat, and Alex Suen, graduate students at Wilfrid Laurier, and at the University of Waterloo for much useful research assistance in assiduously tracking down key sources in diverse scholarly literatures and, in Alex Suen's case, helping compile the bibliography and index.

I have drawn inspiration and insight from numerous discussions at the Centre for International Governance Innovation and the Balsillie School of International Affairs, and from numerous students who have attended my seminars on climate, security, and environmental governance in recent years. Preliminary versions of many of the arguments in these chapters were presented as papers, seminars, and lectures to audiences in Ottawa, Boston, Greensboro, Oslo, Lund, Tucson, Atlanta, London (Ontario), Exeter, Milton, Toronto, Chicago, Eugene, Kitchener, Victoria, New York, La Paz, Newcastle, College Park, Miami, Linkoping, Los Angeles, Mayne Island, San Diego, and Waterloo. I am indebted to numerous colleagues, audience members, and friends at these events for useful questions and suggestions that have shaped my thinking. My apologies that I can't name you all but neither my memory nor my notes are up to the task of compiling what would be a very long list indeed.

Thanks to Cara Stewart for tracking so many of the themes of this volume in contemporary online media; her continued affection and support for my academic efforts makes all this much easier. The Balsillie School of International Affairs is an unusually conducive intellectual environment to think about matters of global governance and contemporary innovations. I am indebted to my numerous academic colleagues there, and to Tiffany Bradley, Kelly Brown, Andrew Thomson, and Joanne Weston, the people who keep the whole place running so effectively. Thank you one and all.

My thanks, too, to the staff at the University of Ottawa Press for turning my text into a book so efficiently, and also to Edward Burtynsky and his colleagues for permission to use his iconic image of a California oil field as the cover illustration for this volume. His inspiring visual examinations of the Anthropocene have done so much to interrogate the contemporary transformation of the Earth, and I am honoured to use one of his images here.

Much earlier versions of many parts of this volume have appeared in print in diverse places and I thank all the publishers listed here for granting permission to reuse and update the following material: Parts of chapters 1 and 8 have been revised from "Geopolitics in the Anthropocene" in Al Bergeson and Christian Suter (eds.), *The Return of Geopolitics,* Zurich: Lit. 2018, 149–166; parts of chapters 2 and 8 have been revised from "Climate Security in the Anthropocene: 'Scaling up' the Human Niche" in Paul Wapner and Hilal Elver (eds.), *Reimagining Climate Change,* New York: Routledge, 2016,

29–48; parts of chapters 3 and 10 have been revised from "Contextual Changes in Earth History: From the Holocene to the Anthropocene: Implications for the Goal of Sustainable Development and for Strategies of Sustainable Transition" in Hans Günter Brauch, Úrsula Oswald Spring, John Grin, and Jürgen Scheffran (eds.):, *Sustainability Transition and Sustainable Peace Handbook.,* Heidelberg – New York – Dordrecht – London: Springer-Verlag, 2016, 67–88; chapter 4 has been revised from "On 'Not Being Persecuted': Territory, Security, Climate" in Andrew Baldwin and Giovanni Bettini (eds.), *Life Adrift: Critical Reflections on Climate Change and Migration,* London: Rowman and Littlefield, 2017, 41–57; chapter 5 is revised from a "Bordering Sustainability in the Anthropocene" in *Territory Politics Governance;* chapter 6 is revised from "Climate Geopolitics: Securing the Global Economy," *International Politics* 52(4),2015, 426–44; chapter 7 has been revised from "Anthropocene Formations: Environmental Security, Geopolitics and Disaster," *Theory, Culture and Society* (special issue on 'Geosocial Formations and the Anthropocene,' edited by Nigel Clark and Kathryn Yusoff), 34(2/3)., 2017., 233–52; chapter 9 has been revised from "Anthropocene Discourse: Geopolitics after Environment" in Stanley Brunn and Roland Kehrein (eds.), *Changing World Languages Map,* Heidelberg: Springer., 2019.

CHAPTER 1

GEOPOLITICS REVISITED

> The fraying thread that connects our past to our future is not limited to the flux in the natural order. The ecological shake-up wrought by climate change is also shaking up our economic and political-order. In the financial realm, as in the natural realm, the past provides fewer and fewer clues to our future. Like the migration patterns of songbirds that no longer correlate to the hatching patterns of their insect prey, or the mountain snow packs that no longer store water for the dry summer months, the economy is facing miscues born of the feedback loop between tumult in the atmosphere and tumult on the earth. Rapid changes in the weather and temperature are outpacing our traditional ideas for assessing risk, redefining the calculus for economic success, shaking up the geopolitical status quo. (Mark Schapiro 2016: xi)

GEOPOLITICS RETURNED?

Alarming headlines in recent years suggest violent rivalries are, once again, the order of the day in global politics. Discussions of migrations and boundary walls and fences, military interventions, and the use of nationalist tropes, especially by the Trump administration, have raised the rhetorical temperature in international politics, not least in the much-discussed China–U.S. rivalry (Allison 2017). But well before Donald Trump's election, commentators and politicians were focused on rivalries, nationalist priorities, and concerns about migration, in particular in Europe and North America. Walter Russell Mead (2014) was concerned antagonistic politics between at least some great powers suggest a return of geopolitics after a period in which it was apparently absent. If the term is used to refer to territorial disputes, and the use of military force or the threat thereof, then clearly the conflicts over Crimea, Ukraine, Kashmir, Palestine, and Yemen, various islands disputed by China and Japan and by various states in the South China Sea, or Russian and Turkish actions in Syria, suggested geopolitics was indeed back. Opportunistic populist politicians frequently respond to crises with xenophobia and threats of force rather than intelligent policy. Robert Kagan (2015) was worried the "weight of geopolitics" is now reducing the role of democracy in global governance as authoritarian states flex their political muscles.

In response, and in stark contrast, John Ikenberry (2014) was equally convinced the liberal order of recent decades remains intact and that regional skirmishing and nationalist rhetoric isn't undermining globalization. Geopolitics hasn't returned apparently, at least not in the sense that force and great power rivalries are the most important matter in international politics. Nonetheless, there has been a fractiousness to international politics, and nationalist logics and increased border controls, walls, and fences are being used to try to reinforce territorial modes of power. Ominously, geographical verities are being invoked in the language of many nationalist politicians suggesting mobility and migrations are a threat to supposedly stable political entities. What really is alarming for scholars and commentators worrying about global governance is the failure of contemporary modes of governance to deal with many complex interconnected changes in a timely fashion.

These political developments also occur in the context of the persistence of formulations that invoke classical notions of geopolitics, of the world arranged in particular geographical ways that shape, if not determine, the conduct of foreign policy and strategic history (Sloan 2017). While Samuel Huntingdon (1996) gets pride of place in most such discussions with his infamous mapping of global culture regions, Robert Kaplan (2012) and others also use geographical language to suggest that context determines destiny. The classical writings of Mackinder and Mahan are back in vogue in discussions of Chinese policy in the United States.

> Whether it is because of their simplicity and ease of intelligibility, or the rhetorical power of charismatic and idiosyncratic advocates, or simply their play to an audience receptive to reassurance and stasis in times of rapid change, these geopolitical visions refuse to dissipate. It is through underplaying the role of global trade and finance, a disregard for the multiple versions of sovereignty and power that exist in the world, and a denial of the possibility for alternative perspectives in world politics that have allowed Mackinder, Mahan, and Monroe back onto the centre-stage of the globalist regime. (Richardson 2015: 236)

In Europe too, classical geopolitics has undergone a revival with political thinkers invoking geographical formulations as the context for policies in the new century (Guzzini 2012).

These intellectual and political developments fly in the face of much recent scholarship and commentary emphasizing the growing interconnectedness of the global economy and the dynamism of globalization, which repeatedly changes patterns of production and trade (Agnew 2009). The revival of concerns with geopolitical matters in scholarly investigations over the last few decades, as opposed to just in the recent foreign policy commentaries, involves a more profound engagement both with the forms of geographical representation that structure policy discussion as well as with these rapidly changing geographies of global political economy.

But little of this discussion so far explicitly links up with matters of the rapid transformation of the environment, another pressing and directly related matter in global politics. This chapter argues that linking geographical representations, and the changing global political economy with discussions of the contemporary transformation of the Earth System, and focussing on the rapidly growing debate about the Anthropocene, is necessary to grapple with geopolitical change. Geological language, as in the use of the term Anthropocene, may be helpful here not least because conventional forms of environmental governance have fallen so far short in tackling global change. Relying on traditional geopolitical thinking may have some considerable political utility for populist, nationalist, and, more expressly, fascist politicians, but insofar as such notions structure policy by emphasizing separation, competition, and conflict, they are making it much more difficult to address the dangerous global transformations of our times.

THINKING GEOPOLITICALLY

In his encapsulation of geopolitics, Klaus Dodds suggests three things are key:

> First, it is concerned with questions of influence and power over space and territory. Second, it uses geographical frames to make sense of world affairs. Popular geographical templates include 'spheres of influence,' 'bloc,' 'backyard,' 'neighbourhood', and 'near abroad'. Third, geopolitics is future orientated. It offers insights into the likely behaviour of states because their interests are fundamentally unchanging. States need to secure resources, protect territory including borderlands, and manage their populations. (Dodds 2019, 3)

Geopolitics thus concerns the contextual matters shaping politics at the planetary scale, about struggles for power, and the rivalries of big states and empires which have played out over the last few centuries as the global economy grew and technologies ushered in new human possibilities (Agnew 2003). It is also about the related attempts to divide the world politically into various spatial configurations, empires, blocs, and such things as the Grossraum formulations of Carl Schmitt (Minca and Rowan 2015) used in Nazi thinking. Schmitt's *Nomos of the Earth* (2006) suggested various divisions of the world and the superiority of European modes of law and authority but relied on an anachronistic fixed geography and a limited view of the transformative effects of the global economy. These notions contrast with other historical modes of geopolitics, the much more obviously vitalist formulations in other writings, which viewed states as organisms struggling and competing with each other (Klinke 2019). Schmitt may have been a more influential thinker in Nazi Germany than Karl Haushofer, who frequently gets the blame for introducing Adolf Hitler to Friedrich Ratzel's thinking on states in competition for space, and the hence indirectly the pernicious ideas of lebensraum, of living space, that informed Nazi ambitions for rearranging the map of Europe by force (Snyder 2015).

Contemporary geopolitics is about rivalries of states, attempts to dominate, if not directly rule, places, and control spaces both near and far. Material capabilities matter in terms of states' military policies and ability to shape international orders, not least such things as trading arrangements and energy supplies. Geopolitical rivalries are about, in Grove's (2019) terms, modes of life and their often-violent imposition and extension across territories. Geopolitical rivalry is frequently a matter of geoeconomics, and influence frequently relates to economic capabilities and development strategies much more than military ones (Essex 2013). Crucially, geopolitics is now about the quest for security frequently understood in terms of how to facilitate the extension of modes of modern economy through practices of development (Power 2019).

Geographical scholarship of the last few decades often under the rubrics of post-modern or more specifically "critical geopolitics" have investigated how this geographical language has important political consequences (Toal 1996). Even a fairly limited reflection on recent history suggests geographical entities in global politics are not permanent and immutable but rather temporary, contingent, and relational: the Berlin Wall has been dismantled; Checkpoint Charlie is now a tourist destination. However, geographical representations frequently pass without this critical interrogation precisely because they are apparently obvious and appear to be permanent. This "geopolitical culture" specifies a state's role in relation to other states both in terms of how geographical language frequently structures particular nationalist narratives of the homeland, but also in how such language shapes larger interpretative frameworks of supposed territorial autonomy, grand strategy and justifications of the use of force in international affairs (Toal 2017).

Such formulations often tie into technological fantasies of geographical control, to territorial sovereignty, and to the supposed sanctity of national boundaries (Brown 2010). Linked to the invocation of martial vigour these are a heady brew in political rhetoric, which links fear to the necessity of strength to provide security in troubled times. Invoking external threats to supposed internal stabilities is a powerful mode of geopolitical discourse that is repeatedly used in American politics (Dalby 2013a), notably in Donald Trump's rhetoric of wall building as a solution to the supposed problem of migration. At more or less the same time, in the Brexit referendum, the rhetoric supporting the leave side emphasized fear of the influence of immigrants on the British state. Once these cartographic entities become the hegemonic assumptions of how the world is organized—frontiers appearing as "natural" and permanent features (Fall 2010)—then these geographical categories become powerful tools for policy makers anxious to emphasize differences and dangers on a variegated planetary surface.

Benjamin Ho's (2014) examination of Chinese exceptionalism points to the risks of assuming permanent fixed identities in geopolitical thinking there, too, and making assumptions that geography presents eternal verities. In a world of rapid change and globalization, this assumption is likely to be misleading in many ways. The relations between places are crucial and have been changing rapidly due to the processes of globalization that involve changing geographical patterns of manufacturing and trade linkages. These are much more important than the military rivalries that usually get so much attention in geopolitical thinking related to foreign policy. Yes, military conflicts matter, and Second World War-era technologies were key to setting in motion the contemporary acceleration of globalization first in the period of the Cold War and then subsequently (Farish 2010). But military matters have been a minor factor in the overall pattern of the global economy although some regional industrial strategies were clearly involved in the cold war period on both sides of the iron curtain.

John Agnew's (2015) more recent discussion of geopolitics and globalization is analytically helpful in explaining these important but much wider formulations. As with other scholars who have been back over the history of geopolitical thinking of late (Kearns 2013), Agnew notes that the early twentieth-century formulations of geopolitics in terms of naturalized assumptions of spatially autonomous competing geographical entities obscured a larger body of historical thinking that emphasized the interconnections between places, the flows of resources from colonies to imperial centres, as well as larger concerns with geographical settings, trading arrangements and cultural exchanges. Looking back to Montesquieu and Voltaire's reconstruction of Alexander the Great's imperial efforts to enhance cultural interactions and trade among the regions he conquered, Agnew (2015) crucially argues that the narrow territorial sense of competing entities in late nineteenth-century thinking obscured this larger sense of geopolitics and, in the process, set up a false dichotomy of geopolitics versus globalization.

As populist politicians have recently being suggesting—forcefully in some cases—the promise of sovereignty, the geographical logic of supposedly-separate spaces, should be the ordering principle of world politics. Invoking globalization as the danger to this order, and foreign economies as threats to domestic prosperity, plays well with xenophobic fears and simplistic place-based identities. Contemporary populism is in part about mobilizing the economic fears of numerous people whose jobs have been eliminated, or whose aspirations have been thwarted, by rapid innovation in the global economy (Derber and Magrass 2019). Blaming others, rather than economic change or corporate behaviour, works. The neat coloured boxes of nation states in political maps of the world belie the complexity of these interconnections; both economic and ecological processes are now about connections across these supposedly separate spaces.

Agnew's (2015) analysis shows that the processes of geopolitics are part and parcel of the growth of globalization over the last half century. U.S. efforts to promote trade and investment in at least some parts of the global economy, a "geopolitics of globalization," interacts with the very different colonial histories of various forms of statehood, a "geopolitics of development," and most recently with the rising new international agencies in what he terms a "geopolitics of regulation," something loosely akin to the processes Zurn (2018) summarizes in terms of global governance. These processes have shaped how world politics operates. In Panitch and Gindin's (2012) terms, American foreign policy has made the world safe for capitalism and, in the process, greatly advantaged American-based industrial and agricultural interests. American "soft power," in terms of its ideological appeals of freedom and the attractions of a modern consumer lifestyle, has also helped extend this mode of life to many parts of the world.

The Anthropocene formulation makes it clear that these globalizing forces of state, along with economic development, are also geomorphic and environmental forces responsible for rearranging landscapes, damming rivers, and moving huge amounts of material to build roads, railways, and cities—all done with the intention of connecting the state into a global economy. The scale of the biosphere's transformation, caused by the history of the expansion of European power over the last half millennium, has only become clear in recent decades. Humanity has been remaking its planetary home on a more drastic scale than has been understood until very recently (Bonneuil and Fressoz 2016).

Dodds' (2019) third facet of geopolitics—his suggestion that states have permanent interests—has long been assumed to be case by people invoking geographical language in politics but, as the critical geopolitical literature emphasizes, rapid technological change, economic development, and shifting alliance structures frequently make this a dubious assumption. Instead, the rapid scale of the transformation of the biosphere and the increasing importance of the novel technosphere in the Earth System (Haff 2014) are dramatically shifting many states' interests. In the long run a relatively functional biosphere is essential for all states; having access to such things as petroleum or coal supplies is no longer in their long-term interest in a future post-carbon fuel world.

This transformation, and the struggles over how it will play out, is the new context for geopolitical thinking even if its profound consequences have been slow to challenge contemporary geographical imaginations (Dalby 2018). In part, this may be because spatial assumptions about the world are frequently divorced from discussions of economy and, in turn, from issues of environment and nature. These distinctions obscure crucial interconnections that now are key to the trajectories of global change. As Neil Smith (1984) made clear, the uneven development of global capitalism is about the production of nature and space simultaneously. Anthropocene geopolitics is now much more a matter of the unfolding consequences of production decisions made by the dominant states and corporations in the planetary system than it is just a matter of territorial rivalries in a supposedly stable geographical configuration.

Rapidly changing climate, rising sea levels, and the melting of Arctic Ocean ice are only the most obvious symptoms of change, and they have yet (despite progress in Paris in late 2015) to be seriously tackled by the processes of global politics. All this has made it abundantly clear that classical geopolitical thinking that once suggested that climates in various parts of the world determined the fate of human communities is now backwards; geopolitics is now shaping future climates, not the other way around (Dalby 2015a). Thus, it no longer makes sense to see the world just as an external backdrop to the human drama, or a source of resources and a sink for wastes. The Anthropocene brings an end to these distinctions of nature and humanity. We live in an increasingly artificial world in which the choices are between a reasserted politics of dominance with increasingly militarized borders, or comprehensive attempts at economic innovation which recognize that policies of separation, and the invocation of sovereignty as a rationale for evading responsibilities across borders, are untenable.

REINTERPRETING GEOPOLITICS IN THE ANTHROPOCENE

The point about the Anthropocene and why it matters to geopolitics is that humanity is now shaping its context on the global scale much more profoundly than modern formulations emphasizing technology, the promise of development, and supposedly the domination and control of nature have traditionally encompassed. Modernity has been about rapid change, and nowhere more so than in military technology. That said, it is important to recognize that the relative power of states in the world system is much more about their economic production and wealth than it is about military capabilities; hegemony is mostly about shaping the global economy (Agnew 2005). Yes, military capabilities matter, and in peacetime the threat of the use of force is always latent in the system. Frequently, however, military power is derived from productive capabilities, especially in recent years as enormously expensive "high-tech" weapons have come to dominate strategic considerations. Wealth is crucial to their acquisition and twentieth-century style mass conscript armies are now much less important. But over the long term the rise and fall of powers is mostly about economic capabilities.

This would seem to continue to be the case even though rivalries between states and the conduct of struggles to shape the future are increasingly being played out in the new networks of cyberspace. From the initial weaponization of malware, in the Israeli and American use of the Stuxnet computer virus, through subsequent attempts by numerous state actors to infiltrate infrastructures and manipulate politics, it is clear that state conflicts are escalating in the rapidly spreading electronic world of the internet and artificial intelligence (Sanger 2019). The key point here, which parallels the argument about climate change in the following pages, is that interconnections, networks, and distant consequences, the so-called "tele-connections" (Benzie et al. 2018) are the geography that increasingly matters in human affairs. In so far as future conflicts may involve sabotage of infrastructure to create artificial disasters (Briggs and Matejova 2019), then the interconnectedness of environmental matters and international security is only emphasized as the new Anthropocene context. But the finer points of online misbehaviour or outright aggression by cyber means are beyond the scope of this volume, important though they likely will be in coming decades.

Rising sea levels, potential agricultural disruptions, the dangers of wild fires, droughts, and extreme weather are changing the calculus of international relations. This is geopolitics in the sense that political decisions about modes of economy, and in particular decisions about energy sources (Global Commission on the Geopolitics of Energy Transformation 2019), are now directly shaping the future context for humanity, quite literally remaking substantial parts of the "geo." Decisions about whether to enhance fossil fuel extraction capabilities versus producing more solar panels, or to use regenerative forestry practices instead of clear-cutting, now have such large-scale consequences that they are changing how the Earth System works. This is the new context of geopolitics.

If serious policy decisions about moving toward renewable energy and ecological economic strategies are taken, and enforced, the future will be very different than if the priority remains the continued expansion of fossil fuel use. These two paths lead to very different outcomes for future generations: the world is headed either onto a hothouse pathway or one towards a stabilized Earth System (Steffen et al. 2018). Energy systems and the use of firepower are not just a matter of relative power in the international system, the traditional theme of geopolitics, but are now a matter of shaping the future configuration of the Earth System. If renewable energy and phasing out of fossil fuels are priorities, the future context for humanity might be relatively stable. However, pursuing a strategy of using firepower—both in terms of military capabilities and economic activity based on fossil fuels (Dalby 2018)—will lead to accelerating disruptions, with rising sea levels changing many things and more extreme and unpredictable weather patterns, droughts, storms, and disrupted infrastructure and agriculture.

This question of shaping the future adds this new Anthropocene dimension to traditional understandings of geopolitics; that's what this book explores. It is but a beginning; much more thinking needs to be done about the implications of these new Anthropocene formulations. In these circumstances, traditional notions of security—both national security for individual states and global security for the system as a whole—need a fundamental rethink, something that is beginning to percolate through numerous parts of contemporary society as the scale of climate change impacts becomes increasingly hard to ignore. Nothing less is necessary in these newly recognized circumstances encapsulated by the term Anthropocene, hence the title *Anthropocene Geopolitics.*

Coupled with this is the insight informing much of the critical work on geopolitics for the last few decades: geographical assumptions about the nature of the world political order are crucial to security policy making (Dodds, Kuus, and Sharp 2013). This has been highlighted by the Trump administration's formulations of international politics as an arena of competition, and its implicit rejection of suggestions that there is an international system of any consequence. While this is consistent with Trump's own presuppositions of competition and dominance as the way the world is, the consequences for the Earth System will be profound if the fossil fuelled mode of economy he champions dominates the global economy for much longer. Trump's policies require both a rejection of an international system, and of the ecological consequences of fossil-fuelled development—directly in terms of climate change and indirectly in terms of the global extinction crisis that ever-expanding resource appropriations and land use changes are causing.

Resisting this contextualization of the planet as an arena of competition is key to any form of geopolitics that takes the insights encapsulated in the Anthropocene formulation seriously. The interconnected nature of people and places, and the role of current economic activity in transforming the ecological context at the global scale, now has to be integrated into any analysis of geopolitics. Related to that is the key ontological shift that embeds humanity and its products in a changing Earth System, rather than as a separate entity, somehow apart from the rest of nature, either trying to dominate it or being endangered by it. As a set of geographical premises for human conduct, these separations simply won't work for sensible governance arrangements in future. Traditional territorial strategies, where security is understood as preventing encroachments on defined space, are premised on a stable world and relatively autonomous spaces. Neither stability nor autonomy as traditionally understood now apply to contemporary transformations, but as yet the profound political implications of this are not widely recognized.

This new context of the Anthropocene requires a conceptual shift from notions of environmental protection to one of geological scale production. Industrial humanity is adding a new element to the Earth System, one now frequently called the technosphere that is expanding and, in the process, is demolishing or reorganizing many parts of the biosphere (Zalasiewicz et al. 2017). It is powered mostly by fossil fuels that are adding large quantities of greenhouse gases and hence causing climate destabilization. Failure to slow the pace of climate change, and try to facilitate migration of numerous species, humans included, to adapt to environmental change will only make matters worse. A politics of separation, of sovereign states with fixed boundaries and exclusive jurisdictions, insisting on their individual prerogatives regardless of the cross-boundary consequences, is anathema to both policies of mitigating, as in avoiding future climate change, and adaptation, as in dealing with what changes are already in the system.

BOOK OUTLINE

This book sketches out the security implications of this novel appreciation for the changing human context: it contrasts new insights with the modern notions of geopolitics that formulate matters in terms of struggles to dominate spaces and assert primacy in the rivalry of great powers. A failure to respond to the novel circumstances of the Anthropocene suggests clearly a trajectory toward rapid climate instability. Unless the causes of climate disruptions are tackled in the immediate future, and appropriate international institutions are put in place to deal with the disruptions that are already inevitable, the long-term prognosis for this world is poor: a potentially disastrous series of conflicts as elites attempt to violently maintain control. Recognizing this as the context for humanity in the future will be key to implementing innovations in global governance; doing so inevitably challenges the modern geopolitical imagination as one of using energy to build technologies to dominate one's surroundings in a world of competing states.

To think through how globalization—as the enhanced and accelerated connections between places, people, and products—now threatens ecological integrity at the planetary scale and, hence, the traditional assumptions of state rivalry as the given context for humanity, the argument that follows this introduction is presented in nine further chapters. The rapid changes in the Earth System require an analysis that doesn't take stable geographies and permanent nation states as the given context within which globalization operates. Now we also need to understand that the struggles over sustainability don't follow traditional fault lines between rival empires either. Anthropocene geopolitics is about how the Earth System is being remade with disparate consequences for people and places depending to a very large degree on how they are connected into the global economy, and what threatens them because of their location in these processes.

Chapter 2, on "scaling up the human niche," tells the increasingly familiar story of the Anthropocene, and how we now understand humanity as a force that has fundamentally transformed how the Earth System operates. The roots of this go back to matters of the emergence of homo sapiens, crucially to the domestication of fire and the enhanced power this gave early hominids in changing landscapes. The spread of agriculture, metallurgy, and such things as the invention of concrete accelerated these transformations. It is entirely possible that early agricultural activities prevented another glacial period in recent planetary history. It is also possible that the destruction of native human populations after the European conquest of the Americas caused enough reforestation, and hence reduction in the carbon dioxide levels in the atmosphere, to cause the little ice age of the seventeenth century. It is clear that the subsequent spread of European colonization and its capitalist economy, in the early iterations of globalization, fuelled increasingly by coal, oil, and gas, has generated rapid climate change as well as, due to fishing and farming, a major extinction event in the planetary system. The Holocene period is over; we now live in new circumstances of the Anthropocene.

Chapter 3 explores this new understanding of the context that globalization has wrought. New perspectives in Earth System science suggest that sustainable development now has to consider the possibilities of rapid phase shifts in the biosphere. These new circumstances are as a result of the great acceleration in human activities in the last few generations, especially the activities of the most recent period of enhanced globalization. The planetary boundaries framework focusing on where the potential thresholds for the Earth System are, and that emphasizes the importance of keeping human activities within these boundaries, is now the key intellectual framework for thinking through matters of global governance. Constraining human activities to within a safe operating space defined by key ecological boundaries in the Earth System is key to sustainability, but planning has to recognize that rapid shifts are probably coming. The implications of this suggest that sustainability transition proposals have to move beyond notions of national security to recognize that human actions are shaping the future configuration of the planet, and hence changing the geopolitical context.

Chapter 4 focuses on how the twentieth century created a geopolitical order of territorial states and related claims to space premised on sovereignty within fixed borders. This solution to political identity questions also reduced the significance of territory as a cause of war by effectively prohibiting geographical expansion as a legitimate political activity. In doing so, however, arbitrary colonial boundaries and accidents of history have shaped much of the world political map. As climate change accelerates, this stable political cartography is presenting a major problem because migration, the most basic mode of environmental adaptation to changed circumstances, is now understood as a potential threat to at least some parts of the stable order of modern geopolitics. The human consequences of rising sea levels, droughts, and floods are mediated by complex global political economies of agriculture, land use, and ownership; for those forced to flee, territorial sovereignty is now a major obstacle to their security. Thus, the implicit modern assumption of a stable geography as the backdrop to political order premised on territorial sovereignty is now challenged by the unintended material consequences of environmental transformation, which suggest that what needs to be secured now is the ability to adapt, not the perpetuation of the geopolitical status quo.

This discussion of geopolitics also relates to other modes of border construction many of which are key to resource governance and oxymoronic attempts at wildlife management. Chapter 5 shows that while environmental matters rarely respect political boundaries, efforts to govern resource, pollution, wildlife, and numerous other matters are often profoundly shaped by territorial jurisdiction. Direct regulation, trade restrictions, and forms of international cooperation have all shaped global efforts at environmental governance while fortress conservation ideas frequently invoke territorial exclusivity. The context for these measures has been changing both as a consequence of the growth of the global economy and as a result of the biophysical transformations that are integral to this expansion through the period of the great acceleration. Climate adaptation practices frequently invoked practices of enclosure and expulsion that are often counter-productive. Novel circumstances due to accelerating Anthropocene change now shape the policy landscape while numerous policy makers grapple with how to implement the Sustainable Development Goals. These require rethinking the bordering practices that govern environmental matters and the relationships of territory to ecological function. This is necessary now, not least because of increased natural system instability, the new condition of non-stationarity, and the inadequacy of stable base line assumptions for dealing with rapid change across boundaries.

Despite the pressing needs to think about sustainability, and the inadequacies of either sovereignty at the state level, or practical measures for bordering numerous phenomena to deal with the new circumstances of the Anthropocene, chapter 6 shows how discussions of energy and climate security remain mired in long outdated modes of thought and policy prescription. Climate has become a matter of security deliberation in the last few years due to the gradually dawning realization that change is happening already and has the potential to severely disrupt states and economies in coming decades. Thus, what "security" has been securing is now transforming the material circumstances that made carboniferous capitalism possible in the first place. Now security requires a reformulation of the basics of fossil-fueled capitalism to attempt to overcome the worst aspects of the metabolic rift that underlies modernity, a challenge that at least so far seems more than either state planners or security thinkers are capable of dealing with effectively, despite attempts to use market innovations to transform energy systems. International political economy and security studies are thus inextricably linked once the material basis underlying the climate crisis is clearly engaged.

Failure to deal with the new context for thinking about security and energy implies that disasters and disruptions are likely to continue preoccupying policy makers. Thinking through the multiple formulations of what needs to be done requires engaging with these policy discussions, which is done in chapter 7. Disasters such as the Fukushima nuclear plant meltdowns, and potentially disastrous plans to geoengineer the climate in coming decades, highlight that the human environment is being remade in the Anthropocene, and conventional notions of state sovereignty are not an appropriate framework for their governance. Humanity is now a geological scale actor, not just a biological one; disasters help clarify this key point and its significance for considering these new so-called geosocial formations.

The revival of explicitly geopolitical thinking, of nationalism in the case of Brexit, right-wing populism in Europe and Brazil in 2018, as well as the election of Donald Trump in the United States in 2016, brings with it a powerful reassertion of the modern geopolitical assumptions of state rivalries as the given global situation and the efficacy of borders to deal with contemporary crises. Chapter 8 looks more closely at these arguments and the importance of getting the geographical premises in policy discourse clear in the face of globalization's legacy. The implications of all this are that the populist articulations of identity, and nostalgic articulations of a golden age of petroleum-powered modernity, make dealing with climate change in particular ever more difficult. The reassertion of borders in a rapidly changing biosphere is a retrograde invocation that undermines efforts to provide environmental security for an urbanized humanity. Thinking more explicitly in terms of Anthropocene categories is now essential if sustainability is to be taken seriously. If it is not, then the future for humanity is bleak.

Connections and change are crucial, but recognizing the trajectories discussed in the opening chapters of the book is the key to policy thinking: Chapter 9 emphasizes the necessity of putting this new contextualization explicitly into the discussion. Thinking about the future of the world that globalization is remaking is a task for all concerned scholars and policy makers. The discussion of the Anthropocene has proliferated across scientific, scholarly, and popular culture genres and raised numerous questions about how the future might be imagined. This discussion has also spun off numerous other terms to describe current transformations: in many ways they reflect the intellectual and cultural contexts brought to bear on the current debate that need consideration in discussing the politics of the Anthropocene and whether the outcome will be good or bad for much of humanity. It is far from obvious that invoking the Anthropocene will necessarily lead to useful innovations and policies that facilitate transitions to more sustainable modes of human life—whether novel modes of cosmopolitan thought, which invoke human universals in productive ways, or those reimposing imperial "top-down" modes of rule matters in how the future unfolds. Regardless, the Anthropocene merges history and geology in novel ways that demand much more careful reflection on the implications of academic formulations in larger realms of cultural politics. Much more than has been the case with environmental politics for the last half century, the Anthropocene formulation focuses on the planetary scale transformations currently under way; having the appropriate intellectual tools to tackle the contemporary politics of transformation requires careful consideration of what Bruno Latour (2017) calls "geostory."

Finally, in light of these insights, the concluding chapter 10 revisits issues of security and war metaphors related to environmental security. Adopting a perspective of political geoecology with a focus on global economic production rather than only on traditional ideas of environmental protection is key to the future if planetary stewardship of the Anthropocene is to be successful. Borders matter, but they, too, must be subject to a substantial rethinking if sovereignty and political rivalry is to be further constrained in the interests of building a sustainable global economy for future generations. Doing so requires further restraints on the use of violence because, as *Our Common Future* asserted in the crucial document that established sustainable development as a key theme in global political discourse, warfare is antithetical to sustainability; environmental security is the necessary prerequisite for human flourishing in a globalized world. Crucially, as the divestment movement makes clear, the questions of who the antagonists are in the new geopolitics of sustainability need clarification. If fossil fuel companies are the primary source of greenhouse gas emissions, and they actively try to stymie climate change policy initiatives, then they can easily be framed as the new enemy against which many social actors have to mobilize; a very different contest from those of twentieth-century state rivalries. The new discussions of climate security, and the need for innovation in the global economy to facilitate human welfare without relying on ever larger consumption of fossil fuels, are gaining traction in many policy circles; thinking carefully about the Anthropocene can helpfully reinforce efforts to make more sustainable futures in many places.

There are numerous other ways to think about the Anthropocene and the vulnerabilities and dangers that it presents to people in different locations. But to make this text manageable as a single volume, and to tease out the multiple ways geopolitics and the Anthropocene intersect, many other approaches have been omitted from this book. Traditional thinking about states as organic entities in competition, a theme from the nineteenth century, and the legacy of Friedrich Ratzel's formulations of political geography in particular, are not investigated in detail here, although some links back to Nazi formulations do intrude in later chapters. The profound effects of the contemporary global political economy on indigenous peoples is not discussed in detail here either; my earlier critique of environmental security discourse owes a considerable intellectual debt to indigenous peoples, and the Mi'kmaq of Nova Scotia in particular (Dalby 2002), but those themes are not reworked here. The history of colonization is discussed in chapter 2, but the themes of colonization and the violence implicit in these processes (Davis 2001), which provide the historical backdrop for the contemporary globalization, are tackled indirectly in chapter 5 on bordering processes, rather than as an explicit engagement with imperial history, something Grove (2019) has recently reworked.

The related issues of racial politics tied into climate change are also germane to all the themes in this volume, and have been dealt with in terms of geopolitics by Chaturvedi and Doyle (2015) in particular, but these too are downplayed to keep the focus in this volume explicitly on the Anthropocene formulation. Climate change in particular is linked to larger issues of governance and justice (Stoett and Mulligan 2019), and while some of the themes in this debate are touched on, it is not a major focus of this book. Likewise, while much of this volume has direct connections with debates in global political economy and the issues of war, peace, and development (Bieler and Morton 2018), this book engages only indirectly with this material. Chapter 9 does touch on some of the other social theory engagements with the Anthropocene, and much more needs to be said about how political theory is now influenced by its encounter with Earth System science (Arias-Maldonado and Trachtenberg 2019). That said, novel discussions in many fields are emphasizing the point that the modern formulations of autonomous individuals, and the promises of escape that development presents, are no longer tenable political narratives in light of numerous forms of ontological critique (Walker 2010). The Anthropocene discussion adds another powerful line of argument here, and does so by radically reworking the implicit assumptions of separate spheres of being in modern thinking.

Challenging these modern dichotomies—nature and culture, rural and urban—has generated a number of neologisms, not least alternative terms to the word Anthropocene, and these terms are briefly invoked in the latter stages of this volume. Terms like geopolitical ecology, geosocial formations, geostory, and political geoecology all appear in the following pages, and they do so because the contemporary scholarly literature uses all of them in various ways while grappling with the conflation of natural and artificial arrangements in the rapidly changing world. These are not discrete analytical terms, at least not yet; in what follows they should be read only as neologisms crafted by a diverse range of scholarship to try to gain better analytic purchase on contemporary transformations.

CHAPTER 2

SCALING UP THE HUMAN NICHE

> By redefining the roles and relations of humans, Earth, and cosmos, the origin story of contemporary science challenges some of the most deeply held traditional beliefs of societies around the world. There is no role for an all-powerful God or any other mystical force. Humans play no central role in the universe. The Anthropocene goes even further, not only confronting these traditional beliefs, but also by revising the classic origin story of contemporary science. In the Anthropocene, humans are put back into a central role on Earth, as planet shapers. (Earle Ellis 2018: 6)

ANTHROPOCENE CLIMATES

Since Paul Crutzen made his now famous statement in 2000 that we are no longer living in the Holocene (Crutzen and Stoermer 2000; Crutzen 2002), but rather in a geological period better termed the Anthropocene, the debate about the term has grown and spread into many genres. Concerned that the scale of human activities was such that a new designation for present times was necessary, in no small part because of the dangers that contemporary transformations present to the future prospects for much of humanity, Crutzen's contention has been worked over thoroughly in the pages of academic journals, in the conference halls and seminar rooms of Earth System sciences, and increasingly in popular culture and the media. Climate change is a substantial part of the discussion, but far from the only factor that is being considered. Numerous other aspects of human activity, and the extraordinarily rapid expansion of our capabilities, are also part of the Anthropocene formulation (Lewis and Maslin 2018). All of which suggests that while climate change is a pressing issue for humanity, care must be taken to understand it as a subset, as it were, of the Anthropocene if political innovations and cultural changes are to be clearly formulated and appropriately implemented in coming decades.

Climate change is part of a larger quite fundamental transformation of the biosphere and of the human condition, one on a scale large enough that Earth System scientists are now seriously discussing the addition of this new geological epoch of the Anthropocene to their long established scheme of the stages of Earth history (Zalesiewicz et al. 2019). If humanity is causing transformations on a scale similar to those that ended the age of dinosaurs, then clearly climate is an important matter; it is also part of a number of simultaneous transformations set in motion by the rapid expansion of the human population since the last ice age and, crucially, by its appropriation of ecological and geological entities to remake its habitat on a scale that is now truly global. Globalization is much more than a process of enhanced trading across state boundaries or accelerated cultural interchange; it is a key process in the geophysical transformation of the Earth, one whereby a new entity in the system is rapidly expanding, a process of economic production that in physical terms has generated a technosphere within the Earth System, one that is, as it expands, now altering how the Earth System functions (Dongas et al. 2017). The expansion of humanity into the dominant species in the biosphere, in effect the process we frequently term globalization, has led to its reorganization to suit the most powerful parts of the species, a process of reordering human affairs in the often-inadvertent process of reordering many other things.

Much of the discussion of these matters is told in tropes of fear, alarm, and various registers of human immorality. The world as we know it is being destroyed (McKibben 2012); catastrophe looms! Violence and warfare caused by environmental disruptions will doom civilization (Wallace-Wells 2019). In more explicitly religious tropes, we have sinned and will be punished by floods and droughts; plagues and famine will once more spread across the Earth to punish us for our hubris. We are killing off many of the species that matter globally; humanity is the terminator species. There is no such thing as a wild world anymore; defaunation is triumphant (Kolbert 2014). The Anthropocene is the end times. Degradation and destruction is the future and even if intelligent planning does emerge soon, it is probably too late to save the world. These pessimistic renditions all rely on at least some clear understanding of particular downward trajectories, of civilization in decline. These "declensionist" narratives are a popular part of modernity, often driven by the assumptions of the end of empire that pervaded European political narratives in the twentieth century coupled with the economic specification of the human condition as one of scarcity. The cultural politics of end times, in Slajov Žižek's (2011) terms, are a matter of hopelessness and defeat for progressive forces loosely understood.

However, some other readings of the Anthropocene put the climate change arguments into a rather different context, one of "next-times," rather than "end-times." One sees this kind of thinking in, for instance, James Lovelock's (1979, 2014) recent reworking of the Gaia hypothesis coupled to the common futurist argument that humanity is merely a means to the end of an electronic intelligence that will emerge to regulate the planet (albeit one that may not have need of humanity once its tasks are accomplished). More generally, the optimistic or "eco-modernist" version of the Anthropocene, epitomized by the work of the Breakthrough Institute (www.thebreakthrough.org; Nordhaus and Shellenberger 2007), is that while the Earth is being remade by humanity, it isn't just a tale of destruction, but one of new human opportunities and remade ecological processes, in which industrial artifacts are an increasingly large and productive part of the new assemblages we are making. Yes, pristine nature no longer exists, as humanity has imprinted its signature everywhere and has become a geological force in its own right. But new, attractive, horizons exist in a post-natural world. The Anthropocene represents a potential bright promising future, especially as humans embrace their role as governors of the Earth (Ackerman 2014). Critics of these techno-utopic visions of the world point to the unevenness of its likely benefits and the huge costs that are likely to be paid by poor and marginal peoples in the global economy (Hamilton 2017).

This chapter reimagines climate change beyond the post-political technical formulations so common in what Wapner and Elver (2016) call "Climate Inc.," the policy community that has grown up around the issue mostly concerned with "post-political" market measures and incremental technical regulations to deal with climate change. In doing so, it underlines that humanity's role in changing the biosphere dates back long before contemporary concerns with climate change. The chapter suggests that ever since humanity started living in cities and practising agriculture in extensive ways, it has assumed a geological scale role in the Earth System. Thus, making sense of climate change as the consequences of long-term and large-scale human activities, greatly expanded in recent decades, requires coming to terms with urbanization, the agriculture revolution, and all that these have involved. Put differently, climate change is simply one, albeit large, wrinkle in the Anthropocene's protracted unfolding, and it is best understood in this context if a larger debate about the future of globalization and the possibilities of sustainability for most humans is to be engaged. But that said, this does not in any way diminish the need for tackling climate change as an immediately urgent priority.

Climate change poses many dangers to both the human and more-than-human worlds. For many, it presents a threatening challenge to security in general terms as the protection of humans from harm. Policy makers, activists, and ordinary citizens have tried to understand this challenge and propose responses that minimize climate suffering and enhance widespread safety. Such efforts have been inadequate in part because they have failed to see climate change in the broader context of the Anthropocene. They have thus proposed at best stopgap measures that offer merely the veneer of security; protecting the existing fossil-fueled, unequal social order is, at least so far, a much higher political priority for the rich and powerful than is ensuring that a relatively stable biosphere can provide conditions for sustaining billions of humans for the long-term future.

METHANE, AGRICULTURE, AND CLIMATE CHANGE

Discussions of humanity and its "forcing mechanisms" in the Earth System inevitably raise questions of the origins of these new geological processes. When, in other words, did the Anthropocene start (Braje 2015; Davies 2016)? There is a parallel discussion of how it might be understood in geological terms, and specifically what might serve as a geological marker of the age, the fossil golden spike marking it in the geological column (Smith and Zeder 2013). Once a species emerged that had the arrogance to term itself *homo sapiens*, one could argue its presence on Earth would inevitably have consequences. But these were not of a scale to be geologically significant; not until at least the end of the last ice age have we left a noticeable record in sediments around the planet.

Much of the Anthropocene discussion is about climate change, perhaps the most obvious facet of the current transformation, but humanity has been changing other matters on a geological scale too. A clear geological marker of human making in future sedimentary layers across the planet is likely to be on a scale large enough to be noteworthy in terms of history as well. This point is made clearly by Bruno Latour (2017) in his attempts to come to terms with the Anthropocene using Gaia (Lovelock 1979, 2014), the formulation of the Earth with life as a major player rather than a superficial entity on a geological substrate. Latour (2017) suggests that we now need other neologisms such as "geostories" to understand recent geology as a matter of historical change, and vice versa. Such reformulations suggest we are starting to rethink theological themes; ones that have profound implications for how life is understood and, hence, how discussions of what life is for—and how one ought to live—are now conducted.

A key part of the discussion relates to the question of what is so significant that it is worthy of being considered as the start of the Anthropocene. There is much more to this than just the matter of technical geological criteria, although if the term is to become a formal part of the geological sciences a clear stratigraphic indicator will be needed (Zalasiewicz et al. 2019). The die-off of megafauna at the beginning of the Holocene is one candidate for the emergence of human impact on a global scale. If the mammoths and other large animals were the victim of human hunting, then the terrestrial species mix had been dramatically altered even before agriculture became a substantial part of the human condition. Elizabeth Kolbert (2014) describes the story of the Anthropocene as *The Sixth Extinction*, a matter of ecocide on a global scale and a consequence of human activities. But if the immediate post-ice age die-off is the beginning of the Anthropocene then the category of the Holocene is made redundant. Or rather, given that the Holocene is understood as the most recent part of the Quaternary, then it refers to the period of human Earth System modification anyway and there is no need for a new term such as the Anthropocene.

Lovelock (2014) has suggested that the beginning of the Anthropocene can be precisely dated to 1712 when Thomas Newcomen patented his ideas for a steam engine. This technology eventually allowed miners to pump water from mines and hence to dig deeper and more effectively. Crutzen's (2002) initial suggestion located the start of the Anthropocene closer to the end of the eighteenth century pointing to James Watt's innovations with the steam engine, dated to 1784, which made it much more practical as a power plant for manufacturing. It subsequently underpinned locomotion with the advent of railways and steam ships, both of which propelled the expansion of global trade. The extraordinarily rapid recent expansion of the global economy, powered largely by coal and petroleum, began after the Second World War. This period is now widely known among Earth System scientists as "the great acceleration." Perhaps the Anthropocene could be more usefully dated from then (Steffen et al. 2011a)? In geological terms, the introduction of artificial radioisotopes into sediments worldwide, the consequence of the manufacture and use of nuclear weapons, coincides with this dating too.

These discussions focus on carbon from first coal and then petroleum, and most recently natural gas, as key to the Anthropocene. There is good reason to do so, not least because the technologies that set the extraordinarily rapid recent expansion of humanity in motion relate first of all to steam engines and, subsequently, in the great acceleration phase of globalization, petroleum-powered propulsion units of various sorts. Insofar as most of the discussion of contemporary climate change is about the consequences of carbon combustion, all this makes sense. But another debate in the Earth sciences on the questions of the origins of the Anthropoceneis also worthy of attention, one that suggests that focusing only on carbon fuels misses the larger story of the emergence of humanity as a geological force. Methane matters too in terms of climate change (Reay et al. 2010). It is getting much more attention as a potent greenhouse gas recently both because of growing alarm about leakage from natural gas wells and pipes and because, as the planet warms, it is being released from thawing permafrost in the Arctic.

Methane may have had historical effects on climate too. William Ruddiman's (2010) research into historical dimensions of climate change suggests methane was critical in the climate after the last ice age. In previous "inter-glacials," geological intervals of warmer global average temperature, the world had slid back into a further period of glaciation fairly quickly. Looking through the geological record, Ruddiman noted that the level of methane in the atmosphere is apparently higher early in the current "inter-glacial" than in previous ones, and that this coincided roughly with the emergence of agriculture.

Methane from agricultural activities, forest clearing, paddy fields, and domestic livestock might have had a significant impact. In atmospheric terms these are trace amounts, but in terms of the thermal balance of the planet, it is enough to make the difference between a trend to cooler times or not.

If this thesis continues to hold up to further scientific scrutiny, and there are indications that it will (Lewis and Maslin 2018), then the question of the origin of the Anthropocene can be formulated in terms of the emergence of agriculture, not of industrialization. Agriculture apparently gave us the Holocene, stabilizing a climate that had been rapidly fluctuating between glacial and inter-glacial episodes. Indeed the argument that the Anthropocene is a redundant geological category, because such things are already implicit in the designation of the present period as the Holocene, gains traction by such considerations. After all, as Smith and Zeder (2013) emphasize, changes to the human niche, dating from the domestication of animals and plants in its early millennia, stretch through most of the Holocene. The formation of artificial soils constructed by agriculture through processes of land clearing, planting, and fertilization—the so called "anthrosols"—provide a clear and novel geological marker in the sedimentary record.

However, this discussion suggests a couple of further points that are key to thinking about the origins of the Anthropocene, and how such a formulation at least nuances the climate change discussion. Agriculture has usually required both the selection of particular species for cultivation and, once selected, efforts at breeding versions of those species to emphasize attributes that produce food for humans. It has also required clearing "natural" vegetation and artificially moving plants and animal species around, and in the process changing the species mix in particular ecosystems in ways that have dramatic ecological effects (Ellis 2011). Effectively this has involved "scaling up" the human niche in the biosphere. This suggests much more than climate change is resulting from human activities, even if climate change is the most obvious large-scale consequence. This "scaling up" is a global-scale phenomenon, given that it has already had the effect of at least postponing the next ice age, something that it did long before the current concerns with fossil fuel-generated global heating.

Recent estimates suggest this earlier intervention in the global climate system may be as cumulatively significant as the emissions in the last one hundred and fifty years, effectively doubling the impact of human climate activities over the long run (Ruddiman et al. 2014). According to the logic of this argument, if humanity had not started doing agriculture thousands of years ago, the planet would probably be in the midst of a further period of glaciation. Sea levels might be hundreds of feet lower than at present—perhaps the North Sea would be dry land—and the boundaries of most coastal states as we know them would be unrecognizable to cartographers. No doubt much of central North America would be under thousands of feet of ice, and the university where this author is based, in what is now called Southern Ontario, would have to be...well, it wouldn't exist at all!

Early farmers were unaware their animal husbandry or rice cultivation practices were preventing the planet from undergoing another "ice age," but if the Ruddiman thesis about the early effects of humanity is correct, this is indeed the consequence of their actions. Such ruminations run directly contrary to most human assumptions in modern culture that humanity has been a relatively small factor in ecological considerations until recently. Environmental determinist arguments, ones suggesting that climate patterns and environments have shaped, and even caused, the course of human history, turn out to be misconstrued even more than earlier critiques infer (Dalby 2015a). Above all, this argument tells us the focus just on carbon fuels and the present climate change crisis, while very serious and extremely urgent, requires further recontextualization to emphasize that humanity is an actor in shaping the planet in geological scale terms. It requires a clear understanding that the biosphere is a much more dynamic entity than most environmentalists assume.

Extending this argument further, Lewis and Maslin (2015; Koch et al. 2019) suggest the Anthropocene might be designated as starting in the early sixteenth century as a consequence of what they term the "orbis hypothesis." The conquest of the Americas by Europeans caused a huge die off of the native human population, the result of diseases introduced by the invaders. The indirect consequence was the abandonment of much of the agriculture practiced on the continents, and a rapid reforestation as trees grew on the newly-untended fields. This, in turn, may have reduced carbon dioxide levels in the global atmosphere enough to induce what has been called the Little Ice Age, a period of colder climate in the seventeenth century related to numerous calamities and human disruptions caused by bad weather and poor harvests (Parker 2013). If this argument holds up in the face of further discussion about climate change over the last few millennia (for why it might not, see Neukom et al. 2019), then, once again, agriculture has turned out to have unanticipated global consequences. This insight suggests a much greater human impact on the global system than most environmentalist thinking usually encompasses.

In addition, the conquest of the Americas caused a transfer of key species across the Atlantic—the so-called Columbian exchange—where, in addition to the diseases mentioned above, horses, rabbits, European earthworms, crops, and other species were brought to the Americas. Potatoes, tobacco, corn, and numerous other species were taken back to Europe and later Asia. In global terms, this intermixing of species has changed ecosystems so that even those understood to be relatively pristine show a substantial human imprint. Plantation agriculture was part of the European colonization of the Americas as elsewhere, too (Crosby 1986), and these activities linking ecology and imperialism have to be worked into discussions of the Anthropocene. This global mixing of ecosystems is another clear indication that the natural world has been dramatically altered by human activity long before the emergence of the fossil-fuelled industrial revolution. The global capitalist economy has subsequently accelerated these transformations (Moore 2015), and its rise in the aftermath of the orbis spike in carbon dioxide is a key factor in the contemporary human condition, but the origins of human transformation of the Earth System lie in a much longer process.

The consequences of this argument suggest part of the problem with climate change discussions is that environmentalists' premises, and the assumption of a fairly stable ecological system that recent human activities are destabilizing, isn't contextualized accurately enough to be helpful in formulating appropriate political and policy responses. Protecting a stable system, assuming change as a problem, and human interference with a naturally functioning system as necessarily something to be avoided is predicated on a modern assumption of humanity as separate from a given nature (Wapner 2014). The argument about methane and "early" human causes of climate change, in the sense of preventing an ice age, suggests this premise needs to be reimagined in how we address climate. None of this in any way reduces the need to curtail the growth of greenhouse gases in the immediate future to slow the pace of change so humanity can cope better with what is coming. But it does firmly suggest that while climate is a matter of human actions, humanity's impact on the planet is not as novel as many of the discussions of contemporary climate emergencies infer. What is novel is the scale, and crucially the speed, of contemporary changes over the last few generations. This crucial point is essential to any serious discussion of sustainability for future human societies.

HABITAT CHANGE: THE URBAN QUESTION

Humanity has become an urban species. Numerous commentators in recent years have noted that since the first years of the new millennium more than half of us reside in towns and cities. The significance of this is profound for all sorts of reasons, not least that it suggests a fundamental shift in the human condition that has happened simultaneously with the rise in carbon dioxide levels in the atmosphere. In so far as climate plays out in terms of more extreme weather, floods, heat waves, and the like, the new habitats that humanity has constructed—the towns, cities, and related infrastructure—are the context in which people experience, and often suffer, the direct consequences of change (Dalby 2009a).

Of course, it is precisely that infrastructure—the long commodity chains that bring food, fuel, and consumer goods to the cities, and the pipes and electricity lines that power urban life and take away its wastes—when disrupted, that makes us vulnerable to extreme weather. Disaster security is now a combination of weather events compounded by the failure or success of complex infrastructures to cope with disruptions (Briggs and Matejova 2019). The increasingly artifactual nature of our urban existence, and the necessity for the networks to function if our lives, jobs, and the contemporary economy are to continue, make our world increasingly artificial. This is the context in which the current concern with climate change is playing out. Imagining climate in these terms raises a number of questions about cities, their origins and the significance of urbanization for how we think about climate.

Many of the discussions of our contemporary predicament are posed in terms of the survival of our civilization, and whether prior human experiments with civilization that ended in apparent decline or disaster have lessons to teach us in terms of the failure to consider resource exhaustion, agricultural limits, or vulnerabilities to climate change (Diamond 2005). Most of the understandings of civilization are ones that presuppose urban existence; indeed, the roots of the term refer to ways of life made possible by city life; modes of existence distinguished from rural and agricultural life ways. Many of the discussions of city life, and of the rise of civilizations, rely on unquestioned assumptions about an evolutionary path for humanity from hunter-gatherers through subsistence agriculture, where surpluses gradually accumulated allowing for the emergence of villages and later towns, to the growth of cities and then the emergence of civilizations. But recent discussions about the beginnings of urbanization suggest an alternative sequence, one that tells a different story that may have further useful insights into how we reimagine climate change and the politics of security in contemporary times.

In his work on the rise of the global economy as networks of cities, Peter Taylor (2013) suggests the conventional assumption of cities emerging only after the gradual rise of villages and towns may be misconstruing the historical record in at least one crucial dimension: Following Jane Jacobs's (1994) work in thinking about innovation and economic growth, Taylor suggests the stimulus for agriculture came from early urbanization. Demand for food and other commodities was, he argues, a key part of the emergence of agriculture. The nascent division of labour in early societies drove the beginnings of commerce, and this is key to the rise of cities and the gradual transformation of ecosystems to producers of agricultural products. Commerce in Jacob's terms is key, and supplying the warriors', or "guardians'," demands for food, weapons, and other items is part of the emergence of divisions of labour and demand for commodities over distance.

Urban innovation, the division of labour at the heart of specialization of economic function, the rise of commerce, and the emergence of agriculture are, in this view, integral parts of one story, not a sequence of happenstances giving rise to civilization. The focus on single cities, and on the rise of states as the political drama of our species, is also reformulated here, suggesting that trading along networks of cities is integral to innovation. That innovation was frequently interrupted by the conflicts among emergent political elites, the "guardians" who struggled for territory in military rivalries between various cities. But these long-distance trading connections, a form of nascent globalization, are key to human innovation, while also distancing the consequences of many human activities from their immediate locales. (These phenomena are loosely analogous to what we now think of in terms of teleconnections in matters of climate risk (Benzie et al. 2018), or long-distance shadow ecologies of consumption (Dauvergne 2008).

If this argument is then linked to the Ruddiman thesis about the emergence of agricultural activities and the slight elevation of the global levels of methane a few thousand years into the Holocene, it follows that economic innovations, based in cities that generate demand for commodities from both immediate hinterlands and indirectly through trading networks, are a key part of the story of the Anthropocene. Economic activities can then be directly linked to the construction of new urban habitats and thus to changed atmospheric circumstances. Viewed in this way, climate change is an accidental side effect of economic activity, but one with a history much longer than the conventional story of recent carbon combustion as the culprit in a new set of urban and globalized circumstances. The upshot is that we are involved in terraforming the Earth, but have yet to act in a way that makes this explicit.

SCALING UP THE HUMAN NICHE

Understanding ourselves as geological actors allows a more careful linkage of geophysical matters of atmospheric composition with such practical matters of crop choice and architectural design. Understanding geopolitics as relating more to the necessity of arranging international trade matters for the future of the human habitat that we are all reshaping, rather than to the traditional "guardian" games of prestige, status, and influence among heads of state, will be key to security in any meaningful sense in coming decades. Humanity has scaled up its niche, and in the process changed both its immediate practical contextual arrangements, effectively becoming "hive" dwellers in Lovelock's (2014) terms, and indirectly set in motion a much larger transformation of the biosphere. Getting these contextualizations clearly in focus is necessary if climate change is to be appropriately understood as part of the human condition. Then we can think about security in terms of innovative ways of building low energy consumption cities and facilitating biological adaptations and migrations. This is not how security has been understood in recent decades, but climate change demands that we understand the security context in these new ways and act accordingly.

The geopolitical categories of the Westphalia system, and its guardian functions in terms of states, national security, and violence, are clearly in need of a very substantial overhaul in the face of climate change (Harris 2013). Cities provide both the possibilities of innovation, and a more prominent place for commercial rather than guardian modes of behaviour for the next phase of the Anthropocene. None of this gives licence for the unconstrained market logics of neoliberalism. What it does suggest is that rethinking the human niche, as part of a rapidly changing world that urban humanity is remaking and how it might be made differently, is a key part of what needs to be reimagined in the climate change discussion (Trachtenberg 2019). This requires thinking well beyond the conventional policy views of "Climate Inc.," which, at least so far, fail to question fundamental assumptions of contemporary collective life (Wapner and Elver 2016). Instead we need to reimagine security in ways that slow down climate change and adapt our modes of urban life to deal with changes that are now unavoidable. Thinking of humanity as a geological scale actor is a key part of this rethinking without which sustainability fails to live up to its promise of living very differently in future. Given that sustainability frequently implies a sense of continuity, dramatic rethinking is necessary now that the scale of the transformation humanity has set in motion is becoming clear.

Without such reimagining, apocalyptic fears of imminent catastrophe might come to pass (Wallace-Wells 2019). Given the abilities of cities in particular to innovate quickly, however, the global economy might yet be reshaped to slow greenhouse gas emissions and, hence, make adaptations easier in coming decades. The longer such innovations are postponed, however, the more difficult adaptation is likely to be, but adapt we will. Whether humanity will do so relatively easily and embrace forces that lead to a more just, humane, and ecologically sound future, or do it the hard way—with much human suffering—in part depends on how the appropriate contextualization of what needs to be secured is now imagined—hence the importance of understanding climate change as part of the production of new urban habitats that have been key to scaling up the human niche. These habitats now have commodity chains that stretch around the world in a global technosphere that has become a new entity in the Earth System.

The necessary focus has to be on what should be secured for urban humanity in the next stage of the Anthropocene, one in which our role in Gaia is now dramatically enhanced and the role of planetary stewardship is foisted on the rich and powerful whether they recognize this or not. Thinking in these terms means sustainability has to be understood in global terms as a series of processes that shape the future configuration of the biosphere in ways that make human flourishing on the large scale possible. The alternative pathological pathway in Dryzek and Pickering's (2019) terms is towards a "hothouse earth," a nightmarish climate-disrupted future for much of humanity.

CHAPTER 3

PLANETARY BOUNDARIES

> Our analysis suggests that the Earth System may be approaching a planetary threshold that could lock in a continuing rapid pathway toward much hotter conditions—Hothouse Earth. This pathway would be propelled by strong, intrinsic, biogeophysical feedbacks difficult to influence by human actions, a pathway that could not be reversed, steered, or substantially slowed. ... The impacts of a Hothouse Earth pathway on human societies would likely be massive, sometimes abrupt, and undoubtedly disruptive. (Will Steffen et al. 2018:6)

What comes next is a matter for humanity to decide: a planetary stewardship would seem to be the desirable next phase of the Anthropocene (Steffen et al. 2011b), but if the Earth System is to be sustained in something roughly approximating Holocene conditions, many things will have to change, not least the understandings of environment and humanity's place in it. In terms of international relations, what should be secured to facilitate a sustainable Earth is rather different from what has been seen as essential until very recently; geopolitics can no longer operate on the assumption that the playing field of international politics is a given (Hommel and Murphy 2013). The key point about the Anthropocene perspective is that climate change and other ecological changes are remaking the context of international politics and doing so in ways that conventional discussions of international politics, and the rivalries of great powers, fail to grasp (Dalby 2014b). While political economists have long understood the importance of changing production systems in the relative success of states in the international system, this now needs to be supplemented by a recognition that the material context for this is being fundamentally transformed by the global economy.

While Earth System science cannot provide a blueprint for a sustainable future, it has developed a loose framework for what is called a "safe operating space" for humanity in light of key ecological functions of the biosphere (Rockström et al. 2009a). This chapter reviews these prior to returning to the questions of what is needed in terms of transitional strategies and how international security needs to be rethought if a sustainable Earth is to be produced in coming generations. In the words of the unofficial report to the United Nations Conference on the Human Environment in Stockholm in 1972, there is *Only One Earth* (Ward and Dubos 1972). How we think about it now differs from that early environmental view of what needs to be done, not least because we have come to understand humanity as a geological-scale actor in the Earth System (Hamilton 2016). While Earth System science does not provide answers to the key political questions facing humanity, it does provide a framing of the options that is increasingly influential.

This chapter turns first to Earth System science and the discussion of phase shifts, tipping points, and the key question of the boundaries of a safe operating space for humanity in the Earth System. These boundaries involve more than climate change, which gets most contemporary attention; it is important to consider other ecological changes that humanity is making if the context for sustainability is to be adequately formulated. Later sections of the chapter emphasize that notions of stewardship and transitions have to be understood in light of these new global ecological understandings. The final section suggests any consideration of peaceful transitions or sustainability now has to include a recognition that any proposed transition involves decisions about what kind of ecology its strategies imply and, crucially, that rapid ecological change may be the context in which the transitions happen. Any plans for a transition to a new less rapacious mode of economy will also have to include thinking about how to peacefully cope with rapid and sometimes unanticipated ecological change. Earth System science has profound implications for how social sciences now understand their task (Schellnhuber et al. 2004);

taking these seriously is essential for all strategies for economic sustainability; environmental security is now about nothing less than the future configuration of the Earth System and how the crucial decisions are made that will shape it.

EARTH SYSTEM SCIENCE

Human actions are often viewed as external drivers of ecosystem dynamics; examples include fishing, water extracting, and polluting. Through such a lens the manager is an external intervener in ecosystem resilience. However, many of the serious, recurring problems in natural resource use and environmental management stem precisely from the lack of recognition that ecosystems and the social systems that use and depend on them are inextricably linked. It is the feedback loops among them, as interdependent social–ecological systems, that determine their overall dynamics and sustainability (Folke et al. 2011). With much more attention now placed on the question of sustainability, and given increasing concerns regarding a wide range of large-scale ecological changes and climate change in particular—well beyond the World Commission on Environment and Development (1987) concerns in *Our Common Future*—the possibilities of transitioning to a sustainable mode of economic life on the part of developed economies extend the conceptual framework of sustainable development further. The 2015 United Nations Sustainable Development Goals explicitly frame matters in terms of transformation.

Earth System science has emphasized how difficult it is to clearly define the parameters of "physical sustainability," the term preferred in *Our Common Future*, while also confirming the necessity of understanding social considerations as an essential part of the biosphere (World Commission on Environment and Development 1987). While in the 1970s environmentalists had often looked to the discussion of "the limits to growth" in terms of pollution and resource availability (Meadows et al. 1972), now the Earth System science literature nuances these matters by looking to a more wide-ranging series of boundaries to what has been called the "safe operating space" for humanity (Rockström et al. 2009b). Climate change in particular has raised questions about how we might now understand "physical sustainability" given that human actions are already changing some of the key parameters of the biosphere.

Lewis and Maslin (2015: 178) note that while earlier scientific discoveries may have reduced the centrality of humanity to understandings of our place in the cosmos, the Anthropocene discussion is different in at least one crucial sense:

> In 1543 Copernicus's observation of the Earth revolving around the Sun demonstrated that this is not the case. The implications of Darwin's 1859 discoveries then established that Homo sapiens is simply part of the tree of life with no special origin. Adopting the Anthropocene may reverse this trend by asserting that humans are not passive observers of Earth's functioning. To a large extent the future of the only place where life is known to exist is being determined by the actions of humans. Yet, the power that humans wield is unlike any other force of nature, because it is reflexive and therefore can be used, withdrawn or modified.

While this may not imply that Gaia has become self-conscious, clearly the extraordinary times we live in, encapsulated in the term Anthropocene, involves a profound shift in understanding humanity's place in the larger cosmological ordering of things. Just as the proof that Earth orbited the sun shook human conceptions profoundly as modern science began its investigations, now Earth System sciences are making clear the planet is a dynamic system that humanity is profoundly and rapidly changing.

Physical sustainability is not a stable given context for humanity; human systems are actively shaping the future geology of the planet, directly altering terrestrial ecosystems and indirectly changing many other aspects of the biosphere, and need to be contextualized that way in any serious thinking about how to address the needs of future generations (Ellis 2011). We are in this new epoch of the Anthropocene, one where human actions are leaving traces in the sedimentary record in many remote places, a geomorphological record of the age of humanity (Brown et al. 2013), a distinctive geological footprint on the history of the planet (Clark 2012). Even if the geological legacy we leave may not be this epochal when viewed from millions of years in the future, the rapidly changing context is more than enough to raise profound questions for societal stability and how to provide human security in coming decades for at least most of us (Scheffran et al. 2012).

As a result of the enormous complexity of the system as a whole, it is not possible to precisely predict the outcomes of rapidly increasing human pressures on the Earth System, but it is clear that thresholds have been or are being reached, beyond which abrupt and irreversible changes occur. These changes will affect the basic life-support functions of the planet (United Nations Environment Program 2012: 210). Addressing climate change is especially urgent as the Intergovernmental Panel on Climate Change (2018) made clear in its report on what it will take to prevent the global average temperature increasing by more than 1.5 degrees Celsius. Beyond this threshold, rapid changes to the global system seem inevitable.

ECOLOGICAL PHASE SHIFTS

In Earth System science terms, the transformations humanity has set in motion amount, in some accounts, to an approaching phase shift in how the biosphere functions, not least because of a rapid expansion of the new entity in the Earth System—the so-called technosphere (Donges et al. 2017). Ecological thresholds have either already been crossed or are in danger of being crossed with the consequence that ecosystems will likely operate in new and potentially unpredictable ways (Huggett 2005). The shift from one state to another can be caused either by a "threshold" or "sledgehammer" effect. State shifts resulting from threshold effects can be difficult to anticipate, because the critical threshold is reached as incremental changes accumulate and the threshold value generally is not known in advance. By contrast, a state shift caused by a sledgehammer effect—for example, the clearing of a forest using a bulldozer—comes as no surprise. In both cases, the state shift is relatively abrupt and leads to new mean conditions outside the range of fluctuation evident in the previous state.

These shifts can occur at various scales, and while the overall effect may be global, it is important to emphasize that the cumulative effects of many small changes may cross thresholds at larger scales (Barnosky et al. 2012). In the context of forecasting biological change, the realization that critical transitions and state shifts can occur on the global scale, as well as on smaller scales, is of great importance. One key question is how to recognize a global-scale state shift. Another is whether global-scale state shifts are the cumulative result of many smaller-scale events that originate in local systems or instead require global-level forcings that emerge on the planetary scale and then percolate downwards to cause changes in local systems. Examining past global-scale state shifts provides useful insights into both of these issues. Those past events suggest the current transition is more rapid than previous dramatic changes in the Earth System, the most recent of which was the transition from the last ice age.

While transitions happen very quickly relative to the fairly stable states that precede them, the pace of human adaptation of numerous aspects of the biosphere may be unprecedented. "Global-scale forcing mechanisms today are human population growth with attendant resource consumption, habitat transformation and fragmentation, energy production and consumption, and climate change. All of these far exceed, in both rate and magnitude, the forcings evident at the most recent global-scale state shift, the last glacial–interglacial transition" (Barnosky et al. 2012: 53). This is one of the worrisome factors in our present circumstances: there are few clear geological analogies to draw upon to anticipate how the Earth System will respond to the new forcing mechanisms humanity has created.

However, the question of whether there are global tipping points, which will mean the Earth System in total will rapidly tip into some new format, is disputed; much remains to be studied on potential linkages between different drivers of system change (Hughes et al. 2013). For at least four of the main drivers, a phase shift in the immediate future is unlikely, at least for terrestrial ecosystems.

> Our examination of the evidence suggests that four principal drivers of terrestrial ecosystem change—climate change, land use change, habitat fragmentation, and biodiversity loss—are unlikely to induce planetary-scale biospheric tipping points in the terrestrial realm. Criteria that would increase the likelihood of such a global-scale tipping point—homogeneity of response over space at a short timescale, interconnectivity, and homogeneity of a causative agent across space—are not met for any of these drivers. Instead, terrestrial ecosystems are likely to respond heterogeneously to these variable forcings and, with a few exceptions, show limited interconnectivity" (Brook et al. 2013: 399–400).

In part this is because humanity has already transformed so much of the terrestrial ecosystem that there is no longer a natural state that might tip in terms of land use. All of which makes the case for great caution in predicting global ecological consequences of further changes. It also emphasizes the key point that ecological change is highly geographically variable in the Earth System; human vulnerabilities in particular places are dependent on this coupled with the increasingly artificial circumstances in which most of us live (Dalby 2009a).

The most worrisome dimension to all this is not that the world will gradually change as a result of human activities, but that the Earth System will be rapidly changed in ways that are not conducive to human flourishing. This may happen if the whole Earth System enters a rapid phase of non-linear change that results in a new relatively stable configuration, but one very different from that so far familiar to human societies. While many forecasts have suggested that this may be unlikely in the immediate future (Committee on Understanding and Monitoring Abrupt Climate Change and its Impacts 2013), exactly how many ecosystems will respond to accelerating climate change is a crucial unknown. That said, the rapid melting of Arctic ocean ice, and glacial ice, especially in Greenland, is happening far more rapidly than most earlier forecasts suggested would be the case. The question of the Anthropocene, as posed by Rockström et al. (2009a), is nothing less than "What are the non-negotiable planetary preconditions that humanity needs to respect in order to avoid the risk of deleterious or even catastrophic environmental change at continental to global scales?"

Such planetary preconditions are not easy to establish, not least because ecological matters rarely work in simple linear processes. They often have very considerable abilities to function while key drivers of important facets vary considerably. Many are resilient, too, being able to bounce back after serious disruptions. Not all ecosystems function in patterns that are immediately obvious and they are sometimes interconnected over distances in ways that are hard to clearly analyze. Many have threshold values that, once surpassed, lead to systems changing dramatically as they cross a tipping point (Lenton et al. 2008). In the case of the global ecosystem, human and ecological systems are so interconnected and enmeshed they have to be considered together if any discussion of sustainability is to make sense. "Because ecosystems are variable, one must focus on the risk, not the certainty, of exceeding an objectively defined target or threshold" (Bennett, Carpenter, and Cardille 2008: 132). Calculating such things is rarely easy, but clearly many Earth scientists are convinced some boundaries have already been crossed, and others may well be in the next few decades, with consequences that are potentially disastrous to the contemporary modes of human existence.

Specifically, ecological change has to be understood in terms of potential non-linearities, thresholds, and tipping point responses to stresses that drive systems in particular ways. Ecosystem attributes, such as species abundance or biological carbon sequestration, can respond in three (stylized) ways to biotic and abiotic drivers. The first type of response is characterized by being consistently proportional to the magnitude of the driver, thus exhibiting a "smooth response" pattern, where no single critical point can be determined. In the second class of ecosystem change, the response, at some critical level of forcing, is amplified by internal synergistic feedbacks and, thus, becomes nonlinear in relation to the driver, changing the slope of the response curve. Similarly, the third class involves nonlinearity, but exhibits hysteresis, in which at least two stable states exist, implying limited reversibility. The term 'tipping point' applies to the second and third class of ecosystem change and refers specifically to the inflection point or threshold at which the ecosystem response becomes nonlinear or the rate of change alters steeply (Brook et al. 2013: 397).

Rapid and unpredictable change worries most political decision-makers: the potential for drastic disruptions to increasingly artificial social-ecological systems is what has stimulated seemingly endless invocations of environmental security since the Brundtland Commission explicitly raised concerns that environmental disruptions could potentially cause military conflict (Floyd and Matthews 2013). Such considerations have become all the more urgent because scientific evaluations of current transformations are identifying thresholds in many systems. Theoretical or empirical evidence of tipping points, manifesting on decadal to centennial time scales, exists at local and regional scales for many subsystems of the Earth System, including the cryosphere, ocean thermohaline circulation, atmospheric circulation, and marine ecosystems. In the terrestrial biosphere, tipping points involve ecosystem attributes such as species abundance or carbon sequestration responding nonlinearly, and potentially irreversibly, to proximate drivers like habitat loss or climate change (Brook et al. 2013). The interconnected nature of these clearly suggests that any attempt to think carefully about sustainability, and strategies for transitions towards more sustainable human systems, will face fraught interpretive tasks in terms of the science. These will be just as fraught as potential governance arrangements if, in the next few decades, humanity seriously tries to shape a functional biosphere for future generations.

All of this is made more complicated by the simple but unavoidable point that multiple stressors are working simultaneously on most systems.

> In a related area of concern, we are struggling conceptually with how to propose robust boundaries for issues that are spatially distributed heterogeneously around the world. Part of the answer relates to the potential geographic specificity of process and function—the primary concern is not the physical intervention in the structure itself. Thus, for instance, deforesting the equatorial/tropical Amazon basin really might be more of a planetary cause for concern than land use change over an equivalent area elsewhere, not because of what it materially consists of nor the area involved, but because of the interplay of that particular patch of vegetation with the processes influencing global water and energy balance. (Cornell 2012: 2)

Thus, while global boundaries are suggestive, specific ecosystems in particular places matter, and trying to ascertain which of these are most important in terms of ecological function is essential—though not easy—for Earth System governance (Biermann 2012).

To even think in such terms requires a conceptual shift from modern notions of a nature external to humanity, to formulations that understand at least the affluent fossil-fuel-powered part of humanity as a key ecological actor in what effectively are geological processes. Such considerations suggest humanity itself be understood in geological terms given the scale of its actions, a discussion that has given rise to various prior formulations of present times in geological terms before science settled on the informal use of the Anthropocene in the last decade (Davis 2011). Nonetheless, what is clear is that human actions are now transforming the biosphere; unless great care is taken not to cross crucial thresholds, we may change it in ways that threaten human civilization profoundly. Not crossing these thresholds is a key part of any strategy aiming to transition from current economic practices to ones remaining safely within the planetary safe operating space. The alternative future, one that if left unchecked climate change will undoubtedly usher in, is the prospect of a hothouse Earth (Steffen et al. 2018). This will be one of rapid largely unpredictable change driven by climate disruptions, with enhanced levels of greenhouse gases playing out on an increasingly artificial terrestrial surface, and with warming and acidifying oceans. If we go that way, we will be in a much more volatile world than the world humanity has known throughout history.

PLANETARY BOUNDARIES

Industrial human systems, in just two centuries, have already introduced at least three clearly novel biospheric processes: the use of fossil energy to replace biomass fuel and human and animal labour, revolutionizing human capacity for ecosystem engineering, transport, and other activities; the industrial synthesis of reactive nitrogen to boost agro-ecosystem productivity; and, most-recently, genetic engineering across species (Ellis 2011). In attempting to provide at least a preliminary answer to questions about how far such transformations can be taken while keeping essential biospheric processes and working in more or less the conditions with which humanity is familiar, the initial formulations by Rockström and others (2009a) of a safe operating space for humanity suggested that nine planetary boundaries need to be especially carefully monitored. While these are obviously not precisely definable technical measures, they are postulated as conditions short of those that might plausibly be thresholds that, if crossed, might shift ecological conditions from the present desirable state into one much less desirable from the human point of view. Thresholds are defined in terms of coupled human natural systems and non-linear transitions, and the example given in the initial papers is the then recent unanticipated retreat of Arctic ice caused by anthropogenic global warming (2007 was a year of especially dramatic reduction in the Arctic Ocean ice cover).

Given the complexity of Earth System processes, simple definitions are very difficult to operationalize in terms of practical metrics. "Some Earth System processes, such as land use change, are not associated with known thresholds at the continental to global scale, but may, through continuous decline of key ecological functions (such as carbon sequestration), cause functional collapses, generating feedbacks that trigger or increase the likelihood of a global threshold in other processes (such as climate change)" (Rockström et al. 2009b). While these may occur at smaller scales (in particular biomes), they may become a matter of global concern when aggregated if their occurrence is widespread. Determining the boundaries prior to such thresholds is not easy and depends on judgments in the face of numerous uncertainties.

Three of the nine boundaries are systemic processes at the planetary scale, namely, climate change, ocean acidification, and stratospheric ozone depletion. While the first two are processes with global-scale thresholds, in the case of stratospheric ozone this is less clear. The other boundaries deal with aggregated processes from local and regional changes. The associated thresholds here are less clear in the case of global phosphorous and nitrogen cycles, atmospheric aerosol loading, freshwater use, and land use change. Biodiversity loss and chemical pollution are also listed: they are clearly slower processes than the others and lack obvious global-scale thresholds. From such categorizations, climate change and ocean acidification, both of which are predominately caused by the accumulation of carbon dioxide due to human use of fossil fuels, as well as deforestation, are the immediate cause for concern, being both planetary processes and ones that are happening quickly. All the others listed matter as well, as they are important parts of the life support systems for humanity even if there is no way to establish precise thresholds yet. Even more complicated is that these processes interplay and connect in numerous ways; changes in one may cause other processes to cross boundaries. As the next few sections of this chapter briefly summarize, scientific efforts to clarify each of these boundaries have elaborated the details of Earth System functions.

The initial planetary boundaries framework was updated and extended in 2015 (Steffen et al. 2015). The new version added updates to the initial scientific estimates, and added an additional discussion of what they termed "novel entities" a category that encompasses the new products of industrial civilization which has added numerous new things to the biosphere, the consequences of which are at least so far less than clear. The revised formulation also emphasized the geographical diversity of boundaries, noting that some boundaries are transcended in some regions, but not elsewhere, a matter that makes the framework more precise, but adds difficulty to the task of aggregating the local boundaries into global calculations. Johan Rockström (Rockström and Klum 2015) argues it is still possible to have a civilization based on abundance within these revised planetary boundaries; but critics are doubtful whether there is the necessary clarity concerning what needs to be done to stay within the climate change boundary in particular (Anderson 2015). Despite the widespread agreement in Paris in late 2015 that led to the Paris Agreement on Climate Change, global emissions of greenhouse gases have continued to increase, making dealing with climate change all the more difficult in coming decades.

Climate Change

The most high-profile theme in the discussion of the Anthropocene is climate change: the body of science related to this topic is now huge. The consensus, widely adopted at the Copenhagen climate negotiations in 2009, is that any warming above 2 degrees Celsius is to be avoided as it will be dangerously disruptive. Subsequently the 2018 IPCC report has focused on limiting warming to 1.5 degrees Celsius and emphasized the importance of moving rapidly to constrain greenhouse gas emissions. What is less clear is the long-term level of carbon dioxide in the atmosphere that will keep the climate below this threshold. Concentrations first reached 400ppm briefly in 2013, and while environmental activists suggest that perhaps 350ppm is the maximum level that should be maintained in the long run—approximately the level in the atmosphere when *Our Common Future* was written—there are as yet few serious suggestions as to how the atmosphere can be brought back to such a level, one already reached after the first few decades of the great acceleration.

With the Arctic Ocean ice cap already melting and warming the northern hemisphere as a result of increased albedo, one of the positive feedbacks that concerns climate science is clearly already in operation. The rapid melting of ocean ice and new phenomenon of fires burning across many parts of the terrestrial Arctic in the summer of 2019 confirmed many of the worst projections of rapid system change. Enhanced methane emissions from melting northern permafrost also suggest accelerated warming in this region. The trend to ever-greater emissions of carbon dioxide from combustion and further destruction of forests suggests rapid climate change. Considerations of rapid climate change have become part of the scenario planning exercises for the future over the last decade (see Anderson and Bows 2011) and increasingly a matter of concern to financial planners who have belatedly (Network 2019) but only gradually begun to consider the consequences of climate system disruptions, despite major studies pointing to the urgency of adding these to forecasts (World Bank 2012). These concerns have become an annual issue in the high-profile economic forum meetings in Davos and show up repeatedly in their annual risks report (World Economic Forum 2019).

In terms of the boundary debate, climate is one of the key potential drivers that might cross significant tipping points this century with potentially serious disruptions to human systems. Lenton et al.'s

(2008) summary suggested Arctic sea ice, the Greenland ice sheet, the Atlantic thermohaline circulation, the West Antarctic ice sheet, the El Nino–Southern oscillation, Indian summer monsoon, Sahara/Sahel and West African monsoon, Amazon forest dieback, and possible boreal forest dieback were all contenders for major changes as a consequence of accelerating climate change. While this is far from encompassing the whole Earth System, these components are substantial parts of it and they raise the alarm about potential climate security risks very clearly, especially as the monsoons are key to feeding much of Asia and Africa. But as Lenton's (2013) subsequent investigation of environmental shocks makes clear, all this change also matters in human terms: as a matter of how vulnerable people are in particular places and, related to that, a matter of institutional preparedness—or the lack thereof—in particular societies. Crucially, some of these tipping point features are fairly directly being shaped by investments made by major actors in the global economy and as such amenable to decisions being made by current political and economic forces. In particular how investments in boreal and tropical forests are handled matters because of their potential functions as sinks for carbon if they are managed appropriately (Gaffney et al. 2018).

All this is especially important because, despite repeated warnings that this boundary is one that humanity is on track to transcend, some key scientists are warning that scientific projections of what is needed to prevent global heating are still not being taken anything like seriously enough by politicians. The 2018 Intergovernmental Panel on Climate Change report on what is needed to keep the planet at close to 1.5 degrees emphasizes the point that rapid decarbonization is essential to prevent heating above this level. Time is short and the political process set in motion by the Paris Agreement is nowhere near tackling the issue with the necessary urgency.

Ocean Acidification

One of the so-called "carbon sinks" that removes carbon dioxide from the atmosphere is the ocean where the gas is absorbed in surface waters. But this process is itself a matter with profound ecological consequences: nearly one-third of the carbon dioxide released by anthropogenic activity is absorbed by oceans; but for this fact, current atmospheric CO_2 concentrations would be higher than they already are. However, CO_2 uptake lowers the pH and alters the chemical balance of the oceans, in particular the solubility of calcium salts. This phenomenon is called ocean acidification and is occurring at a rate faster than at any time in the last three hundred million years (Gillings and Hagan-Lawson 2014). The solubility of calcium salts is a key factor in the success of coral reefs and other marine creatures dependent on shells; if the water is too acidic, coral skeletons or shells may dissolve and cause reefs to stop functioning and shellfish to die. The ecosystem consequences of this phenomenon and other disruptions of marine life may be crucial to the future of the biosphere.

In the final analysis, protection of the ocean may be more important than protection of atmosphere or land because it stores more carbon, mediates climate variability, and provides essential ecosystem services. This point is especially important given the obviously global dimensions to the oceans. Despite the large-scale implications of shifts in oceanic functions, they frequently remain a low priority for environmentalists, whose focus is on terrestrial systems, which are perceived as a more immediate matter of human experience. Indeed, the focus on greening things in environmental politics and the formulation of green policies suggests a focus on chlorophyll that is key to growing plants. But the Earth System perspective, and a focus on Anthropocene life, suggests that (given the importance of the atmosphere, oceans, and ozone layer) a focus on blue formulations, following from oxygen in ozone and in water in particular, might be more appropriate. Correcting this inherent terrestrial bias is one of the key implications of Earth System thinking. Ocean acidification, correlated with earlier global extinction events, is now being done rapidly as carbon dioxide from human actions is being absorbed by sea water, another worrisome trend in the Anthropocene.

Stratospheric Ozone Depletion

If there is a success story in global environmental management and international cooperation, it is clearly the Montreal Protocol and its subsequent additional amendments and extensions (Benedick 1991). These mandated the end to the production of chlorofluorocarbons (CFCs) and the gradual reduction of the use of other halocarbons. While they remain in the atmosphere, and will for decades more as they gradually decay, the annual ozone holes over the poles are not increasing—although, in 2014, detection of new chemicals in the atmosphere in small quantities raised concern about the efficacy of this regime (Laube et al. 2014). Coincidentally, the reduction in CFCs in the atmosphere has been a useful climate change measure given their potency as greenhouse gases. While other chemicals such as nitrous oxides will still have some detrimental effects on ozone levels in the stratosphere, the immediate danger of destroying the essential ultraviolet filter from the upper atmosphere, something essential to terrestrial life, has been removed.

However, while this success is worth emphasizing, so too is the point that the combination of easily identifiable dangers, the availability of technical replacements for the outlawed gases, and the relative simplicity of the technical issues allowed for a relatively rapid evolution of policy. Likewise, financial compensation to Southern states for difficulties they might have encountered in making the transition was forthcoming and was not a prohibitive cost to signatories to the agreements. But this regime, frequently invoked as a model for dealing with other "global" environmental matters, and a prominent part of the discussions about climate change in particular, may not be a good fit for more complicated issues where numerous technologies operate and where substitutions are much more difficult to identify and implement (Hoffman 2005).

Phosphorous and Nitrogen Cycles

One of the keys to the rapid transformation of rural landscapes has been the availability of artificial fertilizers that have, when coupled with tractors and other farm machinery, facilitated industrial-scale monoculture farming. While the fossil fuel subsidy to natural systems has boosted productivity dramatically in the so-called green revolution, it has done so by disrupting rural social systems and ecologies and by dramatically increasing the circulation of nitrogen and phosphorous through the biosphere. "Nitrogen flux through the biosphere is primarily a biological process, while phosphorus availability arises slowly through geological weathering. Humans sidestep the phosphorus bottleneck by mining and distribution of fertilizer onto agricultural lands, thus inadvertently increasing the flow of phosphorus into the oceans" (Gillings and Hagan-Lawson 2014: 5). Eutrophication and other ecological disruptions result from the addition of artificial fertilizers into aqueous environments; ocean anoxic events that have caused large-scale die-offs may have been caused by phosphorous being washed into the ocean.

However, the boundary on this ecological change is distant when considered at a global scale, despite the fact that phosphorous run-off rates may be significant for some coastal waters. An important consideration with managing phosphorous is that it is geographically heterogeneous: while the application of fertilizers in some places may have eutrophication effects on terrestrial waterways, phosphorous deficiencies elsewhere limit ecosystem productivity. This means a global boundary for phosphorous is very difficult to calculate even if specific ecosystems have transcended boundary conditions (Carpenter and Bennett 2011). Nitrogen pollution also has regional effects but as yet does not seem to be close to any global threshold (de Vries et al. 2013). The nitrogen cycle is more complicated to assess as, in the form of nitrous oxide, it is an important greenhouse gas and hence also counts as part of the climate change calculations.

Atmospheric Aerosols

Burning fossil fuels and, in particular, their inefficient combustion, leads to particulate matter and various chemicals in the atmosphere producing numerous effects (Tsigaridis et al. 2006). These have been of particular concern recently in terms of their immediate pollution effects in Asia where both Beijing and Delhi have frequently had especially bad air quality, and the possible effects global warming may have on disrupting the Asian monsoon. Monsoons supply the key rainfall for agricultural systems in the region, thus helping feed a large portion of humanity (Kitoh et al. 2013). Ironically, aerosols also act as cooling agents in the atmosphere, shading the ground from sunlight. This effect is clearly visible in studies of the consequences of volcanic eruptions and has become one of the proposed ideas for geoengineering to artificially cool the planet in coming decades if climate change becomes an immediately hazardous phenomenon. As such, aerosols are both a pollution and a health hazard, but also potentially an artificial sunshade if practical attempts to cool the planet are undertaken—hence the great difficulty in assessing the total impact of aerosols on global heating as well as other related human effects.

Freshwater Use

Human activities divert large quantities of surface and ground water for farming, industrial use, as well as for basic human needs such as drinking, bathing, cooking, and household use, making discussions of water security for humanity very complicated indeed (Grey et al. 2013). Potable water is key to basic hygiene and disease prevention and, as such, a key dimension to human functioning in many increasingly artificial ecosystems. Water supplies are both a matter of natural supply (as in rain and snow), but also, given the extensive plumbing systems that now supply cities in particular, very much a matter of artificial hydrology. Many rivers no longer flow all the way to their estuaries due to the volume of water diverted en route. Groundwater aquifers are also being pumped dry in many places. While this may not have many direct ecological effects beyond the locations where aquifers feed water springs and hence provide water for ecosystems and human use, the effects matter once the water is depleted and the unsustainable activities dependent on that water source have to be discontinued.

Climate change may alter rain and snow patterns, causing droughts and forcing ecosystems and farming arrangements into new configurations. The California drought emergency of 2014 suggested difficult political choices concerning the allocation of remaining water supplies. Such decisions regarding prioritization have practical, social and philosophical implications for the communities and actors affected. Water is an essential part of human politics, contested and used in numerous ways that defy easy categorization, but an unavoidable necessity in all human activities no matter how humans try to govern its use (Linton 2010). It is clear that human use of fresh water is rapidly increasing due to food cultivation requirements in particular. As such, governance issues will be an important part of sustainability transitions. "This indicates that the remaining safe operating space for water may be largely committed already to cover necessary human water demands in the future" (Rockström et al. 2009b: 16). Ironically, all of this is compounded by climate change-induced extreme flood events, which provide too much water in specific places in short time periods.

Land Use Change

Humanity cleared land for agricultural purposes throughout much of the Holocene period. Indeed, part of the argument that the Anthropocene started long before the industrial revolution is related to the release of methane from agricultural activities (Ruddiman et al.

2014). The scale of the transformations that have already taken place are such that ecologists have suggested that traditional classifications of the world's large geographical designations of natural areas in terms of biomes now needs to be updated with the addition of various "anthromes" (Ellis et al. 2010). Deforestation reduces carbon sink capabilities, at least in forests where trees do not decay quickly and return their carbon to the atmosphere. The albedo of bare land is very different from that of a tree canopy. Forests' water retention functions also affect other hydrological functions. Clearly, terrestrial land cover is key to many ecological matters and it is very hard to aggregate these into any one meaningful global threshold.

That said, humanity is already using much of the most fertile parts of the planet's land surface and we will need to implement many changes in how land is used if the ecological footprint of agriculture is to be reduced while its efficiency is simultaneously increased to feed a still-growing population (Foley et al. 2011). Part of the concern about land use change is the question, "Can a threshold for habitat clearance effects on biodiversity be defined on a global scale?" (Brook et al. 2013: 399). The answer would seem to be negative not least because "thresholds are deeply context dependent" and "tipping points might differ between scales" (Brook et al. 2013: 399). Beyond that, it is also worth emphasizing again that, given the diversity of terrestrial land cover, it is unlikely that terrestrial ecosystems will universally respond to a global tipping point crossing some other boundary; they are more likely to react heterogeneously in the event of major disruptions.

Biodiversity Loss

The huge changes to landscapes, including deliberate land clearing as well as inadvertent habitat disruption, in combination with hunting and fishing, has already led to the extinction of many species. The rates of extinction are much greater than the normal background rates of species disappearance in the geological record, suggesting that we are living through the sixth global extinction event in the planet's history (Kolbert 2014). While many species have disappeared, other artificial species, such as farm animals, have expanded greatly. These, however, are dependent on human systems and not a replacement for the diverse species that make up "natural" ecosystems. The rate of extinction is the key consideration: the alarming pace of extirpation has been driven by most of the other ecological processes in addition to direct human predation on particular species (Ceballos, Ehrlich, and Dirzo 2017). Given the diversity of species in tropical rainforests, many of them with very limited geographical ranges, forest clearing is an especially damaging human activity in terms of reducing species diversity. Further complicating efforts to stem biodiversity loss, conservationists warn that assuming that these ecosystems have already been radically disrupted may undercut important conservation efforts that can still protect many species, especially in tropical areas less immediately susceptible to climate change playing out more intensely in polar regions (Caro et al. 2012).

While possible food and pharmaceutical derivatives are being destroyed, the larger concern is that unknown future possibilities for life are being precluded. In the long run, the planet will no doubt replenish life forms, but humanity faces an impoverished range of life forms in the centuries ahead. It is important to note that not all species are equally important in ecosystem function: removing "top predators and structurally important species such as corals and kelp, results in disproportionately large impacts on ecosystem dynamics" (Rockström et al. 2009b: 15). As such, while an overall reduction in the rate of extinction by several orders of magnitude is needed to push biodiversity loss to a level within the safe operating space, specific species may have a disproportionate effect on particular ecosystems and their functioning. Consequently, it becomes clear that managing the global scale must be balanced with micro-scale interventions.

The overall pattern of biodiversity loss in comparison to previous mass extinction events is not clear (Condamine, Rolland, and Morlon 2013), even if the trend in particular places due to sledgehammer clearing effects is observable and better understood. This remains the case in the updated version of the planetary boundaries framework where matters of biodiversity loss are nuanced by dealing with them in terms of biosphere integrity, and focusing on functional and genetic diversity in specific biomes (Steffen et al. 2015). The lack of clarity about baselines in terms of species numbers and extinction rates remains a measurement problem in terms of the precise location of the boundary even if the trajectory of rapid extinction is clear. This is especially the case with recent alarms about dramatic insect population reductions in diverse parts of the world where there is serious doubt about whether the causes of the decline are pesticide or other chemical disruptions or more general environmental change (Jarvis 2018). Unseen trajectories among species that are not well studied may have more severe consequences than relatively well understood large mammals. In addition, one of the key implications of climate change is that ecological conditions conducive to specific forms of ecosystem functionality are in motion. Species need to migrate, and assuming conservation in situ is the appropriate policy framework may be to badly misconstrue what needs to be done in the face of contemporary transformations (Kareiva and Fuller 2016).

Chemical Pollution

While pesticides and their consequences for insect and bird populations were a central driver in the rise of environmentalism in the United States in particular, inspired by Rachel Carson's (1962) book *Silent Spring*, other forms of industrial pollution have long been a problem both for ecosystems and as a direct cause of human health issues. Recent smog events in China are reminiscent of the situation in London sixty years earlier when the death of thousands as a result of smog caused by coal fires in the 1950s finally led to comprehensive efforts to reduce smoke. Many of the environmental campaigns of the 1960s and 1970s in the developed world led to technological innovations that removed pollutants from smokestacks and effluent pipes. Such "ecological modernization" provided numerous technical fixes to pollution problems but only rarely led to more fundamental social change (Mol 2001). With the rise of globalization, industrial production frequently moves to states with less rigorous regulations, effectively outsourcing pollution rather than permanently and directly addressing the problem. Of great concern are the very low-concentration toxic substances that may have effects on particular species and thus alter whole ecosystems indirectly. These include such substances as endocrine-disrupting chemicals. Where the thresholds on such activities might be is not yet clearly known.

BOUNDARY PRIORITIES

The most immediate concerns are with atmospheric greenhouse gases. Nonetheless, as Steffen, Rockström, and colleagues (2015) emphasize, the nine factors identified as safe operating space boundaries interact and interconnect in complicated ways. It is worth remembering that chlorofluorocarbons, the most obvious cause of stratospheric ozone depletion, are also powerful greenhouse gases. The regime to curtail their production is effectively also an agreement to deal with climate change even if it is not designed explicitly to do this. Crossing one boundary may have many serious and unpredictable consequences for others: this simple but difficult point is key to any serious consideration of how to facilitate transitions to sustainability.

Sustainability usually implies a fairly stable context for humanity but, as the Earth System science analyses briefly summarized here suggest, in the present context sustainability of societies has to be considered in terms of the rapidly changing context for humanity and the simple fact that societies have been changing quickly as rural transformations and urbanization interact. Viewed as a totality, the planetary boundaries perspective suggests humanity has effectively taken its own fate into its hands in terms of the future configuration of the planetary system. Or, to be more precise, the rich and powerful who decide on what gets made and built, and how the global economy is powered, are now shaping the future configuration of the biosphere. This is the key insight that Earth System science adds to the discussion of globalization, and this novel context presents discussions of sustainability with a series of dilemmas, not least of which planetary boundaries need the most immediate attention.

However, while we have clearly crossed the boundaries in terms of biodiversity loss, the artificial production of nitrogen in the atmosphere, and climate change, it appears human action has at least halted the dangerous trend of ozone depletion and limited it to the areas within the high-altitude polar vortex wind systems. Although depletion will remain a problem until at least the middle of the current century, given the existing inventory of ozone depleting substances already released, it is important to remember that the boundary has not been crossed nor does it seem likely that this will happen given the widespread agreement that chlorofluorocarbons and related chemicals are too dangerous for more than very limited use. Dealing with this boundary has been relatively easy given that the components necessary for a solution were practical and political opposition to agreements was relatively weak. Other boundaries are much more difficult to deal with, even if it is clear where they might be and how close we are coming to some of the thresholds.

The update of the original planetary boundaries formulation published in 2015 (Steffen et al. 2015) is clear that biodiversity and climate change are the two most important boundaries, each of which is capable of causing a phase shift in the operation of the planetary system. Hence, these two need priority attention, not least because many of the changes involved with these ecological processes are irreversible, as in the case of species extinction or, as in the case of climate change, given the lengthy time lags in dealing with reversing carbon dioxide accumulation, irreversible in terms of contemporary human lifetime. The key to both is the rapid expansion of the fossil-fuelled globalized economy of the present (Dalby 2018). Neither the Convention on Biodiversity nor the United Nations Framework Convention on Climate Change (UNFCCC) have yet operated in ways that suggest that global political systems are taking these two boundaries anything close to seriously enough.

While these forms of boundaries are key to the discussion of the Earth System and sustainability at the global scale, very different modes of boundary making are key to politics and governance. Hence the current institutions that might be employed to deal with the Earth System boundary transgressions that the global economy has set in motion in recent decades operate on very different notions of how boundaries matter in human affairs. While economic globalization is frequently understood as a matter of trade arrangements and trans-national rule making, international law and a diminution of state sovereignty, the Earth System sciences and the larger discussion of the Anthropocene make it clear that the processes of globalization are a much more fundamental challenge to human governance and its presuppositions of stable geographical entities as the basis for politics and policy (Angus 2016). This is especially clear when the debate about climate change and migration is engaged.

CHAPTER 4

TERRITORY, SECURITY, MOBILITY

[I]f the relationship between political and scientific atomism has been disrupted by the emergence of more recent science, it may be worthwhile considering whether such disruptions bear any implications for the fundaments of not just the physical but also the political world. If sovereignty is premised upon an atomistic conception of the state of nature, then surely a more interconnected understanding of nature raises the question whether the basic presumption of autonomy that undergirds sovereignty should shift in favour of a politics of interdependence. (Chantal Thomas 2014: 57)

New Zealand has deported a Kiribati man who lost a legal battle to be the first person granted refugee status on the grounds of climate change alone. Ioane Teitiota, 39, has argued that rising sea levels in his homeland meant his family would not be safe there. ... His deportation on Wednesday night follows a failed appeal against a New Zealand high court decision that he could not be a refugee as he was not being persecuted. (BBC News 24 September 2015; http://www.bbc.com/news/world-asia-34344513)

TERRITORY AND SECURITY

The geopolitical order of modernity is apparently one of states, of a fixed territorial arrangement, and supposedly stable arrangements where state sovereignty is tied to an agreed set of fixed boundaries. All else follows from this mode of governance; this system of states is sovereign, the overarching principle that orders humanity's affairs. It's an especially elegant resolution to the political difficulties of reconciling universal aspiration and political particularity (Walker 2010). We can all be modern and exercise our human rights within the boundaries of our state; citizenship understood in geographical terms as related to distinct, exclusive territorial states is the most basic political identity for people. From this elegant arrangement, the modern "global covenant" in Bob Jackson's (2000) terms, all other questions of politics can supposedly be derived. Stable states may be threatened from abroad by military and other dangers, or internally by subversion, sedition, and domestic protest, but the category of the permanent territorial state is unquestioned most of the time.

This territorial fixity norm underpins much of the United Nations system, and insofar as it has operated to reduce the frequency and severity of international warfare has, despite the protestations of the United Nations' frequent critics, been an important matter in the reduction of large-scale, if not persistent smaller-scale, violence. This key theme in contemporary geopolitics suggests both that state boundaries are stable, and that minor demarcation readjustments are possible but major boundary changes or accretion by aggression are no longer acceptable parts of state practices.

In part, this territorial state cartography is premised on arguments that states represent nations; culture is, following the Wilsonian principles of self-determination, a geographical matter. Ethnicity, in the form of a common identity, supposedly resides in places that can be at least approximately mapped into bounded territories.

> This confused imaginary [of pure ethnicity] was born with a territorial basis that was then spread materially throughout the world via Western imperialism. This territorial legacy of the Peace of Westphalia of 1648 renders it that much more difficult to think through, or outside of, this confused imaginary as distinct 'nations' become affixed to distinct 'states' in an elision which

> essentializes non-essences (nations) thereby according 'them' agency. (Archer et al. 2007: 120)

Politics is thus now fundamentally a geographical matter; territory is key to this even if as a category it was slow to emerge as a key organizing principle in human affairs (Elden 2013). That said, the United Nations has been reluctant to link nations explicitly to territories in the neat Wilsonian cartography. Peoples, relating to residents of the territory rather than members of a specific ethnicity, are frequently the entity understood to be sovereign within specified borders.

Here and there are to be distinguished by drawing lines and demarcating spaces in which certain forms of jurisdiction are paramount and where certain cultures and ethnicities reside and are to be administered in terms of residential location. One's geographical address is key to one's identity; 'where do you come from?' is very much more than a conversation opener in many parts of the world. The United Nations arrangement in the 1940s codified the tentative League of Nations aspirations to non-intervention and fixed state boundaries in the 1933 Montevideo Convention on Rights and Duties of States. Decolonization and practices of boundary drawing, partition, and population relocations were frequently violent in the aftermath of the Second World War, as the cases of India and Pakistan as well as Israel and Palestine made clear. Huge numbers of people in the category of displaced persons in Europe had to move too in the late 1940s where major boundary changes were part of the post war settlements.

But at least in theory, once these disruptions were accommodated and people's papers put in order, permanently fixing boundaries removed a major cause of warfare (Zacher 2001). Irredentism and further territorial adjustment by violence were outlawed; military interventions were only allowed in matters deemed as self-defence and supported by United Nations actions to protect the new territorial order. Honoured in the breach frequently, nonetheless this arrangement has become the geopolitical norm of modernity. The lines on the map will remain, and if adjustments must be made, they are done on the basis of antecedent administrative arrangements and fixed territorial jurisdictions. The fact that the cartographers who dreamt up some of these lines may have been inebriated, incompetent, or both—as has frequently been suggested in regard to the 1884–5 Berlin congress where European colonial powers divided up Africa—is an unfortunate reality in many cases. As this chapter shows, all this is now made more complicated by global environmental change.

After the Cold War this system of states, while specified as the given geopolitical arrangement, has been beset by frequent anxieties about globalization, economic sovereignty and cultural nationalism. While patriotism may indeed be, in Dr Johnston's famous phrasing, the last refuge of the scoundrel, nationalist anxieties have been a recurrent part of geopolitical discourse driven by globalization and its militarized version in the war on terror, including European and American concerns about jihadism and Islamic threats of various sorts. Distinctions between us and them, locals and foreigners, those worthy of moral solicitude and those beyond the ambit of responsibility, rely on such categories to the degree that the territorial fixity assumption that underlies this isn't usually questioned. In Oscar Wilde's dark rephrasing of Dr Johnston, patriotism is the virtue of the vicious. In these terms, security is about the invocation of culture and territorial identity in ways that assert a sovereign right to exclude those specified as different, from somewhere else, regardless of the consequences for those so excluded.

NON-TRADITIONAL SECURITY

There is, however, much more to the questions of sovereignty and security than these ideal types and overarching view of the system of states suggests, however elegant and persuasive their categories are in establishing the terms of political discourse. In the aftermath of the Cold War, security has been challenged in terms of the dominance of the state-centric formulations. After all, national security premised on the promise of mutually assured destruction in the cold war provided a very dangerous form of political order. Nuclear issues continue to overshadow international politics and the potential for all-out warfare due to miscalculation continues to haunt the international system even if the dangers seem much less immediate than they were in the Cold War period.

The inability of states to protect their own populations and the vulnerabilities of people to various global disruptions generated a large discussion of matters in terms of global dangers and the possibilities of a human security agenda (Kaldor 2007). These formulations have subsequently fed into discussions of a responsibility to protect and more general discussions of non-traditional security threats (Hameiri and Jones 2015). The term non-traditional security is of course somewhat of a misnomer because security has never been only about narrowly defined national interests, but nonetheless the term encompasses a broader agenda than the earlier focus on military rivalries and the supposed dangers of domestic subversion. Crucially, with the rise of international trade and the rivalries that go with it, economic matters have been discussed in terms of stability and security. The largest threats to domestic populations in Europe, in particular recently, and earlier in terms of the Asian crisis of the 1990s, the Argentinian debt crisis and other events came when international financial arrangements caused economic disruptions.

Beyond this focus on economic and political matters there is a growing realization of just how dramatically humanity is changing the material circumstances that provide the context for the state system. Global environmental change now challenges the principles of territorial stability—admittedly it is mostly at the margins so far—with long-term implications for how geopolitics will play out. Climate concerns have become the predominant theme in this discussion. Sustainable development has been recently supplemented by discussions of resilience, adaptation and environmental security. Much of this has been a reworking of earlier themes of economic development as a necessary strategy to pre-empt peripheral insecurities and disruptions threatening metropolitan order. This is especially ironic given that environmental change is driven predominately by metropolitan consumption rather than peripheral activities (Dauvergne 2008). But this isn't a new pattern; environmental security has long been about metropolitan fears of those dispossessed by the expansion of its political economy (Dalby 2002).

Nonetheless, the implicit assumption that the metropoles do provide an order that has to be perpetuated is key to the formulations of security that currently purportedly address climate change (Boas 2015). Epitomized by the repeated focus on climate as a threat multiplier, where environmental disruptions will supposedly aggravate political instabilities, or in the worst cases cause states to degenerate into violent conflict over diminishing water and food supplies, and become "failed states," the security agenda remains in danger of perpetuating a focus on symptoms of climate change rather than its causes (CNA 2014). Its metropolitan consumption that is changing the climate but focusing on peripheral political symptoms rather than metropolitan root causes obscures the key causal relations while the victims are portrayed as a security threat to the perpetrators (Buxton and Hayes 2016).

Most glaringly, the contradictions of this show up where discussions of climate refugees enter the picture, and where the fate of low-lying states in the face of rising sea-levels is addressed. If mass migration is portrayed as a threat to national security, then the possibilities of military responses loom (Smith 2007). Modern geopolitical assumptions of stable state arrangements and in-situ political solutions to complex security problems are directly challenged by environmental change in the new period of the Anthropocene (Hommel and Murphy 2013). Just as the territorial fixity norm has become hegemonic, climate change threatens the existence of some members of the United Nations quite directly, and also challenges the assumptions of state solutions to global problems. Building fences to stop migration, as numerous governments are now doing, especially in areas where economic discrepancies across boundaries are dramatic (Jones 2012), runs directly counter to the most basic ecological adaptions to environmental change—for species to move to more suitable circumstances.

Sources of these migratory species, whether human or otherwise, are often specified in terms of the dangers of failed or failing states.

> This matters because labelling a country as a failed state is more than merely a rhetorical exercise. It delineates the acceptable range of policy options that can be exercised. States called 'failed' are therefore primarily those in which such crises are perceived to threaten Western interests; in other cases, conversely, these features of state (mal)functioning are not only accepted, but sometimes almost encouraged. (Bøås and Jennings 2007: 483)

With this goes the implicit assumption that sovereign authority has effectively been suspended in a "failed state," which by definition can't provide order and isn't effectively occupying its territory. Sovereignty here is, in Elden's (2009) terms, contingent; the absence of effective sovereignty invites interventions from abroad to provide order; the international community now has a "responsibility to protect" (International Commission on Intervention and State Sovereignty 2001). The implicit, although frequently misleading, assumption in the notion of a failed state is that internal causes lead to failure but, in the case of climate change and the extreme case of state extinction due to rising sea levels, this isn't an appropriate way to frame the issue. The causes are nearly entirely external. Insofar as state failure leads to an exodus then responsibility cannot easily be assigned to the origin state. But, at least so far, the responsibility to protect doctrine doesn't apply to people set in motion by climate disruptions.

Discourses of invasive species and migration threats reproduce the territorial fixity assumption in terms of security precisely where innovation to adapt to changing sea levels and weather patterns is needed. Ironically in human terms, the elegant formulation of fixed boundaries is now, even more than in the past, running directly into the simple fact of contemporary environmental transformation (White 2011). For those in need of sustenance, health care, employment, and housing, the borders and fences of the current order are the security problem. For those, like Ioane Teitiota, faced with impending inundation of their homelands, these difficulties are especially acute. How does the international system, premised on a precise and fixed cartography, deal with the fact that anthropogenic climate change is rendering that fixed cartography something at best temporary? At least so far, the answer is, not very well. The Montevideo convention may need an update!

SOVEREIGNTY IN THE ANTHROPOCENE

What sovereignty might mean in the face of disappearing territory is a fraught question in the climate discussion, not least because as globalization seems to be leading to a diminishment of sovereign control, states are, ironically sometimes, responding precisely by building walls (Brown 2010). As the Montevideo convention made clear, states have territories. While India, China, and the United States all face considerable coastal inundation issues in coming decades, it is the small island states built on coral reefs that face the immediate prospect of elimination from the system of states, and hence have been the focus of a rapidly growing literature on climate adaptation and international law (Gerrard and Wannier 2013; Yamamoto and Esteban 2014). These are also the states possessing the least material capabilities in terms of the traditional measures of power, financial, diplomatic, and military capabilities. They can't physically protect their territorial integrity from rising seas despite the growing popularity of the slogan "we are not drowning we are fighting" with its explicit refusal on the part of those facing inundation to be treated as victims and refugees.

Insisting on their collective rights as citizens of states raises the crucial questions of how they might be understood once their territory disappears under the waves. If not drowning, at least some of these people will indeed become *Lives Adrift* (Baldwin and Bettini 2017) as they take to the seas in search of dry land. What is to be done about the elimination of these states in future decades? What legal remedies might apply, and with what implications for the implicit assumptions within the state system about the persistence of states?

None of these questions can be answered by simple invocations of state sovereignty; power and political practices have always operated in complicated patterns that evade neat encapsulation in theories of state sovereignty. That said, the geography of trans-boundary issues, and the so-called new security agenda dealing with non-traditional threats, usually start with the invocation of statehood in some form even if much of the discussion is about the limited capabilities that individual states have for dealing with the problems identified as new ones for security (Hameiri and Jones 2015). Understanding these as global phenomena usually quickly follows. The point is made that the larger political economy of globalization emphasizes that economic policy is key to security (Stiglitz and Kaldor 2013). But such formulations usually require a very considerable amnesia concerning earlier historical situations, the migrations implicit in imperial colonial practices of the nineteenth century in particular. Indeed, the migratory patterns that currently reflect the anxieties of globalization are fears about what might happen if "they" come "here." The historical consequences for "their" societies when, uninvited, "we" went "there" earlier are not to be remembered, much less considered, as part of the globalization discussion.

When it comes to questions of who is subject to what treatment at contemporary borders, or points of immigration, the questions of jurisdiction remain tied to matters of location and citizenship even as the rights and responsibilities of states for non-citizens have become more complicated by United Nations arrangements regarding human rights and refugee convention, and the larger overarching rationales of the responsibility to protect. This is especially the case where matters of forced migration are in play, even if not the outright political persecution for which the refugee regime was initially established (Mountz 2010). There is a longstanding argument about whether a category of environmental refugee is appropriate in dealing with current transformations (White 2011).

The distinction is also frequently made between voluntary and involuntary migration, the latter being a matter of necessity as a result of persecution or imminent danger. But, as Ioane Teitiota discovered in New Zealand, the refugee convention doesn't apply to many people who are forced to move but who are not directly persecuted. There is, it seems, a need for some additional category of "survival migration" (Betts 2010). In the New Zealand case, discussions of a new category of humanitarian visa in 2018 have followed from the Teitiota case as it becomes clear that migration for many Pacific Islanders will be necessary in coming years. While states that face inundation are one very obvious case of climate-induced difficulty, elsewhere the distinction between someone forced to move because of poor crop results caused by climate change and poor rural economic performance because of matters of political economy is not easy to sustain; migration, especially from rural to urban areas, is a key part of the contemporary changes of the human condition even if much of it happens within national boundaries. It is playing out in spaces changed by the practices of the global economy, and agricultural transformations and the consequences of global property markets in particular (Parenti 2011).

Clearly species are in motion, either autonomously in search of more conducive ecological conditions or being moved by gardeners, pet owners and agricultural corporations. New modes of conservation are attempting to "rewild" spaces in part to facilitate adaptation to Anthropocene conditions (Lorimer 2015). Such movements don't apply to humans who are not bound by the ecological niches they need for sustenance but, instead, by the cartographies of power that is the contemporary geopolitical system of state territorial jurisdiction. Thus, the palpable contradiction, whereby the floating fences used to allow the structures to rise and fall with the changing dune patterns on the Mexican American border also allow the landscape to change, quite literally, while preventing people and presumably at least some other terrestrial species from crossing.

These complicated and contradictory geographies are the context for discussing climate migration; simple assumptions of either stable material circumstances or stable institutional arrangements are no longer useful premises for trying to grapple with the questions of migration. While there are many difficulties with suggesting that climate change is setting migrants in motion as a result of environmental transformation, there is one case where this is very clearly, and obviously, what is happening. This is the situation of low-lying island states where rising sea levels in some cases are either, already, or soon will be threatening states with extinction. If they are to live, citizens of these states will have to move and live in the jurisdiction of other states. What then matters of sovereignty as a principle for organizing human affairs?

The admittedly limited number of cases of impending state inundation do pose key questions for sovereignty in the Anthropocene: bluntly put, the issue is simply "what happens when states are permanently failed?" In the case of island-state inundation, the failure comes from abroad, from the failure of advanced industrial states to address climate change and by their explicit failure to live up to their implied responsibilities to at least not harm others, if not actually protect citizens of other states. Related to that is the question of whether principles of compensation or rights of the internally displaced inform discussions of what happens when sovereignty is extinguished? What then does all this mean for post-sovereign politics if some notion of global justice prevails rather than brute force, and if some notion of a human collectivity is seen as a necessary entity to which rights continue to be extended even if the territory in inundated (Nine 2012)? Can humans be understood as such first and foremost, rather than only in terms of their territorial state defined citizenship?

DISAPPEARING STATES, MOVING PEOPLE

All these questions relate to the key matter posed in the first epigraph to this chapter regarding the scientific basis of sovereignty, and its long-held presuppositions of a stable context within which autonomy operates (Elshtain 2008). This is now being undercut by new understandings of the interconnectedness and contingencies of ecology, and at the largest scale by the rethinking of the human condition in the discussion about the Anthropocene. Rising sea levels challenge the assumptions of stable physical contexts; the implicit geography of modernity can no longer underpin adaptation to climate change and other Anthropocene phenomena. This chapter is not the place to engage the finer points of legal argument on these issues. Nonetheless, a few key points are germane, not least because they raise crucial matters about whether sovereignty can be disconnected from territorial states. If that is done in the case of, say, Kiribati and Tuvalu, it might have implications elsewhere for the new geopolitics of the Anthropocene. "The mortality of a state is no longer a far-fetched hypothetical: the 'theoretical' possibility of state extinction via emigration of its entire population and the complete loss of territory may come to pass in the foreseeable future" (Wong 2013: 44). What then is sovereignty?

Obviously only a few states face complete inundation, although many face partial territorial loss in coastal areas; the case of the small island states emphasizes the key point that geographical change is upon us and the premise of stable territorial entities as basic units of governance can no longer be accepted as applicable to all state situations (Vidas, Zalasiewicz, and Williams 2015). Migration will be a necessity for some peoples' survival, but sovereignty in terms of territorial fixity doesn't imply an obligation to receive those who have to move. There is as yet no clear path forward in resolving these tensions, but some thoughtful suggestions have been forthcoming in contemporary scholarship that highlight the dilemmas posed by migrants from failed states in a world where sovereign territory is still the key governance arrangement.

The questions posed most starkly by the prospect of rising sea levels inundating existing states relates to whether states have obligations to either the endangered state as a legal entity, or some kind of ontological entity, and who has the responsibility to accommodate the people moving from the former state. Are there circumstances whereby territory will be granted to migrants, or is it the case that they may do little better than purchase property in states to which they migrate without the transfer of legal powers that go with claims to territorial sovereignty. In such cases, if the destination state grants citizenship to the immigrants, then the specific identities of the migrants, and their claim to sovereignty, will presumably at some point be extinguished unless innovations are made that perpetuate sovereign claims among descendants of migrants.

Vaha (2015) ponders whether states can be disconnected from territory, whether a state right to exist as part of the system of states rather than just as a territorial entity might be formulated given the likely inundation of some island states. Nine (2010) emphasizes that states are mere institutions; it's the political collectivity that matters, but can it persist in the absence of territory? This would obviously require a rethinking of the Montevideo convention, and much international law since, but the point about the relation of members of the system suggests an ontological status not dependent on the continuity of territory in perpetuity. "[O]ne might ask whether and to what extent international community of states has a duty to prevent or react to such state-extinctions, in the same manner as individual morality and duties require us to help the dislocated people" (Vaha 2015: 207). The argument leads to a formulation that "... suggests that there might be a duty on behalf of the members of the international state-system to take measures that guarantee the continuing existence of these states – although this does not (necessarily) amount to a duty to provide them with a new territory" (Vaha 2015: 208). To do so, however, requires invoking notions of ontological and state identity rather than territorial sovereignty as usually understood: "By relying on the concepts of ontological security and state identity, one can now argue that what is essential to the state is not mere physical existence, but rather ontological existence as an entity, as well as a continuing sense of 'the self' as a state" (Vaha 2015: 215–16). This is important because states don't intend to renounce sovereignty. "The intention of island states is not one of renouncing sovereignty, but rather reflective of the reality that movement is necessary" (Wong 2013: 16).

Wong (2013) comes at this point by starting explicitly from the Montevideo convention premise. Crucially, she points out that the extinction of states is not something that will come as a surprise; it's entirely predictable and something for which planning is needed:

> Climate change is not a sudden phenomenon and loss of territory will not occur instantaneously. There are therefore two periods which require consideration. The first is when the people migrate due to the effects of rising sea levels. Crucially, there is still territory but issues relating to abandonments of sovereignty may arise. The second period commences with the complete loss of territory. Here, the question is whether extinction automatically follows from a complete loss of territory. (Wong 2013: 6).

An additional solution, not discussed by either Wong (2013) or Vaha (2015), is state amalgamation, an extension of one state to encompass the citizenry of the soon to be inundated area, one that might give the un-inundated part of the new state access to fishing rights and seabed resource access too if these are perpetuated after the first wave overruns the last rock, a matter that may yet provide imperial temptations, and promises of extended protection in various neo-colonial arrangements. But insofar as law of the sea arrangements for territorial seas and exclusive economic zones are premised on measurements that work outwards from shore baselines, the extinguishment of territory suggests waters surrounding land that has been inundated will revert to the status of high seas, thus removing the temptation for amalgamation. Where this is avoided it is entirely feasible to suggest that sovereignty for sale, in exchange for migration and citizenship, opens up as a possibility. This is effectively an extension of the practices that already provide for tax havens and financial services based on extraterritoriality (Bullough 2019). The alternative, probably most likely in Pacific Ocean cases, is that many of these people will end up as immigrants in New Zealand or Australia, or living in some updated neo-colonial arrangement whereby they have residence rights but not full citizenship rights, as is now the case with American-administered islands in the Pacific.

If such strategies fail to give the citizens of inundated states effective agency to relocate, or find ways to keep their territories above the waves, then questions of compensation, and liability for lost territory, arise. Given that the responsibilities for climate change can be allocated to specific states in terms of the amount of fossil fuel burnt historically—or at least since 1990 when clear warnings about the consequences of greenhouse gas accumulation in the atmosphere were widely circulated, and hence the proportion of the sea level rise attributed to a particular state can be ascertained—then the possibilities of territorial compensation, beyond mere land rights emerges (Dietrich and Wundisch 2015). Compensation for land lost can be imagined in terms of financial measures approximating the value of the lost real estate. Rights to relocate and the obligation of other states to make possible modes of earning a living for migrants are also possible formulations that deal with polluters' obligations. But territorial rights, and with them matters of self-determination and the ability to operate a recognized separate political identity, require more than financial recompense or the provision of new land rights in a new location (Nine 2010).

Dietrich and Wundisch (2015) suggest the particular loss of the ability to operate as an autonomous territorial polity can only be compensated by the provision of that ability on some other territory. Clearly, the worst carbon polluters have the largest obligation to replace the territory that their actions have indirectly inundated. Most discussions of climate justice and responsibility don't include this in-kind compensation, not least because this isn't so easy given the current absence of any vacant unclaimed territory where displaced people could relocate. Hence, territory will have to be transferred in some manner, one that Dietrich and Wundish (2015) suggest must meet at least three criteria: those of 'cultural identity,' 'appropriate size,' and 'population majority' conditions. In other words, the compensatory territory must allow the migrant population to continue living in ways analogous to those of its former homeland, and not be faced with a situation where it becomes a political minority in its new territory.

All of which suggests a sense of, in Nine's (2010) terms, "nested" territorial arrangements, one that challenges simple cartographic assumptions of mutually exclusive sovereign spaces. These are all requirements for appropriate restitution of lost territorial rights. These go beyond normal measures of compensation related to relocation within states as a result of mining or such development projects as dam building and resultant flooding. The mechanisms by which these might be done are not going to be simple, and Dietrich and Wundisch (2015) have various ideas about communities, auctions, and state obligations, none of which are easy to administer and all of which will require international transparency if obvious invidious practices are to be avoided in the process of sovereignty transfer. They argue that states conceding sovereignty over parts of their territory are not obligated to accept displaced islanders as immigrants, a situation that would require migrants to give up their territorial rights, for which they argue there is no possible non-territorial compensation.

Dietrich and Wundisch (2015) don't expect culprit states to respond positively to their suggestion, but the normative claim of territorial rights and in-kind compensation requiring territory transfer puts the questions of sovereignty and security at the forefront of how climate change is now to be rethought. The reallocation of sovereign territory to a migrant state also causes doubts about how the territorial fixity norm will subsequently be adjusted in international practice. Crucially, xenophobic invocations of migrants as threats suggest that invoking security understood in terms of territorial sovereignty in the face of environmental change are likely to make everything worse.

RETHINKING GEOPOLITICS

Politics as a matter of territory thus first raises key questions of political responsibility and the ability of states to act as independent autonomous authorities; in short, the case of territorial compensation, and the difficulties that inevitably arise, quite fundamentally challenge the modern geopolitical assumptions of separate territorial entities as the most effective mode of political action. In Ulrich Beck's (2008: 78) terms regarding European response to contemporary difficulties:

> While the world faces a host of problems—from climate change, global economic interdependence and migratory movements through to issues of regional and global peace keeping— nation-based thinking has lost its political capacity to deal with any of them. Ironically enough, every issue that has helped to fuel nationalism in Europe—the transfer of jobs to other countries, refugee flows, wars, terrorism—is an international issue.

Assumptions of a given geographic context and separate containers for politics are no longer tenable as the premise for either scholarship or policy advocacy; and yet their elegant resolution of the difficulties of universal claims and political particularity have no obvious replacement as of yet.

The frequency with which the question of "why do people move?" is posed in discussions of migration presupposes that this is an aberration, a departure from the norm of stationarity. The history of humanity is one of movement and adaptation, but this is implicitly denied by political actions reaffirming the fixity of boundaries and the presuppositions of a simple cultural geography of nations in particular places (Baldwin, Frohlich, and Rothe 2019). While this provides a principle for international politics, the mobility of people and the rapid environmental changes wrought both directly in terms of development projects, and indirectly by the changing climate, as well as the rapidly enhanced patterns of connection between particular places that is globalization, all operate counter to the simple assumptions of a stable geographic order.

Where authority has shifted from divinity to state and now to individuals as Elshtain (2008) has suggested, the question posed by the rapidly changing environmental circumstances of the present is how notions of authority and legitimate politics are to be disconnected from increasingly untenable geographical premises. Beck (2008) suggests that coordinated action among states is part of what needs to be done, because without the coordination then states are increasingly ineffective. Cerny (2010) suggests that the sources of effective action are dispersed through numerous actors, a neo-pluralist arrangement, not all of which can be specified in geographical terms. It is clear that attempting to deal with such things as climate change and migration is leading to a transformation of many states as cooperation and unilateral measures begin to reshape many state agencies (Hameiri and Jones 2015). Or at least they do so in the absence of nationalist and xenophobic responses to supposedly external threatening migrants.

What is now inescapable is the simple fact that climate change, which is no respecter of territorial boundaries, makes clear that the geographical fixity assumption on which territorial jurisdiction operates is literally being eroded as sea levels rise. The complicated interconnected global geophysical reality that science has been elucidating in the last few decades, now under the label of the Anthropocene, reinforces the point that the political ontology of territorial states, human collectivities, Lockean notions of property rights, and the modern assumptions of autonomous sovereign entities are increasingly ill-suited categories for grappling with contemporary transformations.

The extreme case of territorial extinguishment thus emphasizes the point that global politics is premised on territory and citizenship, not on humanity. Despite the frequent invocation of a universal humanity, a key ontological premise for modern international relations, and one that justifies interventions under the responsibility to protect (Mitchell 2014), nonetheless people in motion are still administered, granted access or not, dependent on the paperwork related to their citizenship, not on the basis of belonging to the species. While the refugee convention was an attempt in the 1950s to deal with this problem, the designation of a refugee and the resultant obligation on the part of states to accommodate such persons, doesn't apparently, as the case of Ioane Teitiota shows, extend to those who are not persecuted.

Security understood in terms of protecting territorial sovereignty isn't appropriate for a situation where adapting to changing circumstances and quite literally to changing geographies is what is needed. What needs to be secured for many marginal peoples in particular but increasingly also for all the rest of us is the ability to adapt. In many circumstances this is quite simply the ability to move out of harm's way. But securing the ability to move is precisely the opposite of insisting that the geographical order of territorial states is the bedrock principle for contemporary governance. Hence, the fate of island peoples facing inundation is both tragic, in the sense that their future is being determined by forces beyond their control that make them vulnerable, and ironic in that territorial fixity, the solution to one key former set of security problems, that of aggressive warfare for territorial gain, is precisely what presents security problems to those now forced to move to ensure their survival.

CHAPTER 5

BORDERING SUSTAINABILITY

> [W]e are entering a new unstable, and unpredictable geological era that will endure for thousands or tens of thousands of years.
>
> In short, the relationship of human beings to the natural world we inhabit has been upended. None of this could have been foreseen a century ago, or even three decades ago. Yet now we must face up to the fact that this situation, an irreversible and dangerous trajectory, is our future and the ideas that we have inherited from the era before the break must all be open to question. (Clive Hamilton 2017: 37)

THE GREAT ACCELERATION

Given the extraordinary scale of human changes wrought in the biosphere and related parts of the Earth, in particular in the last three quarters of a century, Earth System scientists tell us we now live in the great acceleration period of the Anthropocene (McNeill and Engelke 2016). This involves the rapid expansion of the global economy fueled by massive fossil fuel consumption and the rise of international trade. The abilities to transform much of the world by using these sources of energy are key to both the current functioning of the global economy and the ecological transformations of the present, of which the most obvious effects show up as climate change. Under the rubric of globalization these processes suggest that the traditional governance with its focus on boundaries and sovereignty is increasingly outdated as global change shapes most societies in terms of commodities, common online experiences, and international regulations that frequently are implemented far from geographic borders.

In part, it can be argued that the territorial trap in international relations has been sprung by these developments and that "sovereignty regimes" now operate in much more complicated geographies (Agnew 2009). Global governance practices now involve numerous complex international institutions, technical knowledge and standards all enmeshed in contested political claims of legitimacy and authority (Zurn 2018). The Sustainable Development Goals process has added a complex series of aspirational goals to all this too, supposedly emphasizing the importance of environment to everything, but without a comprehensive set of linkages between the goals to ensure that policy measures are efficacious (Dalby et al. 2019).

However, in recent years the assumptions of a borderless world have been repeatedly challenged by the rise of xenophobic nationalisms and protectionist economic sentiments, a topic taken up later in this volume in chapter 8. Despite the rise of supposedly global corporations and the far-reaching impact of electronic technologies and the Internet in particular, sovereign states have frequently reasserted their power in shaping how global phenomena play out in particular places. In the exemplary case of the Paris Agreement on Climate Change, state prerogatives have been reasserted even as commonly agreed-upon goals are set in terms of meeting targets on limiting overall global warming (Falkner 2016). The United Nations Sustainable Development Goals link international aid and global targets to specific national programs for implementation and state metrics for evaluation of progress (United Nations 2015; United Nations Development Program 2016). The contradictions of universal ambitions and local particularities highlight the persistence of the old saying that the Earth is one, but the world isn't. Clearly, matters of property in terms of real estate, local jurisdiction, sovereign spaces, and territorial prerogatives continue to shape governance efforts. Sustainability efforts that ignore the practicalities of these matters, while convincing arguments in many political fora, are unlikely to be efficacious in practice.

Territorial jurisdiction frequently shapes governance arrangements in ways that suggest that globalization is a matter of reterritorialization rather than the removal of borders. It is frequently a matter of re-bordering. These processes were highlighted by the

American response to 9/11 where border controls were imposed under the rubric of homeland security (Andreas and Biersteker 2003), and these procedures have subsequently coexisted uneasily with efforts at economic integration. That said, economic integration has also begun to extend into novel territorial forms in international carbon markets as part of the mechanisms for tackling climate change. While these are notionally global arrangements the practicalities of their management fall on local administrations, re-territorializing matters of ecosystem services and in the process of forestry in particular linking "sink" functions to very specific local geographies (Lansing 2013). Global managerialism is, in these cases, dependent on the application of very local jurisdictional authority.

As this chapter suggests, global environmental concerns are also frequently, but not always, tackled in terms of new forms of territorial organization; climate change governance has invented new forms of carbon territoriality while simultaneously becoming a matter of American national security deliberation too (Dalby 2014b). By framing matters this way, the growth of the global economy can be understood as the expansion of modes of spatial enclosure. Where traditional conservation efforts often used designated spaces, in terms of parks and ecological reserves as a key mode of governance which excluded economic development, landscape change, and extractive activities, these have now sometimes been reworked in terms of ecotourism and the novel arrangements of carbon sinks and the financialization of ecosystem services. Now climate adaptation is also driving some of the so-called "land grabbing" processes in the global real estate market (Sassen 2014).

This is in many ways a long-term continuation of the extension of territorial modes of control over nature that has frequently used force, or the threat thereof, to extend the scope of commercial activities arranged in terms of colonization, commodification, and expanding property arrangements, a continuation of "the great transformation" in Karl Polanyi's (1944/1957) terms. The legal transformation of nature into territory and of commons into property is still frequently a violent business as indigenous peoples and environmental activists in numerous places can attest (Marzec 2015). All of this is now complemented by various international legal arrangements in attempts to tackle environmental matters that frequently apparently evade modes of territorial governance, while triggering numerous attempts to reinstate them in new measures. These processes highlight the importance of how territory and ecological responsibilities might be reconsidered in light of climate change in particular (Dahbour 2017). But now as environmental change accelerates and ecosystems partly adapt by migrating as climate zone shift (Jones 2018), the frequently implicit in situ assumptions of territory are also in doubt—so too the questions of whether local ecological priorities or those tied directly into global adaptation measures will win out in particular locales.

These contradictory processes explicitly add ecological considerations to the discussion of territory, politics, and governance. The rest of this chapter teases out some of the contradictory tendencies in global environmental governance and its territorial dimensions, looking first at traditional matters of fortress conservation, and then to matters of globalization in terms of logistics and enclosures. Later sections show how these practices have been extended in response to climate change and how climate mitigation, adaptation, and migration are entangled with prior modes of territorial governance. The final section emphasizes the importance of the relatively novel recognition that the current phase of the Anthropocene now involves non-stationarity and increasingly unpredictable fluctuations in ecological matters that further challenges governance measures premised on fixed territorial demarcations.

GLOBAL ENVIRONMENTAL GOVERNANCE

Understanding globalization as the extension of these process of the enclosure and commodification of nature, turning land into property (Blomley 2017), with all the related practices of re-bordering the world, suggests that global environmental governance too can be viewed as a series of processes that frequently use territorial strategies in attempts to manage phenomena for which the term 'natural' is increasingly inappropriate. Climate change is only the most obvious symptom of the consequences of contemporary transformations which have generated numerous responses to try to financialize risks and extend commodity relationships as part of both climate mitigation and adaptation strategies (Keucheyan 2016). Those outside these market logics are often rendered even more vulnerable to severe and unpredictable weather events, which in turn play out as disasters in increasingly artificial contexts where infrastructure is crucially important to survival (Dalby 2009a).

Global environmental governance emerged in part as a response to the consequences of the great transformation. Attempts to limit pollution, preserve wildlife, and conserve resources for future generations, while maintaining peaceful conditions to allow development to continue, have structured the discussions of sustainable development from *Our Common Future* (World Commission on Environment and Development 1987) thirty years ago through to the extensive agenda of the Sustainable Development Goals that now, at least in theory, shape government policies around the world (United Nations 2015). But the mechanisms used by governments to tackle global problems are frequently very much about local control, national sovereignty, and border practices, despite the supposedly global dimensions of environmental matters. While the Sustainable Development Goals may be universal aspirations, their practical implementation is mostly a matter of state action (United Nations 2016).

Ken Conca (2015) has summarized this situation as a matter of the United Nations operating in terms of a framework of "law between nations and development within them" in matters of environmental management. "Political elites present at the UN's creation may have failed to see the world as a tightly coupled global ecosystem, but they were quite attuned to the role of natural resources in global commerce and state power" (Conca 2015: 35). The insistence on the part of many states that resources are a matter of state sovereignty has long stymied attempts to think about global environmental matters; territorial imperatives still shaped the development agenda in *Our Common Future* and the subsequent formulation of international arrangements to deal with ozone depletion and other matters in the 1990s. These international regimes worked on matters that spilled over state jurisdictions, with international arrangements shaped by state development policies primarily.

However, while numerous efforts to extend managerial methods, and encompass more human activities within the ambit of environmental regulation, have been undertaken in the last few decades, it's clear that these measures have neither grappled effectively with the scale of overall economic activity or the legacy of destruction of native peoples and their territories by resource extractions and related ecological and human dislocations. The extant measures of governance, in Peter Dauvergne's (2016) terms "environmentalism of the rich," have yet to deal with either the historical legacy of ecological disruption caused by European colonization or the total material and energy throughputs of the current global economy.

SUSTAINABLE DEVELOPMENT AND ECONOMIC GROWTH

Facing this situation discussions of sustainability require much more by way of policy and technical innovation than traditional environmental management measures if they are to grapple effectively with how to shape the future of the technosphere. There are some successes in global governance, as the various protocols dealing with stratospheric ozone depletion in particular suggest. But on the two largest issues within the current discussions of Earth System science, climate change, and the global pattern of extinctions, clearly existing modes of environmental governance are inadequate. Launched a quarter of a century ago at the "Earth Summit" in Rio De Janeiro, neither the United Nations Framework Convention on Climate Change nor the Convention on Biodiversity have effectively dealt with these issues (Steffen et al. 2015). Insofar as they are formulated in terms of environmental protection, they are responses to the dynamics of economic expansion rather than frameworks that direct the future shape of economic activity in ways that respect Earth System boundaries.

As Conca (2015) notes, there was no grand strategy for global environmental governance until the 1980s attempt to develop this under the rubric of sustainable development. Despite the rhetorical umbrella provided by sustainability, and the numerous aspirational targets in the 2015 Sustainable Development Goals, the various international legal arrangements still lack overall coordination or any clear understanding of how they might all fit together in a larger framework dedicated to maintaining a functional biosphere in the face of a rapidly expanding technosphere. Critics have become increasingly forceful in their challenges to the framing of development in terms of conventional economic thinking. They argue that the implicit assumptions of economics, with its premises of consumers and markets as all that matters, are inappropriate given that they ignore the essential biospheric conditions that are key to considerations of sustainability (Göpel 2016).

Linkages are key to complex systems, and this is especially so in a world of globalization where ecological and economic factors cross administrative boundaries so frequently. Conservation of particular species or ecosystems may require thinking in terms of creating such things as migration corridors across state borders and thinking through how animals can migrate through fragmented landscapes transected with linear infrastructure, fences, and other barriers, as well as the enclosures and exclusions intrinsic to much private property (Shafer 2015). It certainly requires thinking about conservation areas that operate based on ecological functions despite state and other administrative borders running through the systems. Urban areas have to be incorporated into these efforts too; biodiversity is far too important to be considered simply as a rural matter best dealt with by making some restrictions on economic activities in landscapes peripheral to core economic priorities (Hartig 2014).

Given the myriad difficulties in dealing with the rapidly changing circumstances of the Anthropocene, numerous new ideas of ecological sustainability, deglobalization, degrowth, and discussions of resilience have emerged (Kallis 2018). Transition town initiatives have focused on reworking urban consumption to emphasize local food and energy sources and hence constrain the climate change impacts of long commodity chains. Innovations are being driven in diverse social locales, not necessarily coordinated with national initiatives (Bernstein and Hoffman 2018). While there have been some successes with global efforts to deal with environmental dangers—the ozone protocols being an exemplary case, insofar as these measures outlaw the production of dangerous substances—discussions of the necessary corollary for developing sustainability, that of directed industrial activity specifically designed to make things in environmentally safe ways, is a much more recent series of innovations (Rockström and Klum 2015). Likewise, economic growth is still seen as essential to the success of the Sustainable Development Goals, despite longstanding critical analyses which show that contemporary production systems need a much more fundamental rethinking (Jackson 2009). This rethinking of economic activity has been reinforced by the need to consider the biophysical constraints that Earth Systems thinking has recently emphasized and the necessity to deal simultaneously with basic social needs for much of humanity while not exceeding the planetary boundaries (Raworth 2017).

FORTRESS CONSERVATION

In many cases, the governance tools for ecological matters need substantial overhaul, not least because sustainability is now about much more than preserving existing environmental conditions and frequently cannot function within the bounds of either parks or reserves on the small scale in terms of larger sovereign national territories. Ecologies don't conveniently follow jurisdictional lines and the history of failed attempts to maintain ecosystems within territorial limits has long been understood (Botkin 1990). Nonetheless, frequently existing modes of governance, and those that presuppose the appropriateness of state vision (Scott 1998), are applied to novel issues with mixed results. Given the vast variety of matters related to sustainability and environmental management, there is no easy way to specify when borders are useful in managing environmental issues and when they aren't. But given the frequency with which states use territorial controls as a mode of governance, this is not surprising, even if the mode of governance would seem to be strikingly at odds with what is ostensibly being managed.

Exemplary in this process is the case of the Convention on International Trade in Endangered Species of Wild Flora and Fauna (CITES) whereby the killing of megafauna for exotic parts, such as rhino horns, bear gall bladders, and ivory, has long been tackled by using traditional trade measures on borders to prevent export (Reeve 2002). Banning the sale of these products is a related measure that at least in theory can be universally imposed by states. The key point is that territorial sovereignty and the imposition of border controls are used in attempts to indirectly manage wildlife by restricting trade. If animal parts can't cross national frontiers, then, at least in theory, this will reduce the financial incentives for poaching. Or, it will at least increase the costs because smuggling will be needed to get these things to markets abroad. Border controls and trade rules are key to managing global matters loosely under the rubric of what has subsequently become known as sustainability.

Direct efforts to stop hunting of wild animals do occur too, often in wildlife management areas in African states in particular. Here the "fortress model" of environmental management, using territorial strategies to exclude people from particular areas in hopes of maintaining a "natural area" in which species can flourish without human proximity, has frequently been tried with limited success, as the classic case of Mkomazi Game Reserve in Tanzania illustrated (Brockington 2002). The implicit assumptions of nature separate from humanity, a long-standing theme in European and North American environmentalism, turned into a geographical strategy for park construction. It has often dispossessed local inhabitants and, in the process caused unanticipated ecological consequences, precisely because of a failure to grasp how local human practices are part and parcel of ecological processes (Duffy 2014).

Replacing the traditional modes of livelihood with paid employment for locals as tour guides, guards against poachers, and employees in facilities accommodating and entertaining ecotourists who fly across the world to see wildlife in a natural state, might be understood as development in strictly economic terms but, given the huge amounts of jet fuel involved in this international tourism strategy, it's far less clear what exactly is being sustained in these circumstances. Linking smuggling to terrorism, and the use of money from illegal trading as a source of funds for weapon purchases, as has been done in a few states recently, only further militarizes conservation and entrenches the fortress model of environmental insecurity (Duffy 2016). Militarizing conservation is often counter-productive as it can feed rural violence and extend the violent logics of counterinsurgencies by states with other agendas. Once again, peripheral places are appropriated into a global economy that remakes places according to distant economic logics and, ironically but crucially, then specifies danger in terms of challenges to this logic (Dalby 2013b) rather than to the key ecological functions that are disrupted in the processes of landscape transformation.

Given the scale of the changes in ecosystems set in motion in the great acceleration period, and the pressures of climate change on most aspects of ecosystem function wildlife, managers are now also working on making new landscapes, which can be re-wilded as an adaptation measure to rapid change (Lorimer 2015). These measures have also frequently involved bordering processes where artificial ecologies are constructed, humans excluded, and a demarcated area allowed to change in response to the species interactions in the system. But problems result here too if species cannot move to adapt to resource shortages or seek new locations to adapt to climate changes and seek shelter from severe weather. Parks cannot function effectively if they are viewed as closed systems; but open systems require boundary crossings that are conceptually anathema to neat jurisdictional divisions that structure many state administrative practices.

At the global scale, fortress model thinking leads to conceptions of environmental security that reinforce boundary drawing narratives and perpetuate the operation of bordered spaces as the dominant modes of administration (Lunstrum 2014). Fears of scarcity and shortages of various resources compound the sense of environmental insecurity and, in the context of neoliberal market logics, drive increases in resource demand and in many places simultaneously perpetuate violent and illegal modes of resource extraction (White 2014). These dynamics in the global economy have a long trajectory in previous patterns of colonial plunder (Le Billon 2012) and are precisely the dynamics that the discourse of sustainable development, with its premises of environmental security, have challenged since these themes were explicitly articulated in *Our Common Future.* But these dimensions of sustainable development have frequently taken a very distant second place to corporate practices of resource extraction (Dauvergne 2016).

LOGISTICS AND ENCLOSURES

If the functioning of the global economy is what has to be secured, which is now the key task of states both in a neoliberal world (Agnew 2009) and elsewhere in more state-directed economies (in Asia in particular), then the continued transformation of nature—directly by resource extraction and indirectly by climate change and pollution of numerous kinds—follows. This logic is especially clear in the case of climate change where consumption demands of contemporary lifestyles are promoted by corporate economic strategies that still, despite the Paris Agreement commitments, include extensive state subsidies for fossil fuel extraction (Coady et al. 2017). State policies among the major polluters are focused on economic growth, and short-term geopolitical rivalries frequently override long-term sustainability considerations (Harris 2013). As a result, trade agreements and international economic policies focus primarily on extending the existing economic system, with the implicit assumption that technological change and improved production systems, still seen as something external to the operation of the consumption economy, are enough to deal with environmental issues.

Trade controls and the security of commodity chains are a key part of globalization. Extra jurisdictional arrangements cross borders; secured areas, sealed containers, pre-clearance of numerous goods are now built into trading patterns, frequently at a cost to local peoples who are in the way of economic developments (Cowen 2014). Much of this is a matter of logistics, and the certification and security of transit arrangements and the increasingly prevalent operation of special economic zones where local control is pre-empted by global market logics supported by state governments anxious to extend links into global supply chains and gain at least some employment income for burgeoning urban populations. Globalization is about these processes of enclosure and exclusion, a matter of complicated local spatial arrangements connecting distant destinations, as Sassen (2018) suggests, with extractivist and predatory operations in financial matters, but also with complicated arrangements for commodity production, and most recently new ecosystem service territorial designations.

Globalization now involves extensive economic activity shaped by global property markets, both urban ones where new high rise residential and commercial arrangements are simultaneously pricing people out of many city centres and residential areas (Graham 2016), and rural ones where the global agricultural economy continues to shape the extension of commercial arrangements that displace subsistence and small-scale production (Dunlap and Fairhead 2014). Global agricultural property markets are driving the transformation of many rural landscapes, especially in Africa where the term 'land grabbing' has been used to describe the processes whereby commercial interests appropriate land and water resources by imposing modern property regimes in place of existing informal arrangements and traditional patterns of use (Sassen 2013). The social consequences for those expelled from local land and economic activities in the process are often severe, and frequently feed the migrations to the urban areas of the global south. Ironically in many cases, not least in Afghanistan (Rasmussen 2017), such processes are aggravated by climate change adding social pressures to already conflictual situations.

In many places local peoples resist the further enclosure and appropriation of traditional lands and resources, articulating local demands with global environmental priorities (Routledge 2017). Protest movements concerning land rights and opposition to commercial exploitation are not a new phenomenon, but now as opponents are frequently met with violence, they starkly pose the question of environmental rights, and the human rights of protest in the face of dispossession. Insofar as rural resistance is connected to insurgencies and rebellions, and these in turn rendered as security threats in the global geopolitics of environmental security, the political tensions involved in the contemporary expansion of the global economy become particularly acute. Activists are being murdered in many parts of the planet; the slow violence of dispossession and landscape transformation (Nixon 2011) supplemented by the direct violence of assassination and intimidation by death squads working to remove obstacles to resource companies. Ironically, such violence, a matter of national security in that it protects businesses, is often justified by claiming that it is an appropriate response to international environmental movement interference with matters of national sovereign jurisdiction (Matejova, Parker, and Dauvergne 2018).

CLIMATE MITIGATION

The sheer amount of fossil fuel used in global trade is a key component of climate change, something that frequently evades national inventories. Aviation and ocean transport along with the sovereign immunity from environmental regulations granted to most military forces that, among other things, operate 'protect' this trading system, are among the most difficult greenhouse gas emissions issues currently facing global governance efforts. Nonetheless, attempts to constrain the use of fossil fuels are being undertaken by many governments, even if, in many cases, these are still on a smaller scale than efforts to subsidize the use of fuels and in particular do so by supporting the corporations that explore and extract them (Coady et al. 2019). The importance of thinking about global carbon use is highlighted by the neglect of international transport and the military systems that ostensibly protect this system. Territorial systems of governance, like so many other nationally based environmental efforts, are, on their own, inadequate methods for grappling with climate change.

Further irony lies in the fact that global climate change mitigation efforts involve numerous territorial strategies where forests are used as carbon offsets, supposedly removing carbon emissions from the atmosphere, and generating revenue, mostly for Southern governments. These programs, and the pattern of payments, play out in diverse ways depending on local circumstances. Sometimes the payments and local administration end up effectively being subsidies to plantation agriculture and related short rotation forestry, with dubious carbon sequestration functionality (Lansing 2013). There are contradictory policy priorities in many of these programs where, despite rhetoric suggesting that payments for ecological services can help poor people, analysis of the first decade of these programs showed that frequently the market logics and payment systems provided greater benefits to wealthier people rather than those for whom the systems are ostensibly designed (McAfee 2012).

In other cases, the United Nations REDD+ and other programs involve forest and land management practices governed by international standards but administered in local spatial schemes which, according to critics, fail to deal with practicalities on the ground in specific places despite the invocation of categories such as "landscape" to structure forestry administrative practices. These generate whole new territorial arrangements, enclosing and sometimes excluding local populations in new bordering practices that apply global rules to local circumstances in ways that seem to reinvent plantation practices from earlier colonial periods. Focusing on the detailed operation of power in specific locations, and the territorial structures of particular places, is key to understanding how payments for ecological services actually work; literally on the ground (McCall 2016). In particular, this requires identifying local people and forest dwellers as key to practices that might optimize forest uses and carbon sequestration, a matter of paying close attention to local political economy.

The complexities of these processes, and the contradictions implicit in trying to use territorial strategies to specify carbon offsets with sequestration functions, are highlighted in the 2017 controversies over diamond mines and deforestation in Brazil. The Surui Carbon Forest Project was established as a certified carbon sink project allowed to sell offsets as part of REDD+. But illegal logging and the intrusion of a diamond mine highlight the difficulties of fixing carbon in such territorial arrangements given the very limited enforcement arrangements that are in place to ensure the forest remains in an ecological state to sink the necessary quantities of carbon (Maisonnave 2017). Ironically, given the importance placed on dealing with climate change by the Catholic Church in Rome, and in particular in its high-profile encyclical leading up to the Paris climate agreement (Pope Francis 2015), the local church opposed the forest scheme given that it explicitly extended the commodification of nature. This may, in turn, have facilitated the illegal mining related to forest destruction.

CLIMATE ADAPTATION

Climate adaptation strategies also involve territorial and bordering practices, only most obviously the construction of coastal protection measures and the re-creation, or novel planting, of mangroves in spaces that local farming and fishing communities have used to gain a livelihood (Taylor 2014). As with mitigation strategies, land use planning for adaptation requires numerous ordinances and restrictions that generate very local geographies invoked in the name of global sustainability. These are now complemented by international operations in property markets and global corporations, and many states have moved to purchase agricultural land abroad as long-term food supply sources to deal with anticipated environmental changes at home. These land grabbing exercises extend global commercial arrangements into rural areas, mostly in the global south, accelerating the conversion of land into agricultural extraction zones, and among other things fueling movements of landless people to challenge state-imposed property arrangements.

These are in part understood as development projects by state elites interested in enlarging the commercial sectors of their states and frequently in terms of personal enrichment simultaneously. Many of these processes are extensions of the above discussion of the continued operation of the great transformation (Polanyi 1957), which has accelerated in recent decades as a result of the expansion of the global economy. Coupled with state vision in Scott's (1998) terms whereby engineering, social, and otherwise are presented as the key to remaking things and securing the state in the process, the development process has now often merged with climate adaptation. Funding is now frequently labelled in just these terms. It is also important to note that states and corporations worried about food and energy supplies in particular have been diversifying land holdings offshore and experimenting with the production of biofuels, which are at least ostensibly less carbon dioxide-producing than fossil fuels (Smith and Ruysenaar 2016).

In Sovacool and Linner's (2016) formulation, climate adaptation has numerous deleterious consequences as a result of four key features in how, at least until recently, it has been conceptualized. They summarize adaptation measures in terms of four explicitly spatial strategies, those of enclosure, exclusion, encroachment, and entrenchment. These operate both as state efforts to anticipate change and respond to disasters, such as floods and storms, which are becoming more frequent and severe in many places and making growing populations in vulnerable places more insecure in the process. Enclosure involves the processes whereby the economy privatizes or incorporates new modes of activity into commercial arrangements. Exclusion is the related process whereby local stakeholders are displaced in adaptation processes and their interests and concerns bypassed or ignored in the development process by international formulations of policy options and local state initiatives driven by development agendas. Encroachment may result as adaptation efforts degrade or damage environments that provided food and resources for local inhabitants. Many of these factors become "entrenched" when economic processes accentuate the differences between those who are excluded or whose environments are encroached upon.

Those who are "expelled" (Sassen 2014) in these processes may resist in numerous ways and, insofar as they are treated as a threat to state efforts or, when dealing with climate issues become the object of state, military, and corporate repression, their vulnerability is accentuated (Buxton and Hayes 2016). Resistance of these sorts is counterproductive to climate policies in that it makes their implementation more difficult, a matter of backdraft effects due to ill-considered local circumstances (Dabelko et al. 2013; Risi 2017). These processes frequently preclude marginal peoples from acting in ways that would make them more resilient; modernization is about displacement, the imposition of new territorial and property borders in landscapes that are being transformed and in the processes of state policy action, frequently impede geographical flexibilities that are needed for social and ecological resilience—all of which frequently follows from assumptions of climate as a separate system from social life. Urban property markets likewise frequently work to further marginalize poor people in the aftermath of storms, floods, and wind damage, accentuating economic inequalities just as vulnerabilities are increasing due to climate change induced weather extremes (Graham 2016).

What is abundantly clear is that climate change requires adapting economic systems to deal with Anthropocene conditions where the global economy in the form of the rapidly expanding technosphere is disrupting Earth System processes. Conventional thinking has yet to encompass the social transformations necessary, not least because the modern distinctions between nature and culture, economy and environment persist despite the implications of Earth System insights. "Far from a clear boundary line between society and climate, in which the former could adapt to the latter, we are faced with complex assemblages of social energies, biological processes and meteorological forces that together produce the world around us" (Taylor 2014: 190). The Anthropocene formulation makes it clear that this is the context in which we have to think about what futures we are making in particular places, and whether it is possible to much more radically rethink economies if the mutual imbrication of society and climate, as well as other natural phenomena, are taken seriously.

Ian Gough (2017) suggests that three key things are necessary in these circumstances: first, a transition to modes of green growth which drastically constrain the use of carbon fuels; second, to a recomposition of consumption to reduce economic luxuries in favour of basic needs; and, third, by the construction of economic modes that flourish without growth. Such transitions are only beginning to be considered as a matter of serious political possibility. Doing so will require rethinking jurisdictions quite fundamentally and, in the process, the questions of what (and more importantly, who) can cross which demarcations in various circumstances will need new answers.

There are signs these innovations are starting to be considered seriously in various places, in particular in relation to climate change where cities, municipalities, and other non-state entities are grappling with adaptation strategies (Bernstein and Hoffman 2018). In part this has been forced on cities given their infrastructure vulnerabilities to storms, rising sea levels and heat waves and the failure of national governments in many places to effectively tackle greenhouse gas emissions. Global climate change is forcing very specific local innovations. However, if the results of local actions simply cause "dirty" industries to migrate to jurisdictions with lax pollution controls, the problems are simply relocated rather than solved. Assigning emissions to states that host production facilities, rather than to those where the consumption actually occurs, complicates this matter further; the geographical designation of emissions sources to particular states is key to the Paris Agreement process, but reducing the consumption of items produced in other jurisdictions is key to constraining overall emissions; once again global managerial efforts are complicated by jurisdictional counting rules, ones built into the international climate science knowledge used in climate negotiations (O'Lear 2016).

MIGRATION AS ADAPTATION

All of these difficulties are accentuated by current patterns of distress and forced migration. The migration crisis of our times is frequently attributed to matters of climate-induced movements by people forced by flood or drought to leave the land in search of sustenance and opportunity elsewhere (Baldwin and Bettini 2017). In particular places, climate change is part of this process but how the social dramas leading to migration happen is set in the context of the global political economy of agricultural property, water resource allocations, and other regulations shaping which commodities cross specific national frontiers. That said, much of the migration currently under way is internal to particular states, and is part of the rapid urbanization processes transforming many societies (Rigaud et al. 2018). Even if alarmist predictions of millions of climate refugees play out in coming decades these numbers are likely to be but a small portion of the populations in motion as a result of other social and economic processes (Koubi et al. 2016).

While climate change gets much of the blame, especially in 2017 in the case of the ongoing humanitarian difficulties and military conflicts in the region of Lake Chad (Carius 2017), other rural transformations and the building of dams and infrastructure in particular, frequently as part of development projects, and now climate adaptation policies in the face of unreliable rainfall patterns too, to supply water and electricity to growing urban areas, are a key part of the processes whereby farmers become migrants. In 2017 considerable media coverage of the rapid drying up of Lake Chad and the displacement of local populations as a humanitarian disaster, but at least some of the transformation of the lake may be due to dams built to supply urban development upstream on rivers that used to fill the lake (Pearce 2017). Additionally, in the case of Lake Chad, it seems that military attempts to deal with the violence in the region by closing borders has by preventing trading and economic adaptation, made matters worse. Coping mechanisms that involved migration and trading were stymied by territorial strategies of security provision (Vivekananda et al. 2019). As with other high-profile lake disappearances, like the case of Lake Urmia in Iran (Dalby and Moussavi 2017), blaming climate change is a convenient political distraction from the practical matters of rural transformation set afoot by the consequences of urbanization and the spread of commercial agricultural arrangements into ecosystems ill-suited for industrial scale production.

The growth of the technosphere involves rapid urbanization that, in tandem with rural transformation, continues apace in many parts of the world. These urbanization processes mostly happen within existing state boundaries, but when a small portion of migrants start to cross international frontiers, and in the aftermath of 9/11 are treated as a security threat by states increasingly looking to border controls as a security measure, then this too becomes part of the global discussion of environmental governance. Care needs to be taken not to impute simple causal mechanisms linking climate change and migration but, clearly, in the case of sea level rise and the inundation of coastal regions—especially in the case of the Atoll island states of the world facing territorial elimination (Storlazzi et al. 2018)—climate change is a key part of the process.

The U.S. military is concerned about how climate change might be related to instabilities, and in particular how peripheral dangers related to climate change might be catalysts for conflict (CNA 2014). This geopolitics of peripheral disruption causing metropolitan insecurity once again maps danger as originating outside the global economy, in the process obscuring the key causal mechanisms. The urgency of dealing with such matters in climate change negotiations is stymied by the refusal on the part of Western governments to accept historical responsibility for causing climate change. It underlies the refusal on the part of Western states to agree to comprehensive measures of "loss and damage" in climate change negotiations, notably at the November 2017 Conference of the Parties to the UNFCCC in Bonn.

The ironies of security understood in terms of geographical fixity, of territorial boundaries as the prime mode of governance by many states, is palpable in the discussion of contemporary migration. Attempts to constrain refugees and limit migration of poor people who try to adapt to the globalized economic forces that frequently render them vulnerable, by quite literally following the money, highlight the limits and the implications of territorial modes of governance in a global system. When migrants and refugees are rendered a security threat, as they are in the fortress models of environmental insecurity (White 2014), borders end up being very violent places that make those who seek succor and shelter even more insecure, all ironically in the name of security (Jones 2016). The territorial state system is being secured, but vulnerable people obviously aren't.

NON-STATIONARITY: THE NEW NORMAL

It is now also clear that traditional planning assumptions of a relatively stable environmental backdrop to human affairs are no longer tenable as the premise for sustainability thinking. Non-stationarity is the new norm and, hence, attempts to think about sustainability must recognize that policies and practices now have to be much more flexible (Milly et al. 2008). Part of this involves local perspectives on larger changing geographical patterns of climate (Jones 2018). The Hadley cell seems to be expanding, with it the boundaries of the tropics are shifting both north and south. Such fluctuations may be seen as droughts in places where dry conditions impose themselves further from the equator than has been the case in the recent past. Care has to be taken in attributing all this variation to human induced change, as natural variation is part of the processes, but clearly human influence is part of what is driving this (Statten et al. 2018). As part of climate change this movement of climate zones requires adaptation in many places where traditional assumptions concerning planting cycles, rainfall frequency, and appropriate agricultural practices no longer apply. In North America, climate changes are clearly evident in the eastward migration of the climate boundary between the western drier part of the United States and the more humid eastern parts. Traditionally the division was close to the 100th Meridian, but this has moved eastward in the last few decades, with obvious implications for agricultural production in the Mid-West in particular (Seager et al. 2018).

These increasingly large fluctuations in environmental conditions mean the past is an increasingly inadequate guide to the conditions human societies will face in coming decades, especially in transition zones from one climatic region to another. In terms of water resources in particular, planning on the basis of past patterns of rainfall, snowfall accumulations and melting schedules, is no longer an accurate guide for current and future circumstances. It is no longer possible to make accurate predictions of the frequencies of extremes, so traditional calculations of such things as one in one hundred-year floods, a widely used benchmark for infrastructure planning, are no longer useful in the face of an increasingly dynamic global ecosystem adapting to the growth of the technosphere. This makes international agreements about water resources management both more important and more difficult (Dinar and Dinar 2017).

In geographical terms, this means species are moving across territorial boundaries as they struggle to adapt to both warmer and less predictable conditions. Human actions are also moving species, but these actions are now partly an adaptation to climate change and mitigation policies too, even if they are not widely understood in these terms at least so far. This new situation requires thinking about how to prepare for continuously changing circumstances given the transformations already in motion (Kareiva and Fuller 2016). But in terms of sustainability, the necessity of dealing with both ecosystem mobility and non-stationarity, where historical records are no longer a useful indication of the likely range of future weather events, simultaneously requires innovations that get beyond traditional notions of conservation in situ, or more recent assumptions that resilience is simply a matter of better preparing to bounce back and reconstruct after inevitable disruptions (Grove 2018).

These processes are adding complications to the geographical assumptions underpinning strategies of sustainable development and attempts at environmental governance; in Conca's (2015) terms the limits of the "law and development" framework of global environmental governance are being highlighted. This adds urgency to matters of global environmental governance, in particular to cross border agreements on shared resource management. In the case of water in particular, it has long been clear that international agreements need to be "climate proofed" to deal with non-stationarity conditions (Cooley and Gleick 2011). In terms of other resource management issues, where agreements are premised on stationarity assumptions, they need an update to specify in advance which measures and procedures will be invoked when the consequences of non-stationarity become apparent. Failure to do so in advance and to clearly anticipate disruptions is to court trouble and conflict that will make adaptations ever more difficult.

Recent discussions of the Anthropocene have emphasized the scale and speed of contemporary transformations (Gaffney and Steffen 2017). In Clive Hamilton's (2016) terms, the significance of the Anthropocene is that we are living in a period where longstanding relationships of our species to the Earth have been ruptured. Humanity has become a force influencing the operation of the Earth System as a totality, not merely changing individual ecosystems. As such, it is important to understand human vulnerabilities and the need to tackle them both in terms of the direct impacts of local disruptions to infrastructure in particular, as well as the larger-scale changes due most obviously to climate alterations and the growth in more severe weather events and less predictable climate patterns.

Attempting to manage these by further bordering practices may be efficacious in some circumstances, but the larger transformations suggest the need for much further thinking about how else human systems can be governed and much more specificity as to what territorial strategies can and can't accomplish once globalization is understood as simultaneously an economic process and a geophysical one that is transforming the context for human societies. There is no indication, even if the Paris Agreement commitments are accomplished in coming decades, that Earth System transformation will stop. At best, rapid decarbonization of economic activity will slow things down allowing adaptation to be done more easily. This requires a notion of security that focuses on ecological flourishing and literally caring for the Earth, a dramatically different conceptualization than those in vogue through the period of the cold war in the capitals of the great powers (Harrington and Sheering 2017).

CHANGING GEOGRAPHIES

Traditional notions of environmental protection in stable local natural contexts now have to give way to policy measures focusing on what is being produced in the global economy and, in the process, which landscapes are being re-bordered to make what kind of future global environment—hence the crucial importance of sustainable development policies that supposedly act to constrain the downward global ecological spiral but which have, at least so far, mostly failed to do so despite the growing urgency to confront multiple interconnected problems of climate change, health, economy, growth, and resource access (Holden et al. 2018). Discussions of adaptation as a global need, and of funding for investments understood as a global effort rather than financial transfers from some Northern states to specific Southern ones, are only beginning (Benzie et al. 2018). A larger framework in terms of thinking about policies for peaceful transition, a "new climate for peace" in the title of a high-profile G7 policy report (Rüttinger et al. 2015), is clearly needed as climate change accelerates.

Insofar as sustainability is a factor in long-term thinking, and the Sustainable Development Goals do institutionalize this theme, the scale of the great acceleration's disruptions of the Earth System and, crucially, the recognition of non-stationarity as the new normal make it clear that attempting to think about transformation, to use the language of the Sustainable Development Goals, requires a recognition that continuous change is simply the human condition in shaping the next phase of the Anthropocene. Non-stationarity is here; effective thinking and planning have to start from this premise. This has implications in particular for Dahbour's (2017) discussion of the relationship between ecological functions and territorial rights. If, as he argues, the right to territory now implies that the area is used wisely, a matter of plenitude in his terms, and such things as food sovereignty are lauded as appropriate in the face of global environmental disruptions, then thinking through how local production changes as climate conditions vary has to be part of the discussion.

Whether local economic considerations triumph over the expansion of commercial export agricultural systems or whether the prerogatives of climate adaptation through distant production for parts of the global technosphere displace local priorities will shape specific places. Do distant consumers have rights to food grown in other jurisdictions if their own states can't feed them? This is a matter of food security rather than food sovereignty. Given the complexities of rural political economies and the expansion of global property markets, questions of food sovereignty loom in numerous places. Is this a matter, as Dahbour (2017) suggests, following Cara Nine's (2012) formulation, that might be considered "benevolent colonization"? But as the analysis above suggests, further enclosures and exclusions, albeit tempting strategies on the part of state planners in many circumstances, especially if they can be rationalized as climate adaptation measures, frequently make matters worse because they don't take the insights of novel ecological thinking or the rights of traditional peoples into consideration.

The conflicts between these may indeed become a matter in need of environmental peacemaking as climate change adaptation ramps up in coming decades. Linking non-stationarity to cross border changes is a key innovation that now has to be added explicitly into the conceptual discussion of environmental governance. Related to that is the point that much of climate adaptation is about humans moving things and reconstructing landscapes, but the politics of this requires taking the unanticipated consequences of these policies into consideration in planning adaptation. Conca (2015) has suggested that peace-building efforts, the extension of human rights to include rights to a functional environment, and establishing principles of state responsibilities to provide environmental protection are a way forward for the UN system in tackling sustainability. Infusing the law and development framework with rights and peace practice might help in countering the worst aspects of the fortress mentality in particular, and in general help further a grand strategy for global governance. In doing so, such initiatives will be all the more effective if they include measures of active cooperation across the numerous boundaries that have effectively stymied previous efforts to facilitate sustainability.

But to do all this requires some fundamental rethinking of the energy systems that power the global economy. Fossil fuels have been key to modernity, making possible the contemporary urban system, consumer culture, and the military strategies that secure its functioning. As chapter 6 makes clear, the assumptions that such security strategies will make possible sustainable futures for most of humanity are highly dubious. Mostly, security has been about protecting the system of carboniferous capitalism, which has produced both the extraordinary expansion of the technosphere and simultaneously the problem of rapidly accelerating climate change. These contradictions, and what they mean for security, are the subject of the next two chapters, 6 on the global economy and 7 on how disasters are now interconnected with the politics of security, and crucially which processes are deemed most important to maintain in the face of dramatic global change.

CHAPTER 6

SECURING THE GLOBAL ECONOMY

> The new energy is rewiring the ecological circuitry of the Earth. It has scrambled ecosystems and is replacing biodiversity with a pyrodiversity – a bestiary of machines run directly or indirectly from industrial combustion. The velocity and volume of change is so great that observers have begun to speak of a new geologic epoch, a successor to the Pleistocene, that they call the Anthropocene. It might equally be called the Pyrocene. The Earth is shedding its cycle of ice ages for a fire age. (Stephen Pyne 2015)

LINKING CLIMATE TO SECURITY

Climate change has gradually become a major factor in discussions of international politics and, as the urgency of the situation and the serious consequences of failing to deal with it become more obvious, a matter of discussion in terms of security (Webersik 2010). While the war on terror focused much security thinking on terrorism and combat in South West Asia immediately after 9/11, gradually concerns about sustainability and climate reasserted themselves in policy making circles. British security planners have long been concerned with the impacts of climate change (Foresight 2011); the Blair and Brown governments initiated both substantial diplomatic efforts on the issue and attempts to change the domestic British energy supply system. German evaluations of security risks of climate change were very comprehensive (German Advisory Council 2008), and linked to industrial strategies to boost the use of solar and wind electricity generation. In the United States, think tank writers warned of the need to tackle climate urgently (CNA 2007; Campbell et al. 2007), the Pentagon began seriously planning to deal with coming disruptions before the Obama administration actively promoted a "green" economy as part of economic stimulus measures to deal with the great recession.

In Berlin, on 19 June 2013, President Obama chose the Brandenburg Gate, the symbolic site of President Kennedy's famous Cold War speech in the early 1960s, to argue that while nuclear weapons were still an important issue, the Cold War concerns with nuclear war and clashing ideological systems were now of diminishing significance in the face of the looming dangers of climate change. As the president put it:

> With a global middle class consuming more energy every day, this must now be an effort of all nations, not just some. For the grim alternative affects all nations—more severe storms, more famine and floods, new waves of refugees, coastlines that vanish, oceans that rise. This is the future we must avert. This is the global threat of our time.

Even discounting the rhetorical flourishes that were President Obama's trademark, this is a very blunt statement of the new security context, albeit a contextualization that his successor frequently dismissed.

However this is not security understood in *national* terms, a matter of defending territorial integrity by traditional military means, bloc politics, or military alliances. Instead, climate change is presented as an emerging challenge requiring a very considerable degree of international cooperation, primarily as a matter of diplomacy and negotiation to deal with transboundary challenges in coming decades (Werrel and Femia 2017). Although, that said, this formulation frequently invokes the very old and persistent geopolitical imaginary of peripheral places threatening metropolitan security (Dalby 2013b). Climate change is thus part of the new security agenda, one that tries to tackle global problems, economic ones prominent among them, without succumbing to the dangers of national protectionist measures. But this geography of nation states and protectionism is precisely the geographical understanding frequently invoked by the

Trump administration in its first two years in office, reiterating security precisely in terms of national priorities and territorial controls. As noted in chapter 1, international politics is understood as an arena of contest, not some kind of community where there might be common interests. The contrast between these geopolitical contextualizations is stark, and the policy priorities that arise from them are very different (Dalby 2018).

Moreover, given the transboundary nature of environmental change and its causes, solutions require efforts in many places, by many actors, in a loosely coordinated series of economic and policy changes. As Obama stated at the Brandenburg Gate: "For the sake of future generations, our generation must move toward a global compact to confront a changing climate before it is too late. That is our job. That is our task. We have to get to work." But precisely how to tackle the issue is not clear; nearly three decades of international negotiations about constraining greenhouse gas emissions have not slowed their overall rate of growth. Indeed, the urgency of tackling the issue, and hence its rhetorical elevation to a matter of security, is precisely because attempts to tackle the matter as an environmental issue, as a problem of pollution to be tackled via emissions limits, have not been effective. This formulation of global security was explicitly rejected by the Trump administration when it entered office. The president proudly boasted in his State of the Union speech early in 2019 that the United States was once again the largest producer of petroleum and an exporting state too.

This chapter links security to political economy to understand the rise of climate change as a threat, the limitations of security as a framework for tackling it, and how new approaches might be formulated. This exploration begins by identifying the material context that has both given rise to concerns about climate change and set the parameters for security: the rise of carboniferous capitalism and the metabolic rift initiated by the industrial revolution. It then emphasizes that security has long been about providing conditions that ensure the social order of capitalism. Responses to earlier environmental difficulties caused by the rapid expansion of industrial capitalist production have frequently taken the form of technological innovations, a strategy of "ecological modernization" coupled with market measures to reduce emissions of various pollutants. Both strategies now figure prominently in attempts to control climate change. These are also linked to the larger themes in neoliberal modes of governance concerned with privatization and the constitution of resilient consumer subjects. However, market mechanisms have not reduced the overall use of fossil fuels, notwithstanding successes in particular places.

This raises the question, with which this chapter ends, as to whether more extreme attempts to invoke liberal market-based modes of governance might work to reduce greenhouse gases in the atmosphere. If not, a more fundamental rethink of security is necessary given the increasing urgency with which climate change needs to be tackled if the biosphere is going to remain in conditions similar to those that have so far existed through human history. Security in these terms is now about rapidly reshaping the future of the global economy.

ENVIRONMENT AND ECONOMY

As previous chapters showed, the roots of contemporary climate change lie in the rapid growth of capitalism since the late eighteenth century, powered first by steam engines and subsequently many other coal and petroleum-using technologies (Malm 2016). The growth in the use of fossil fuels, first coal and subsequently oil and gas, and the transformation of political economy and human geography that resulted, set in motion what Karl Marx called a metabolic rift (Foster 2009). Industrial urbanization disconnected human life from natural cycles and substituted fossil, or ancient organic sources of life, as a fuel source in place of contemporaneous ecological energy sources like wind, water, and timber. Much of the new fuel came initially from rocks formed in the geological period known appropriately as the carboniferous. Lewis Mumford (1934) thus described the industrial revolution as "carboniferous capitalism." With that came the disconnect from nature, celebrated as one of the great triumphs of modernity, but with numerous de-spoliation and pollution problems, where the natural recycling of wastes was overwhelmed by the scale of industrial production and the concentration of human activities in new cities. Climate change is a consequence of this process, now operating globally.

American power in the twentieth century was, to a very substantial extent, built on the basis of a petroleum-powered economy (Yergin 1991). The key technology that boosted U.S. economic growth was the automobile, which used gasoline in large amounts and accelerated the suburbanization of North America. The expansion of suburban living as the preferred notion of the good life involved consumption patterns dependent on extensive use of energy and resources increasingly sourced from all over the globe. This locked American society into a pattern of extensive fossil-fueled energy consumption (McNeill 2000). Industrial production systems in turn greatly extended the scope of the appropriation of resources and the disruption of rural ecologies as capitalism went global (Dauvergne 2008).

The evolution of carboniferous capitalism has generated social, economic, and political developments impinging directly on how security is understood and pursued. The social and political transformations accompanying the rise of modern states involved numerous struggles to extend the material benefits made possible by the new productive technologies. Timothy Mitchell (2011) argues that some of the key struggles to expand the provisions of the welfare state and extend the rights of citizens related directly to the fuel supplies that powered carboniferous capitalism. The alliances between coal miners and transport workers were especially important in forming the industrial unions and working class movements that improved working conditions and extended benefits to wider segments of society in the late nineteenth and early twentieth centuries. Their threat to paralyze the supply of coal, the substance that kept everything moving, was effective, in part, because of the large numbers of workers at the coal face and the relatively local use of coal.

Petroleum, on the other hand, is much more a matter of technical expertise. Its production is capital-intensive rather than labour-intensive; it needs much more processing before use, but its ease of transport gave it flexibility on international markets that coal lacked (Yergin 2011). The Marshall Plan to rebuild Europe after the Second World War was tied into attempts to change the fuel mix from coal to oil, much of which came from the Middle East. Attempts by American companies, and the American government, to control key parts of those supplies were an important part of this geopolitics, but the rivalries between companies, and the attempts to involve governments in support of their various efforts, mattered too. Notwithstanding periodic petroleum supply crises, Mitchell (2011) crucially reminds readers that companies were frequently more concerned to keep supplies off the market, and keep prices up, than they were to bring resources on-stream quickly.

Geopolitics, in the sense of interstate rivalry, thus explains only part of the global petroleum system and attendant security dynamics. Frequent arguments that the U.S. is involved militarily in the Middle East to ensure that supplies of petroleum reach global or specifically

American markets are oversimplifications of a much more complex political economy of oil (Dalby and Paterson 2009). Likewise, restrictions in petroleum supplies, as in the case of the OPEC embargo in the aftermath of the 1973 war between Israel, and Syria and Egypt, have frequently triggered large exploration booms and a subsequent diversification of sources of supply. Energy security is frequently defined in terms of guaranteed supplies to run national economies, but commercial arrangements, pricing, and rivalries between competing energy companies greatly complicate the policy picture.

While petroleum is important, it is also the case that it is little-used for electricity generation; coal is still a major energy source for power stations. This point was emphasized in the 1980s when in Britain, Margaret Thatcher set out to break the power of the coal mine unions, and simultaneously oversaw the rise of natural gas in the fuel mix of the United Kingdom. Supplies of natural gas came on stream in the 1980s partly as a result of the North Sea exploration accelerated by the 1973 OPEC embargo. Given the importance of electricity to all modern modes of living, and not just capitalist production, keeping the lights on is now an essential function of states. Most states have some sort of national grid system. Access to reliable supplies of electricity is seen now as the mark of an effective state; electricity is, in present terminology, an essential service. Modern citizenship is now enmeshed with the notion of a consumption-based lifestyle and states' legitimacy is related to their provision or at least the convincing promise that it will soon be forthcoming. This lifestyle, and the mode of production that enables it, is now what has to be secured, both from external threats to prosperity or disruption of the supplies that make it possible, and internal threats to the order that makes prosperity work for at least a substantial part of the populace—a point developed more fully in the next section.

Modern humanity's proclivities for turning rocks back into air, while simultaneously changing the vegetation and ecological mix of much of the planet's terrestrial surface in search of fibre and food for urban industrial life, have generated ecological transformations on a global scale. The global economy is changing the geopolitical situation, both because new technologies are changing how militaries function and economic rivalries play out, and because larger-scale processes of environmental change and urbanization are literally changing the material context. In turn, the reconfiguration of the global economy in coming decades will shape the biosphere profoundly, only most obviously by determining how much carbon dioxide and methane is added to the atmosphere and at what rate.

The conventional assumption in security thinking—that climate change will have geopolitical effects—needs to be supplemented by a clear understanding that geopolitical decisions and the modes of political economy built in the immediate future will also determine what kind of climate, and planetary circumstances, future generations of humanity face (Dalby 2014a). This crucial point links security studies and international political economy directly. The rapid transformation of the biosphere is changing the context of international politics, just as the expansion of the global economy is generating new social insecurities in many places. Whether security can be rethought to take this dynamic seriously, and to recognize that a functional biosphere is more important than the existing social order of capitalism, is the key question for Anthropocene politics (Dryzek and Pickering 2019).

SECURITY

Much recent literature explains the changing scope of security as reflecting the emergence of new threats that are often simultaneously identified as by-products of and threats to globalization. Arguably, however, security has *always* been about mitigating the contradictions of capitalism and providing the conditions necessary for its reproduction. Critical scholarly work has focused on acts of securitization: how threats are invoked and dangers used to mobilize states to act in particular ways (Fierke 2007). In Buzan, Wæver, and de Wilde's (1998) terms, securitization involves the invocation of dangers and threats to a referent object that is frequently a particular state, and the subsequent mobilization of resources to counter that threat. This may require the suspension of normal politics and the invocation of emergency measures, as in wartime or in the face of a major disaster. This formulation, close in places to Carl Schmitt's (1985) discussions of sovereignty as the ability to suspend the law and declare a state of exception, emphasizes both the performance of security by political actors and the ability to impose extreme measures (Williams 2003).

The difficulty with such discursive formulations of the logic of security is that they frequently occlude the persistent function of security in maintaining the legal, political, and economic arrangements of modern societies (Bell 2011), and thus overstate and misapprehend its recent expansion. Security was understood in the eighteenth and early nineteenth centuries, just as the metabolic rift began to change human circumstances, in terms of providing the legal assurance of private property, the essential prerequisite for the rapid expansion of capitalism (Neocleous 2008). This was crucial to the rise of modern capitalist states, and subsequently of globalization. Thus, while security is obviously about mobilizing to face both immediate emergencies and long-term threats, its more pervasive function has long been to perpetuate the existing social order.

In the realm of international relations, the term security typically relates to defending particular states in the face of competition from other states and, since the dawn of the nuclear age, to arranging matters internationally so that global warfare does not bring civilization to an end altogether. However, this narrow view fails to recognize the longstanding relationship between capitalism and security. American national security, with its global military reach, has long underpinned the current geopolitical order of liberal-capitalist states (Latham 1997), even while ostensibly providing a defence against a supposedly expansionist Soviet Union during the Cold War. Thereafter, in the Clinton administration's foreign policy, this became about the enlargement of democracy and the related spread of economic freedom. Despite differences in emphasis, the subsequent Bush administration maintained that imperial impulse to extend the remit of American-led globalization (Smith 2005). In the Bush doctrine after 9/11, economic freedom had to be spread, by force if necessary, to do nothing less than eliminate tyranny on Earth, as the official White House documents put it (Dalby 2009b). As security was extended widely in the logics of the global war on terror, it has become an explicit mode of governance in many places.

Security studies in its Cold War manifestation—the focus on nuclear weapons and strategies, and the overarching superpower rivalry—frequently failed to consider in much detail the larger social functions of security in domestic terms beyond the concern with subversion, and the internal communist menace to capitalist social arrangements. Maintaining the American-led social order was simply taken for granted in much of the literature, something that required permanent military readiness and a willingness to use force in many places around the world (Bacevich 2010). However, the contradictions of nuclear weapons and "Mutually Assured Destruction" very clearly suggested that such threats of massive violence rendered everyone insecure, generating numerous attempts to redefine security. Much of these were summarized in the very influential United Nations Development Report of 1994, which introduced the notion of "human security," covering numerous things including environment, economy, politics, and community. This formulation recognized that many threats to human security are generated unintentionally by the actions of millions of people undertaking routine activities, not by the malicious designs or aggressive intentions of one state's rulers towards other states, which had been the traditional Cold War focus of national security (Kaldor 2007).

As security expanded beyond military threats, so too the agencies responsible for providing security to themselves and others were extended; security became ubiquitous as a statement of desire and a mode of ruling numerous things, agencies, and peoples (Rothschild 1995). Indeed, given the proliferation of security discourse in the last couple of decades, it has become a prime mode of governance. Linked to the logics of neoliberalism and the presumed efficacy of the market, security has extended its scope to ensure social relations consistent with the further expansion of capitalism into such things as carbon markets, and the production of resilient subjects able to deal with numerous new threats in a way that will not undermine social order (Chandler 2013). Thus, security is increasingly understood—though still only implicitly—as being challenged by the contradictions of capitalist development, which require multidimensional mitigation.

The difficulty with claiming that this formulation of security is new is that many states have long provided at least basic welfare under the rubric of social security. Pension schemes, some health services, unemployment insurance, and public education have been part of welfare state provisions for generations in the world's metropolitan economies. These initiatives were in part necessary to provide for the survival of people in new urban settings without the social safety net of traditional communities, and partly won by working class struggles, with coal miners, key workers in carboniferous capitalism, central to many of these (Mitchell 2011). This helped legitimize modern states and justify their taxation systems. In this sense, states have long provided for key aspects of human security, at least within their borders, by mitigating some of the social, economic, and political disruptions and inequities caused by the rapid expansion of industrial capitalism.

The historical extension of such measures to many states is part of the argument underpinning the principle of "responsibility to protect," which insists that their provision is part of the necessary functions of states (International Commission on Intervention and State Sovereignty 2001). Ironically, this has occurred just as financial globalization has reduced the abilities of many smaller states in particular to raise taxes and deal with related policy issues, and made states more vulnerable to the vagaries of the global economy, emphasizing that the vulnerabilities against which states supposedly provide security are increasingly artificial (Stiglitz and Kaldor 2013). Similar dynamics are in play in terms of environmental matters, as the emerging discussion of climate security illustrates. Paradoxically, extending human security as currently formulated in terms of modern modes of economy, of biohumanity in Dillon and Reid's (2009) terms, involves ecological transformation to provide ever-greater supplies of commodities and energy to support human life and the commodity systems that make it possible. This exacerbates insecurities stemming from environmental change, the processes that Grove (2019) simply calls "savage ecology."

ECOLOGICAL MODERNIZATION

Just as security has been shaped by the contradictions and requirements of carboniferous capitalism, so too have the tools used to pursue security, which often take a market-based form, diverging from the emergency measures anticipated by securitization theory. They also, therefore, shape the limited efficacy of our response to date. Complicated infrastructures and global resource flows now provide the essentials for human living, and they are vulnerable to both weather events and economic disruptions. Ensuring resilience in the face of such challenges is increasingly a function of modern states, and consequently economic policy and disaster preparedness are now part of security considerations. They are also frequently contracted out, enabling capitalism to make profits out of dealing with its own contradictions; the financialization of disaster preparedness continues apace (Grove 2012; Klein 2017).

Current neoliberal modes of environmental security governance are partly the consequence of prior struggles to deal with environmental de-spoliation. The massive industrialization that produced both the automobiles and the rest of the consumer goods, that made the American lifestyle many societies sought to emulate, also produced toxic wastes and atmospheric pollution on a huge scale. This threatened to undermine the benefits of all the new commodities that shaped consumer lifestyles. The subsequent rise of the environmental movement in the 1960s, as a reaction to these contradictions in the developed world, resulted in numerous pollution prevention laws in many states to accommodate political demands to deal with ecological hazards.

Capitalist industrialists responded to these regulations with sophisticated technical fixes. These increasingly portrayed pollution as inefficiency and promised clean technologies as the solution in a series of practices frequently now understood as ecological modernization (Christoff 1996). Systems where externalities were priced and constrained, including in the case of acid rain emissions in the U.S., added market mechanisms to the regulatory agenda, providing financial incentives for corporations to rapidly innovate and reduce pollution. Cap-and-trade systems on sulphur emissions to reduce acid rain and technological substitutions to remove dangerous chlorofluorocarbons from the atmosphere produced more business as usual. More recently, the conversion of some coal-powered electricity generating stations to use natural gas is a form of ecological modernization based on cleaner technologies. Gas is more efficient and cleaner burning than coal; but it still produces carbon dioxide in huge, albeit lesser, amounts.

The logic of such thinking is that, if the market incentives are correctly constructed, economic efficiencies will ensure an optimal outcome and capital accumulation can proceed. Environmental security and the capitalist economy are not necessarily antithetical; configured carefully, so the ecological modernization argument goes, the environment is a key input into economic activity, not an obstacle to it. Such logic has been extended into the sphere of climate in recent decades, suggesting that it is possible to offset the emissions of carbon fuels by sinking them in ecosystems, and using market mechanisms to buy and sell carbon credits, price carbon, and ensure that efficiencies reduce the carbon intensity of economies (Newell and Paterson 2010).

Crucial to the analytical task facing social scientists dealing with such strategies of rule is the recognition that, as Mitchell (2011) argues, while economics abandoned its material concerns in the twentieth century and became a science of money movement, this was premised on an economy fuelled by cheap oil. The material context was simply taken for granted; land, resources, and energy, the previously important "factors of production," in economic analyses were assumed to be available in abundance. The metabolic rift is not entirely forgotten but rather is rendered as amenable to technological fixes, while perpetual material abundance is assumed as the backdrop for ongoing policies of capitalist development.

This focus on the science of money movement is related to the mathematization of banking and the use of sophisticated algorithms, derivatives, and other computational devices to generate profits. But as the financial crisis of 2008 illustrated very clearly, its disconnection from practical material circumstances in the mortgage markets leads to chaos. Climate change presents us with a similar problem: the carbon credits, offsets, and related financial measures tied into clean development mechanisms are premised on promises not to build or produce fossil fuel emitting things, or on assumptions about the ecological services that particular landscapes will fulfill in the future. Carbon credits, ecological offsets like forest plantations, and related financial instruments have thus further extended commodification (Paterson 2014). This system of climate economics also depends on some sort of guarantee that governments will ensure particular forms of land use long into the future, and ironically that the climate changes already in motion will not prevent the survival of precisely such agreed upon ecological systems.

Inter-governmental negotiations that largely treat climate change as a pollution problem, and hence focus on emissions limitations as the solution, and market innovations in updating development, are central to contemporary efforts to govern climate (Harris 2013). Their failures so far to substantially slow the rate of greenhouse gas emissions overall are precisely what is generating discourses of climate security, but it is far from clear how redoubling either existing market or inter-governmental efforts will deal with the rapid transformation of the biosphere—unless, that is, a rapidly increasing price on carbon is imposed across most jurisdictions.

NEOLIBERAL SECURITY

While various market-based mechanisms may have largely failed to produce climate security, they have nonetheless helped accelerate social and institutional changes supportive of capitalist reproduction. Financial globalization has proceeded alongside the erosion of state authority and the marketization of social life. Citizens are increasingly turned into consumers, and the functions of state agencies rearticulated in terms of clients and customers, not democratic political subjects. Neo-liberalism is also a matter of identity politics and interpellations of social status in terms of consumption, but above all a reconstruction of the social into competing entities and a politics of division that repeatedly makes collective responses difficult (Parr 2013). Its ideological formulations emphasizing the rollback of state activities, the supposed efficacy of self-regulation, and the use of market mechanisms are directly connected to the emphasis on the self-governing subject and the economic assumptions of autonomous action to maximize personal welfare.

This emphasis on market rationalities and individual actions has facilitated the privatization of environmental concern. Bottled water has become ubiquitous despite the widespread municipal provision of potable water. In North America, water is frequently more expensive than gasoline, but while fuel prices are politically volatile, fewer objections are heard to the prices for privately purchased drinking water. Air cleaners and numerous commodities for hygiene provision are now standard equipment in commercial and domestic contexts. In Andrew Szasz's (2007) terms, suburbia has constructed an inverted quarantine arrangement where external threatening environments are kept at bay. Security is paramount, but is provided by security companies, and endless devices and modes of monitoring behaviour, everywhere from gated communities to children's playgrounds. Collective action to reduce pollution or prevent environmental degradation has been replaced by people looking to private consumption, rather than acting as political subjects collectively determining the conditions of our lives.

This larger cultural politics of "shopping our way to safety" (Szasz 2007) in North America feeds into both Republican Party opposition to climate change legislation, much less international treaty arrangements, and into the active support for petroleum and coal developments that should provide the energy to allow suburbanites to ride out whatever disruptions may be coming to ecology and economy. The rhetoric of independence plays with the cultural logic of the autonomous consumer encountering a dangerous world. It also feeds further arguments, and state strategies in search of technological innovations that might perpetuate profitable economic strategies while promising to decarbonize the economy (MacNeil 2017). Financial arrangements to facilitate rebuilding commercial and domestic buildings and public infrastructure are to be preferred to preventative action that might curtail the exorbitant lifestyles that have become culturally accepted as a right in the logics of neoliberal subject formation.

The market-based provision of security by both state and private actors has effects in the Global South too, not least due to the frequent presence of carbon offset arrangements there, and the direct and indirect consequences of adaptation strategies by states and corporations attempting to secure access to land and resources in the face of anticipated climate disruptions. These initiatives to make carbon-trading part of the response to climate change were partly because of the emergence of a political coalition that increasingly has vested interests in pushing forward renewable energy, and offset arrangements too (Paterson 2012). Linking environmentalists and the financial industry with innovative international arrangements through the clean development mechanism in particular, where funds are used to buy emissions credits and sink them in development projects in the global South, has also generated a whole new knowledge industry and policy communities dedicated to the provision of technical certification of carbon sink capabilities and related metrics. This is an extension of the market logics applied to governance: capitalism once again shapes the policy instruments developed to deal with its own consequences.

Development projects promoted by Northern states are now being shaped by the priorities of carbon markets and the criteria in the clean development mechanism. Insofar as states in the Global South, where most of the green projects are situated, accept funds under these auspices, their governance is determined by ecological calculations in the global carbon economy, not by indigenous priorities. Such matters have been themes all through the discussions at the annual meetings of parties to the United Nations Framework Convention on Climate Change, although as Nicholas Stern (2009) bluntly suggested at the time of the Copenhagen climate conference, a new "Global Deal" on these matters would need to be much more comprehensive than had so far been the case. A decade later this deal hadn't materialized.

Related to these matters have been unilateral efforts on the parts of states and corporations to make preparations for climate change. In particular, metropolitan states have become interested in ensuring food supplies from abroad by purchasing agricultural land. As noted in chapter 5, such "land grabbing" has been part of the current climate adaptation process, especially in the aftermath of the 2008 financial crisis and the failure of the 2009 Copenhagen climate conference to grapple with the larger political economy issues (Matondi et al. 2011). Persian Gulf states, concerned about rapidly growing populations, and in the case of Saudi Arabia in particular, declining aquifer levels for irrigation, were then starting to purchase land in other parts of the world to ensure access to food supplies in the long run. This too is changing Southern states as elites become more entangled in rural property deals, many of which are coerced or at least violate traditional land tenure arrangements. But such climate adaptation measures may generate political conflict, a case of backdraft where climate adaptation measures are more of a problem than climate change itself (Dabelko et al. 2013).

The extensive use of offsets abroad and the purchase of land, has suggested to Saskia Sassen (2013) that territorial states are effectively being disassembled, with parts of one state territory effectively becoming adjuncts to distant states which use their ecological functions as either offsets or resource supply sources. In many ways such patterns are not new; plantation agriculture has a long history of disrupting local agricultural systems to supply food and fiber for distant markets. The latest "scramble for Africa" (Carmody 2011) is a replication of past colonial patterns, but now run much more by market mechanisms than direct state mercantile actions. Indeed, security has been reprivatized in many parts of the world, and in the process these new extractive systems are tied into the operation of private security companies in a pattern that is reminiscent of at least some earlier colonial periods where corporations ran their own colonies in the absence of formal state control (Abrahamsen and Williams 2011).

State elites are incorporated into these international security and financial arrangements often at the cost of local populations dispossessed by deals over which they have no control. However, once land has been marketized, land price bubbles, speculation, and corruption play a role in how these processes work in particular places (Cotula 2012). This has implications for food supplies locally if land is alienated from local economies, but more generally too if climate change disrupts agricultural production and subsistence systems. Despite all these transformations—and it is difficult to distinguish those that are part of the rapidly expanding global economy—and those that are a direct part of attempts to facilitate climate security, the relentless growth in carbon dioxide in the global atmosphere makes clear that such measures have, at least so far, fallen well short of what is needed to stabilize and, more importantly, begin the process of reducing carbon dioxide levels in the atmosphere.

CLIMATE SECURITY DISCOURSE

Indeed, it was the failure to respond effectively and the increasingly alarming projections from climate sciences concerning what is coming (Anderson and Bows 2011) that made security agencies pay attention to climate matters (CNA 2014; Werrell and Femia 2017). Faced with long-term changes, and required to think about strategic threats to the integrity of states, security planners have been generating technical reports and projection of the risks to states and directly to military infrastructure too over the last few years. The focus on climate has revived the earlier discussions of environmental security (Dalby 2002) and added an immediacy and urgency to addressing these issues (Floyd and Matthew 2013). Once again the arguments were that political instability in the Global South would be caused by environmental change, and fear of hordes of refugees in motion to the North were assumed to present crises that the military might be called upon to address.

Much of this discussion in the U.S. was focused on tropes of national security, asking questions about what climate change would do to American interests and how the American military would be called on to act (Chalecki 2013; National Intelligence Council 2016). The danger here is that traditional rhetoric of national security will be invoked to specify poor, marginal, and endangered populations as a threat to stability that requires military interventions to stop migration or deal with local violence deemed a security threat. Insecurity "over there" might spill over boundaries and disrupt trade or threaten regimes unable to handle the influx. Climate migration is thus on the policy agenda (White 2011). It is important to emphasize that there is little serious research that suggests that environmental scarcities will lead to full-scale war, whatever social vulnerabilities might occur and however frequently neo-Malthusian fears are reproduced in media accounts of imminent catastrophe (Theisen, Holtermann, and Buhaug 2012). But large-scale disruptions of the climate system, and simultaneous global financial crises, might indeed cause conflict if states act unilaterally to try to control food supplies or other key factors that disrupt the often tenuous links in the international system (Homer-Dixon et al. 2015).

Dealing with humanitarian crises, especially in the Asia-Pacific theatre, has long been a growing concern for Pentagon planners (Briggs 2012), given the vulnerability of many island states to both rising sea levels and increased typhoon intensity. These events might cause political instabilities that generate conflict too. But as chapter 4 made clear, in the case of many island states their inundation is a problem that needs urgent attention, and migration is going to continue to be necessary; this is an existential threat to island states but one that has not generated much international sympathy despite repeated calls to understand this as a security threat. This is a matter of survival for low-lying atoll states, a new matter of national security as states face the prospect of obliteration by rising sea water.

MARKET QUICK FIXES?

If climate disruptions become severe, and states and markets fail to adapt to new circumstances quickly enough, the prospect of geoengineering looms in the future and, with that, potential future conflict too. But these are attempts to engineer a solution that once again secures the capitalist order by further manipulating the environment, rather than facilitating social change that might produce less ecologically disruptive modes of human life. Such geoengineering speculation, which will be taken up in more detail in the next chapter, suggests very clearly that humanity has yet to come to terms with the consequences of the metabolic rift. Assumptions that humanity is separate from the Earth, and that engineering can perpetuate this rift, as in seriously planning geoengineering programs, makes clear that the evacuation of the material context of humanity from thinking both in political economy and security studies needs to be tackled directly. But clearly, to borrow Daniel Deudney's (1999) terms, it is time to bring nature back into geopolitical thinking. Society, politics, and economy framed in terms of nation states protecting carboniferous capitalism no longer provide the appropriate categories for thinking about security in a period of rapid environmental change.

Climate change makes it abundantly clear that the metabolic rift has consequences; but which economic categories, and crucially which geopolitical categories, are mobilized to frame policy options matters greatly. Much depends on whether state elites understand themselves as competing over a shrinking pool of resources or as collectively facilitating modes of production that replace fossil fueled capitalism quickly (Dalby 2013c). Failure to transform states so that they effectively deal with climate change may indeed turn new security issues back into traditional ones if states threatened by rapid environmental change and societal disruption attempt to resolve difficulties by using force. But the more immediately important policy implication from the analyses now circulated by the leading international financial institutions is that mitigation is essential to slow climate change, to prevent drastic change that might undermine the stability of the global economy and with it human security in many forms (Network 2019). But it is that economy that is causing climate change; long-term security now means finding ways to change that economy rapidly. In particular it suggests investments need to be rapidly moved out of fossil fuels and into projects, in forestry in particular, that act to enhance their carbon sequestration capabilities (Gaffney et al. 2018).

Moving quickly to decarbonize at least the North American economy, which ought to be a global security priority given the high per capita consumption of fossil fuels, obviously requires political innovation that somehow short-circuits the policy logjam in the American Congress. Rapid decarbonization could become effective by a simple but dramatic innovation such as James Hansen's (2009) proposed fee-and-dividend approach to the fossil fuel industry. This advocates charging fees directly on fossil fuel production to begin making carbon fuels pay some of their environmental costs, and sending the proceeds directly to American citizens as bank deposits. This policy would provide all people in America with the cash to make appropriate changes to respond to rapidly rising energy prices. As Foster (2013) notes, this would be a major policy initiative with valuable redistributive effects that could rapidly make capitalism much less fossil fuel-dependent. Ironically, it remains within the dominant neoliberal logic of market mechanisms, which would make it relatively easy to promote politically. It could work quickly. In Canada in 2018 the federal government proposed using just such a fee-and-dividend scheme as a national carbon pricing system, but with very modest carbon fees, one unlikely to change fossil fuel consumption quickly.

While Hansen's scheme would not solve all the problems of the metabolic rift, it would, if adopted, begin to tackle one of its most dangerous consequences if not the larger pressing issue of formulating new political subjectivities less driven by market logics and status based consumption. However, despite American presidential rhetoric, and Obama's securitization of climate change, any chance for such scheme in the short run evaporated with the election of Donald Trump to the White House in Washington. But the potential for drastic change is there. Panitch and Gindin (2012) suggest the possibilities of reworking the financial systems that now run the global economy into public utilities that facilitate the making of a more sustainable world. Clearly given the ubiquity of fossil fuels, carbon taxes or fee-and-dividend schemes will be the likely measures to deal with climate change in the absence of other policy initiatives, including those explicitly aimed to reduce supplies of these fuels, keeping them in the ground, quite literally (Green and Denniss 2018).

Whether states can innovate fast enough to quickly facilitate new energy systems and, in doing so, take the key insights of the new security agenda seriously enough to rework carboniferous capitalism into a more sustainable mode of political economy, or whether they will fall back on old technologies and older geopolitical understandings of a competitive world where self-help may mean beggaring the rest, is now the key question for Anthropocene geopolitics. If security is to be rethought in terms of keeping the biosphere in conditions analogous to what humanity has so far experienced, it is also clear that political economy scholars will have to reconsider material factors and think beyond the science of moving money.

In doing so they will also have to understand that where earlier versions of modern political and economic thought dealt with scarcity as the human condition, the problem with carboniferous capitalism is the opposite, a matter of the global over-abundance of fossil fuels. As such, many of the security challenges of the present are increasingly artificial, a matter of shaping the technosphere and living with the consequences when parts of it fail. Disasters are increasingly artificial and security is now also partly about the politics of this. How it works with concerns of long-term sustainability relate fairly directly to the question of what is to be secured: fossil-fuelled modernity or a stable Earth. Getting the answer wrong might well prove to be disastrous in ways that are new and difficult to anticipate.

CHAPTER 7

ENVIRONMENTAL INSECURITY

There are no necessities, but everywhere possibilities; and man, as master of the possibilities, is the judge of their use. This, by the reversal which it involves, puts man in the first place – man, and no longer the earth, nor the influence of climate, nor the determinant conditions of localities. (Lucien Febvre, 1925: 236)

As a generalization, people with a commercial cast of mind find it almost impossible to believe they're headed willy-nilly into irreversible environmental disaster. They can't believe there's no way out. It doesn't ring true emotionally. Instead, what does grab commercial people, emotionally as well as practically, is ingenious ways to forestall disaster. (Jane Jacobs 1994: 43)

GEOSOCIAL FORMATIONS

To a growing degree, human insecurity is now a matter relating to the global economy, its economic entitlements, and the technological systems in which those are enmeshed. In the modern cities of the Global North, economic activities and the mundane practicalities of everyday life are directly related to the supply of electricity to homes and workplaces. While disasters and insecurities are not new in the human condition, and volcanoes in particular have seriously disrupted agriculture dramatically in recent centuries, what is now clear is that disasters and human vulnerability are increasingly artificial matters (Hannigan 2012). The expansion of the technosphere intrudes on human lives in numerous complex ways that are increasingly important in the current phase of the Anthropocene (Haff 2014). The meltdowns at the Fukushima nuclear plant in the aftermath of the 2011 earthquake emphasized that so-called "natural hazards" are mediated or enhanced by technological innovations. Simultaneously the rapidly expanding discussion of the possibilities of artificially engineering the climate through solar radiation management, to prevent the worst effects of global heating, suggests new forms of potential environmental disaster given the largely unknowable consequences of such efforts. These processes and outcomes suggest the need to conflate social and geological processes in analyses of the Anthropocene—hence the term "geosocial formations" (Clark and Yusoff 2017).

Insecurity is related to disaster in numerous ways while the natural and infrastructure contexts in particular places shape how vulnerabilities play out to imperil people (Briggs and Matejova 2019). Clearly, the nuclear fallout from Fukushima and the expense of trying to deal with the contamination caused by the radioactive materials that escaped the confines of the nuclear facility are disastrous. Ironically, part of the response to the Fukushima plant's failure has been the increased use of fossil fuels to substitute for the off-line nuclear plants; viewed from a climate change perspective this is contributing to a potential global disaster as climate disruptions cause further insecurities. But these disruptions, and the failure of political elites to respond rapidly to climate change, are precisely the arguments that support advocacy of climate engineering experiments. If political innovation can't manage climate change, so the argument goes, then perhaps solar radiation management might provide at least temporary conditions of environmental security by holding global temperatures somewhere close to what humanity has known for the last few millennia (Keith 2013)?

As carbon dioxide levels rise inexorably in the atmosphere, reaching over 400ppmv on average for a whole month for the first time in April 2014, this is increasingly a key theme in the discussions on environmental security. This rising level of carbon dioxide is a direct result of the use of fossil fuels to power contemporary urban systems and the global economy. Arctic ice is receding and the polar climate is changing rapidly; Antarctic ice sheets now seem certain to follow; geophysics analyses suggest these trends are very worrisome for anyone hoping to live in a relatively stable biosphere later this century (Hansen et al. 2016). The potential for dramatic disruptions has hastened the recent discussions of geoengineering to artificially adjust the temperature of the planet (Burns and Strauss 2013). The prospect of rapid environmental change, and related disruptions to many human modes of living, suggests the need to secure societies from such disasters and evaluations of the scientific possibilities have been proceeding apace for more than a decade (Royal Society 2009).

To environmentalists, the fact that we are even contemplating such things is a disastrous situation already, one that renders the future of all humanity very insecure (Hamilton 2013). Whichever way environment, technology, disaster, and insecurity are linked leads to numerous ambiguities. At least some of these can be resolved if the assumptions of a stable environmental backdrop to human affairs are suspended and a more dynamic and explicitly geophysical contextualization is introduced into the discussion, as is now frequently done in the more thoughtful invocations of the Anthropocene. The geo and the social are increasingly intermeshed in this thinking (Clark 2013). None of this solves the political difficulties of our time, but as the rest of this chapter suggests, taking geosocial formations seriously does re-contextualize current politics in potentially useful ways by challenging its unquestioned environmental assumptions. Questions of who decides the future configuration of the biosphere, and how the technosphere will shape it, are only beginning to be considered. But, clearly, geopolitics is now about geological politics and specifically about geophysics. Security, too, now needs an update not least because the security implications have been a relatively neglected dimension of the geoengineering discussion (Corry 2017).

This chapter first turns to another brief discussion of the history of security which complements and extends the discussion in chapter 6, then picks up the discussion of environmental security from earlier chapters and adds a further discussion of contemporary human insecurities. Given the increasingly artificial conditions of human insecurity, as a consequence of the global economy and the growing technosphere, the argument turns to a couple of the key points in the discussion of the Anthropocene, and the explicit re-contextualization of humanity that it implies. Insecurity is now a geological-scale matter, not a matter of just biology or ecology in a given set of natural circumstances, but rather a dynamic situation in the new contemporary human geophysical processes (Clark 2014). Engineering and ecology are now inextricably interconnected in discussions of security and disaster. They are so because the growing technosphere is becoming an increasingly important part of how the Earth System functions (Dongas et al. 2017). Environmental security now is in part about technological choices and how these shape both immediate contexts for some humans due to the geography of their deployment, and more generally the Earth System.

ENVIRONMENTAL SECURITY

Environmental security was a key theme in the discussions in the World Commission on Environment and Development (1987) and underpins much of the argument in *Our Common Future*. As the Cold War wound down, security thinkers, concerned to rethink geopolitics once the superpower rivalry ended, linked their ideas with those of environmentalists worried about the scale of the transformations to the natural world. Environmental security is thus also a term that subsequently refers to the discussion that emerged in the late 1980s in the Anglo-American world relating changing ecological matters and numerous social consequences, some of which, it was feared, might be new causes of warfare (Floyd and Matthews 2013).

While the term "nature" is ubiquitous, too, it is not accidental that security has been appended to environment rather than nature most of the time. Environment is a complicated term that loosely relates to that which surrounds an entity; its emergence in the latter part of the nineteenth century is a key conceptual shift in modern thinking, which so frequently operates on a radical separation of humanity from nature (Conway 2019). With roots in the term "environs," as in that which surrounds, it has become a ubiquitous term that specifies something outside a human entity, but which is often confused by the link to a natural-environment, or sometimes to a built-environment, and frequently without much reflection on the matter, a conjunction of both. These ambiguities about its meaning allow for both natural and artificial elements to constitute the surrounds, which become a matter of political concern should they impinge or constrain human actions in ways that endanger security, understood usually as the provision of relatively safe conditions of routine modern human life.

While earlier environmental arguments gradually shifted from focusing on themes of population, parks, and pollution in the 1960s through discussions of limits to growth and resource constraints in the 1970s, then into a focus on themes of sustainable development in the 1980s, climate change has gradually come to dominate the discussion in the twenty-first century. (Diez, vonLucke, and Wellman, 2016; Rothe 2016). The earlier discussions of environmental security have been reinvented in the last decade. But the contradictions at the heart of the debate have been perpetuated rather than alleviated because the implicit contextualization in most of the discussion draws much more heavily on traditional thinking about security, with its assumptions of a given geographical context, than on the novel insights of the Anthropocene (Clark 2013; Dalby 2014b).

The implications for this, in terms of a practical discussion of such things as the Fukushima nuclear disaster, emphasize that social formations are very much geological formations, too, and understanding geopolitics in these terms is now unavoidable. The Fukushima meltdown is, of course, a mixture of natural and artificial in that the earthquake and subsequent Tsunami damaged the reactors prior to the dispersal of their radioactivity. But as the official report of the Japanese Diet makes clear, it was an accident that could have been foreseen and prevented and, hence, one that was more artificial than natural (National Diet of Japan 2012). The meltdowns added to the difficulties in dealing with the consequences of the natural disaster of the earthquake, one accentuated by the construction of towns and infrastructure in areas known to be vulnerable to tsunamis. They had occurred before but warnings from earlier generations about the dangers of coastal life were ignored. Coastal facilities were constructed literally in harm's way in environments that are very insecure in multiple senses.

How environment is invoked in the environmental security discussion matters greatly. Much of the original discussion in the late 1980s and 1990s simply assumed a given environment that was being disrupted and, hence, was a source of danger (Dalby 2002). On the contrary, as this chapter suggests, the very notion of environmental security—of a planetary system in need of securing—only arises in the context of the technologies that both provide the risks and the modes of knowing and measuring what we have of late come to understand as the environment. In many ways, technological disasters are part of what constitutes environmental insecurity in the first place; material and social are interconnected all the time (Beck 2009). These fears of technological disruptions have been repeatedly linked to other metropolitan fears of the instabilities in the peripheries, of environmental refugees, conflicts over resources, the destruction of forests, and possible wars caused by such disruptions.

In recent years, spurred on by the increasing alarm about climate change, questions of the environmental sources of conflicts (if not outright warfare) again grace the pages of scholarly journals as researchers try to make links between climate change and insecurity (Gleditsch and Nordas 2014). Environmental threats, we are repeatedly told, supposedly compromise national security. The theme has been distilled into textbooks on both sides of the Atlantic (Chalecki 2013; Hough 2014). However, correlations between conflicts and climate change that supposedly prove environmental causations are at best suggestive, at worst they simply misconstrue interconnections (Selby 2014). More recent research is increasingly emphasizing the point that matters of the global economy, structural violence, and the frequent failures of policy initiatives to deal with the root causes of insecurity are more important in explaining what is happening than exogenous environmental factors (Zografos, Goulden, and Kallis 2014). Clearly, climate change in particular matters in terms of the vulnerabilities of agricultural populations, but issues related to development and political institutions are foremost in terms of when distress turns to violent conflict, or when it doesn't (Mach et al. 2019).

HUMAN INSECURITIES

The global financial crisis of 2008–9 emphasized the fact that numerous people are vulnerable due to the vagaries of the global economy. Precarious livelihoods, fears of unemployment, and the persistence of billions of people living in extreme poverty makes the human condition an insecure one in many ways; matters aggravated by the removal of social safety mechanisms of the welfare state and the dramatic fluctuations in economic fortune render employment prospects in certain places increasingly unpredictable (Feldman, Geisler, and Menon 2011). On the other hand, those living longer and more affluently than previous generations do so in part because the global economy has remade so much of the planet; roads, electrical grids, and buildings of all sizes are the artificial condition of modern life directed and shaped by the global economy (Stiglitz and Kaldor 2013).

The extreme poverty of part of humanity is not unconnected to the affluence of other parts, nor from the transformation of environments by the production of food, fibre, and raw materials that feed and fuel the rapidly expanding urban systems where the majority of humanity now reside (Dauvergne 2008). We are, after all, living in a world where development is supposedly key to providing security. Development is all about modernization, changing people and environments to provide the commodities for metropolitan consumption. All of this suggests that traditional notions of an external environment that is the context for humanity is no longer a useful formulation for any discussion of the human condition and the politics of either preventing dangers or facilitating human flourishing. Indeed, this geography is now being turned on its head as people start demanding climate justice and compensation for the disruptions that modernity has inflicted on poor people, most obviously in terms of climate impacts and forced migrations (International Organization for Migration 2014).

The scale of these processes is transforming matters at an accelerating rate, one raising new modes of vulnerability, most obviously those caused by the misfit between contemporary infrastructures and increasingly severe weather events (Graham 2010). This doesn't mean geophysics is now entirely artificial, or that humanity is in control of plate tectonics, earthquakes, or volcanoes; it does, however, mean humanity is an increasingly prominent player in configuring the future of the biosphere.

While this may be disastrous in the sense of causing events that endanger and kill on a large scale, disaster is also a social condition that challenges ways in which people make sense of their worlds. Nigel Clark (2014: 21) invokes Maurice Blanchot's (1995) discussion of disaster to suggest that it can be understood as a "crisis of such severity that it undermines our very capacity to make sense of the world." While much of the Earth System science accentuates how difficult it is to know the world in meaningful senses, it is also the case that the Anthropocene formulation involves reimagining humanity's place in the cosmos. It requires understanding ourselves collectively as a substantial geophysical presence in contemporary Earth history, not as separate passive victims of a capricious nature (Yusoff 2013). This crucial ontological reframing suggests simply that we are not apart from Earth; we are part of Earth. That said, the lack of clear understanding of precisely how the Earth System operates also suggests forcefully that pre-emptive actions such as attempts at geoengineering may potentially be very dangerous too (Cooper 2010). Nonetheless, extensive evaluations of its possibilities are part of the contemporary climate change discussions (National Research Council 2015a, 2015b). Experiments to test at least some of the physical properties of various aerosols in the atmosphere are being seriously considered as climate change accelerates (Tollefson 2018).

The Earth System science discussion of the Anthropocene poses questions of how to think the artificial circumstances of the present beyond the emphasis on risks that financial planners can accurately stipulate and insure against (Grove 2012), and for which security planners can supposedly anticipate or prepare resilient societal responses within the parameters of existing political economies (Amoore 2013; Cooper 2006). The focus on terrorism and the militarization of policing that attempts to constrain emergent threats by interfering with political phenomena, the biopoliticization of security, focuses on potential future disruptions to the global economy and at least to its affluent residents (Dillon and Reid 2009). The interconnections between human and non-human elements of the planetary system, and their circulations, are thus also key to rethinking security in the Anthropocene if potential future dangers are to be pre-empted. All of this feeds into considerations of geo-engineering and the artificial manipulation of the atmosphere in hopes of preventing the worst consequences of climate change (Baskin 2019).

The rise of Asian economies, and China in particular during the last few decades, has added hugely to the productive capabilities of humanity, but made the term "acceleration" especially apt for our current circumstances. While the global economic disruptions following the financial problems of 2008 slowed the economies of Europe and North America, and temporarily slowed the emissions of carbon dioxide, in the aftermath of these events the upward trend continues. Acceleration has resumed, and with it the alarming concern that planetary boundaries that have marked the relatively stable conditions of the Holocene are being rapidly transcended. While such trends raise numerous suggestions that the Anthropocene is the prelude to a massive crash in ecological systems and that disruptions of catastrophic proportions are looming, some Earth scientists are examining the possibilities of a third phase of the Anthropocene, one that will hopefully be a period when humanity takes seriously the possibilities of a sustainable Earth.

SUSTAINABLE EARTH?

If such a prospect were to unfold, then thinking about the global ecosystem as a single entity that cannot be transformed endlessly without hugely disruptive consequences is essential. While there are obviously some limits to growth, as the 1970s discussion suggested, given the abilities of technology to innovate and make new things and materials in new ways, resource constraints are now much less of an issue than the earlier neo-Malthusian frameworks suggested. In the case of climate change, the problem is too much fossil fuel, not too little. Humanity is now effectively making the future, but has no effective governance mechanisms in place to shape it. To create such institutions requires numerous social and political innovations obviously, but also some clear indications of what the safe operating space for humanity is and what thresholds we need to avoid crossing if the nightmare scenarios of ecological catastrophe are to be avoided (Steffen et al. 2015).

Given the looming possibilities for humanity to dramatically alter how some key parts of the surface of the planet functions, and in the process initiate a phase shift in the biosphere, much bigger questions of how the future will be shaped are coming to the fore (Barnosky et al. 2012). No longer is it a matter of a given set of physical parameters within which humanity operates. Pollution may be a matter of poison or ecological damage, but the larger issues of climate change and the whole-scale eradication of many species in the process of ecological conversion, require a serious discussion of what kind of a planet current policies should facilitate a transition to. All this follows from the fundamental reorientation set in motion by Earth System science, which suggests that humanity is now an active participant in the geological scale processes that shape the future of the planet.

Both the recent discussions of the Fukushima nuclear disaster, and of solar radiation management, have added urgency to the linkage between formulations of human security and vulnerability. They pose the role of technology in the human condition once again, and suggest that the sense of a global setting for humanity that is relatively new in historical terms is becoming more urgent in political and intellectual discussion (Dongas et al. 2017). On the one hand, Fukushima reminds us we cannot assume environmental stabilities in the face of such things as earthquakes, the damage from which is made much worse if nuclear reactors melt down or other technical failures lead to widespread pollution.

While solar radiation management might be disastrous in terms of making things worse for humanity, it might also be a recognition that we are already in a climate disaster to which it might be a partial solution in the sense that it might buy time to allow atmospheric carbon dioxide removal strategies to be worked out (Keith 2013). Geoengineering can be understood as a response to climate change that requires emergency measures. It can also be read as security in terms of the provision of the conditions necessary to perpetuate the present geopolitical order. Of course, miscalculations might cause environmental disruptions attributed to geoengineering actions by one state, with adverse effects for another leading to precisely the kind of conflict that geoengineering is supposed to pre-empt (Urpelainen 2012). Geoengineering might well end up being worse than what it ostensibly responds to.

If the formulation of the Anthropocene is taken seriously, and humanity's role as a geological agent becomes the starting point for thinking, then the implicit contextualization for human action shifts. In which case the future isn't a matter just of environmental degradation, but one of new ecological assemblages and technologies that are increasingly a matter of human choice (Ackerman 2014). Ecological arrangements will be ones composed of dramatically fewer natural species than the recent past; we are living through the sixth great extinction event of our planet's history (Kolbert 2014). There may be unforeseen synergies and thresholds in how new assemblages function or fail. None of this suggests that anything goes, and such crucial ecological transformations as the increasing acidification of ocean waters due to elevated levels of carbon dioxide being absorbed from the atmosphere, cannot be ignored. Instead the re-contextualization implicit in the Anthropocene is that such things are now the result of political decisions, albeit ones with unintended consequences. Geosocial formations are literally about what humanity produces, both directly and indirectly.

As earlier chapters in this book have suggested, the emergence of the Anthropocene as an overarching conceptualization for humanity's present condition likewise suggests that the sheer scale of contemporary changes is now understood as being qualitatively different from earlier discussions. Thinking in terms of a new geological epoch suggests the increasing artificialities of our circumstances—hence these new environmental insecurities—are now what is made, built, and produced. Volcanoes and earthquakes may persist, but the global economy is causing new potentially rapid transformations of parts of the Earth System. Thus, the Anthropocene raises complicated questions about when humanity might be understood to have begun to do things that make possible such a formulation as environmental security in the first place. The Anthropocene makes a discussion of how the future of the planet is to be shaped and what environment it is that will be secured for whose benefit where unavoidable. Geopolitics is now unavoidably about geophysics.

GEOPHYSICS

The knowledge practices of geophysics, which have given us an understanding of the climate system, also help us understand the world in ways that make possible serious discussions of geoengineering. The emergence of a sense of the global is integral to the geopolitics of the Cold War (Van Munster and Sylvest 2016). Climate change is a matter frequently understood through the knowledge practices of physics. The iconic "Keeling Curve" that charts the rise of carbon dioxide levels in the global atmosphere is a product of the International Geophysical Year in the late 1950s and presents a key geophysical measurement in terms of parts per million of carbon dioxide in the atmosphere that is now one of the key geo-metrics at the heart of contemporary geopolitics (Dalby 2013c). Remote sensing satellites that are now used to get such things as proxy measurements of atmospheric temperatures and polar ice sheet dimensions started life as Cold War reconnaissance tools. Concerns about ozone depletion, which emerged as a major issue in the 1980s, also started as a consequence of investigations into the effects of nuclear weapons detonations in the atmosphere. In the early years of the Cold War, the American military was interested in weather modification as a weapon of war. Geophysics and nascent climate science were intimately interconnected with military concerns in the birth of global ecology (Robertson, T. 2012).

These connections remain in the discourses of environmental security: scientific knowledge used to grapple with the effects of nuclear weapons has spun off into the official stories used to calculate the consequences of nuclear radiation in many aspects of its uses. Dose rates and exposures were initially modelled on the Hiroshima casualties, and such considerations continue to shape calculations about the hazards of radiation. In contrast, epidemiological calculations use rather different methods and, as the Fukushima episode suggests yet again, repeatedly raise concerns that official physics-based models are drastically underestimating the casualties (Mangano and Sherman 2012). If this is the case, residents of Japan (and perhaps further afield too) may be in a much more insecure environment than official statements claim.

The consequences of global heating are frequently also measured in physical terms, not only temperatures but in matters of ice volumes in the Arctic and particulate matter concentrations as well as volumetric measures of key gases in the atmosphere. Climate change researchers have generated vast amounts of data concerning physical measurements and fed these into ever more complicated models of global climate (Edwards 2010). These modes of knowledge are, in turn, generating serious discussion of the possibilities of artificially and deliberately changing the atmosphere to reduce global heating—which may become 'necessary' if extreme weather events, rising sea levels, or rapidly changing climate conditions are deemed by the rich and powerful to be so disruptive to ecological systems as to require remediation by solar radiation management.

This argument about geoengineering is among the most controversial topics in the conversation about how to move towards a sustainable planet. Under the loose rubric of geoengineering, these suggestions include many novel technologies (Vaughan and Lenton 2011). The simplest one is to mimic the cooling effect of volcanic eruptions by using aircraft to inject sulphate aerosols into the upper atmosphere. In theory this would effectively provide a sun-shade for the surface of the Earth and marginally reduce the amount of radiation that will cause warming. Such solar radiation management schemes are complemented by ideas for carbon dioxide removal, pulling it out of the atmosphere on the large scale by forestry plantation and other ecological or industrial methods (Meadowcroft 2013). Rephrased as "negative emissions," carbon dioxide removal is now widely seen as necessary to meet the climate change goals of limiting average global temperature change to less than 2 degrees Celsius, and are essential in coming decades if the 1.5 degree target is to be met (Intergovernmental Panel on Climate Change 2018).

All of the solar radiation management, or "albedo modification," techniques are controversial and as yet untried, but the more articulate advocates of the case suggest that, given the trajectory of carbon dioxide emissions, the fact that in planet boundary terms, we have already crossed the climate threshold and show little sign of slowing the use of carbon fuels, then temporary geoengineering is probably going to be necessary to buy time to build new energy systems that don't further aggravate warming (Keith 2013). While advocates are keen to institute at least some principles of governance in advance of the use of this technology (Rayner et al. 2013), there remain great difficulties in governing technologies in advance of their production and deployment. Should they be tried and fail, further questions arise about how they might be terminated without further aggravating climate disruptions (Bellamy 2016)—hence the advocacy of reluctant geoengineering by those convinced that political innovations won't come fast enough to constrain disastrous consequences of greenhouse gas-induced heating (Corry 2017). In the absence of more effective political initiatives, geoengineering may effectively become climate change policy (Luke 2010). If this is the case, the prospects for dealing with other planetary boundaries are bleak given that technical solutions are proffered instead of much more careful thinking about how to collectively live in a rapidly changing biosphere.

Much of the discussion of the engineering of the climate has, because of its focus on technical matters, eschewed a discussion of the geopolitical contexts within which it might be deployed or more specifically the potential security consequences of its introduction (Dalby 2015a). At least implicitly, all this operates on the assumption that when the impacts of climate change become severe enough, political consensus will support active efforts to do solar radiation management. But should that fail and unilateral action be undertaken, the potential for conflict where one state's politicians blame another's geoengineering efforts for weather–related disasters could be considerable. Floods, droughts, and disruptions of the Monsoon rains in Asia are all potential points of contention if active solar radiation efforts are under way. While no one took former Iranian President Ahmadinejad's claims that European and American states were using weather modification techniques to disrupt agricultural production in Iran seriously, the precedent is clear (Dalby and Moussavi 2017).

What matters in terms of human life are the processes that supply food and water and other "ecological services." Without the transportation links and the industrial systems to process the agricultural produce into what humans eat, the majority of humanity that now resides in urban places would not survive. Human systems are changing the ecological context dramatically, but that infrastructure is vulnerable to more extreme events and rapid changes that are beyond its design parameters. This is now an artificial ecological context, a series of assemblages that make modern life possible in the global urban system. The biological changes in the planetary system are noteworthy as a result of climate change, but also very much as a matter of habitat conversion on terrestrial surfaces and the reduction of oceanic species as a result of fishing and coastal pollution, and now as carbon dioxide levels rise, oceanic acidification. Indirectly these threaten the viability of the infrastructure that has disrupted them in the first place.

In contrast to the modern assumptions of a separate nature as simply the background for the human drama, contemporary thinking which draws on ecology, complexity theory, and post-humanist themes is a very different mode of knowing the world (Connolly 2013). How ecosystems adapt to changing circumstances is key to geological sciences, but now science has turned its attention to the most recent geological innovation. *Homo sapiens* have in the last few centuries, by burning fossil fuels, begun the systematic process of turning rocks back into air, reversing the normal natural geological processes of sequestering atmospheric carbon. Humanity has, thus, become a geological actor, and done it in part through the use of technologies that provide both our increasingly artificial lived environment and simultaneously change the geophysics of planetary systems. Life, now in technological form, is changing planetary processes but doing so very rapidly by geological standards.

This is now the context in which we must understand efforts to secure the environment, the *sine qua non* for future human being. No longer can environmental determinists suggest nature causes climate disasters (Dalby 2015a); in part they are of our own making at the largest of scales as well as in terms of the practical infrastructural vulnerabilities we build into our economic systems. The formulation of the Anthropocene neatly encapsulates all these themes. Viewed hypothetically from the perspective of many other species the disaster at present loose in the biosphere is industrial humanity wreaking havoc directly and indirectly on most other species, with the notable exception of those that it has 'domesticated' and bred for its own purposes as pets and food supply.

SECURING DISASTROUS FUTURES?

Thinking in these terms suggests the discussion of geoengineering, and solar radiation management in particular, might be understood both as a response to a disaster and as potentially an exacerbation of the disaster that has been the geophysical extension of human powers. Nuclear technologies are attempts to dominate the world in some particular ways, but just one part of the engineering approach to making futures. Such technological innovations fascinate their adherents with possibilities of remaking the world to better suit the short-term interests of a few sections of humanity. In its early years, for example, American proponents justified nuclear power with the promise of a better life for all with electricity too cheap to meter.

Critics of geoengineering are quick to point out that it, too, involves technology rather than attempts to rethink societies; technical fixes to supposedly technological problems rather than a more fundamental rethink of human societies (Hulme 2014). It fits with the rise of neoliberalism, with the remaking of state power to enhance profitability rather than social justice, as well as with the spatial tactics of controlling peoples and dissidents by all sorts of technologies of security. The assumptions of a hostile and competitive world in need of engineering protections all fit with the ethos of planetary management done by geophysical engineering techniques. Such processes are, once again, beyond any effective democratic control or public oversight and presented in terms of post political necessity, as matters of security rather than some form of democratic deliberation (Swyngedouw 2010).

Regenerating human societies rather than engineering the climate has long seemed a better option to many commentators (Beck 2010). The alternative of rethinking human societies, of political and ecological rather than solar radiation management, might be disastrous for the aspirations of planetary engineers, the putative geophysists of the future. This would seem to be an altogether more promising way of avoiding the potential failure of the geoengineers' technologies should they either miscalculate in how to calibrate the routine operation of their machines, or should those machines malfunction in the kind of spectacular failure that Fukushima's multiple meltdowns now symbolize (Hamilton 2013). The counter argument that it is too late, and that if at least temperature is to be controlled, then more technological interventions will be needed, drives the case for geoengineering.

For environmentalists anxious to stop this pathological path dependency on proliferating dangerous engineering schemes, the fact that there are already serious discussions of solar radiation management under way suggests very clearly that we are living in a situation that is already disastrous. For engineers concerned that environmental change may already be reaching dangerous levels, not actively planning geoengineering schemes to prevent disasters is, well, disastrous! Either way, the Anthropocene formulation makes it clear humanity is determining the future of the planet in many ways that we are only beginning to comprehend. It is tempting to overdraw a distinction between ecological and engineering views, but which kind of engineering is used in future, one focused on using ecological means of carbon dioxide removal and designing human habitats that don't use fossil fuels, or one using solar radiation management in attempts to ameliorate the disruptions caused by fossil-fuelled economies, matters greatly in terms of how the next stage of the Anthropocene is shaped. This is the new context within which we have to make sense of environmental security and think politically about what to produce, and how.

Understood in these terms, the disasters that are geoengineering and Fukushima are but two ways of probing the security politics of the Anthropocene and the consequences of the evolution of the technosphere. This is a geological geopolitics in the sense that what we are making is what will be the sedimentary record of humanity in future eons (Clark 2012). But that geological record is open to being shaped by a security politics that thinks seriously about how to construct a future for humanity in a world that has already been remade by many technologies. The geopolitical temptations to use geoengineering loom large for political elites more interested in maintaining their power and privilege than reshaping a sustainable Earth System (Dalby 2015b). How that future is shaped will, in part, be about trying to avoid disasters, but political judgments about which ones deserve priority are now unavoidable if the focus is on making an Earth that can sustain humanity in the long run in the Anthropocene.

CHAPTER 8

GEOPOLITICS AND GLOBALIZATION

> The world has moved from a global threat called the cold war to what should now be considered the 'warming war.' Our conflict is not being fought with guns and missiles but with weapons from everyday life – chimneystacks and exhaust pipes. We are confronted with a chemical war of immense proportions. (Afelee Pita, Representative of Tuvalu, address to the United Nations, 17 April 2007)

> But for now, notice that the Anthropocene obtained purchase in popular and scientific discourse in the context of ubiquitous urgent efforts to find ways of talking about, theorizing, modeling, and managing a Big Thing called Globalization. (Donna Harraway 2016: 49)

GEOPOLITICS AND GOVERNANCE

The most important point about contemporary governance and the geopolitical challenges of the present is so obvious that it frequently goes unsaid: the organization of the world into nearly two hundred supposedly sovereign territorial states (Jackson 2000), a matter that appears stable and fixed. The United Nations system is premised on this geographical division of the Earth's terrestrial, and by extension, parts of its oceanic surface. This arrangement was, to a substantial extent, an effort to solve one of the key problems of European geopolitics—the longstanding pattern of using military force for territorial aggrandizement. Winners of European wars traditionally got territorial rewards as the spoils of victory but, in the process, frequently sowed the seeds of future conflicts. Fixing the frontiers once and for all, as the United Nations system did after the Second World War, removed this temptation while making aggressive warfare international anathema (Zacher 2001). The apparent violation of this norm in the case of the Russian-Ukraine conflict in recent years is one of the reasons it generates so much international attention.

Globalization is partly about accelerating interconnections, but frequently those interconnections are between the now relatively fixed spaces of territorial states and regional blocs enclosed by various rules, or forms of sovereignty. In the case of non-traditional security threats, such as diseases and environmental problems, states adapt to international arrangements in ways that frequently enhance the power of elites and leading sectors in their economies, a pattern once again suggesting that globalization favours well-connected corporations and their local suppliers (Hameiri and Jones 2015). Simultaneously, numerous complicated matters of international finance slip out of control of national governments but require their collective intervention when matters become too chaotic. Arcane technical specifications govern trading arrangements, and in many cases curtail freedom of action by governments, at least those that wish to remain within the more complicated structures of the international trading system. The territorial state is the dominant mode of administering these larger arrangements of political economy and, seen as such, the proliferation of nation states—while apparently suggesting the supremacy of territorial rule and sovereign jurisdictions—in many ways simply operates as the local instantiation of larger globalization processes.

The scale of material transformation involved in the rapidly evolving global economy—the interconnected world that Montesquieu and Voltaire discussed (Agnew 2015)—needs to be updated to include the transformation of the biosphere and the geophysical consequences that are manifested as climate change. Most terrestrial surfaces that are potentially useful for modern agriculture are now being exploited (Ellis 2011). Rapid deforestation and the rise of plantations for such things as palm oil are emphasizing that environmental change is part of the growth of the global economy. Crucially, the consumption of fossil fuels is both powering the industries of the global economy, often through the use of cheap coal, and by using petroleum facilitating the mobility of both commodities and people linking places in the processes of globalization. But it is precisely this consumption of fossil fuels that is a key factor in destabilizing the climate system and rendering the taken for granted geographies of the world increasingly anachronistic.

As chapters 4 and 5 showed, trying to assert control over contemporary changes by using territorial strategies flies in the face of the basic processes of geographical change—most obviously in case of the current migration crisis. In the case of environmental change, the key mode of adaptation for most species is to move to more conducive climes. But where animals, both two- and four-legged, encounter barriers in the form of fences and walls, this most basic mode of adaptation is thwarted. The would-be migrants are rendered ever more vulnerable by being hemmed in precisely when they need to move (Jones 2016). Now, as the geological scale of contemporary transformations becomes ever more clear, this contradiction between geographical fixity and the need to accommodate rapid change has become acute. The governance arrangements at hand are increasingly inappropriate, and the situation is aggravated by attempts to use force to try to dominate matters in a badly divided world. Rethinking these contextual questions—to use the term from the introduction to this book—is now key to dealing with these counterproductive consequences of the return of geopolitics.

The rapid proliferation of the use of the term "Anthropocene" in recent years suggests it is becoming synonymous for the present, the latest stage of globalization, and one bringing with it threats to numerous aspects of the human condition. Much of the discussion seems, at least so far, to have underplayed the significance of the fact that this is a specifically geological term. The significance of this lies in the scale and longevity of the phenomenon; it is about much more than just globalization (Chakrabarty 2017). The implications of thinking in geological rather than environmental terms suggest much longer term and dramatic transformations are already afoot. Human actions are changing matters profoundly, moving the planetary system out of conditions that have pertained for hundreds of thousands of years and launching the planet into a new and as yet unknown configuration.

Just as the assumption of autonomous spaces is impossible so too is the modern assumption of humanity separate from nature.

The Anthropocene makes this clear, but how to think of humanity as making new spaces isn't so easy. Related to this are the expanding processes of commodification and enclosure as the global economy incorporates ever more processes and products into its circulations; governance and property relations are increasingly commercialized. In the process, as chapter 5 has emphasized, boundaries and borders extend in new ways to privatize and hence price many things. Change generates numerous new modes of bordering, incorporating and governing social and ecological processes—hence the irony of a globalization process that apparently crosses numerous boundaries but simultaneously involves numerous new rules, regulations and enclosures to function. Lengthy commodity chains are the new shape of global economy, ones that require modes of security that transcend territorial boundaries while incorporating their governance practices into commercial arrangements that cross many borders (Cowen 2014).

Above all, the matter of rapid anthropogenic climate change looms over international affairs. In Paris in December 2015, despite high-profile terrorist attacks a huge conference lead to an agreement on a number of measures to be taken to begin, belatedly, to tackle climate change. While this wasn't the binding treaty many hoped for, and the aspirational statements about keeping the average global temperature rise to close to 1.5 degrees Celsius were in stark contrast to the promised commitments to cut greenhouse gas emissions, nonetheless the meetings did convey a clear sense that major powers were at last beginning to think about how to craft a global arrangement to deal with the threat of increasingly severe weather events, rising sea levels, and much more dramatic future disruptions to the existing planetary climate. The Paris Agreement's entry into force in November 2016 is a start in the right direction, albeit one that requires voluntary commitments on the part of state parties to the arrangement. But pretending this agreement solves the problem, or provides an overarching institutional framework for doing so, is clearly wishful thinking (Dimitrov 2019).

CLIMATE WARS?

President Obama elevated climate to the top priority for U.S. national security in his speech at the Brandenburg Gate in Berlin in 2013, and then set in motion confidential negotiations with China to grapple with the issue. The deal between the United States and China in late 2014 made Paris possible; without such a meeting of minds the Paris

Agreement would probably have accomplished even less. What it did do, by incorporating all the major states into a loose framework, was perpetuate the attempt at universal involvement in the United Nations Framework Convention on Climate Change. The United States insisted nothing in the Paris Agreement was to be understood as an admission of responsibility for causing climate change and such language showed up in the final documents. This was one important factor that prevented a binding treaty from being the final outcome. In the process, the U.S. acted as a great power by dictating the terms of its accession to the arrangement. Nonetheless, some notion of universal involvement in the process to grant it legitimacy was maintained. In terms of the climate change process, the argument that geopolitics has returned appears at least partly inaccurate. Clearly, climate has become a key focal point in global politics. Whether one takes climate change seriously, or acts, as in the case of the Trump administration, to try denying it is even happening, geopolitics now revolves around the issue (Latour 2018).

However the growing literature on climate security suggests some of the more pernicious formulations of geopolitics are reappearing in ways that are dangerous to the formulation of intelligent policy (Chaturvedi and Doyle 2015). The climate justice arguments, heard repeatedly in Paris, and key to the justification for the aspirational statements to keep the average temperature rise to no more than 1.5 degrees Celsius, suggest that the developed world, with its long history of greenhouse gas emissions, has primary responsibility for dealing with climate change. The ill-fated Kyoto accord of the 1990s started on the premise that those who had caused the problem should take the lead in trying to deal with it. This garnered no support in Washington where Congress voted in patterns preventing the Clinton administration from even trying to get the accord acceded-to by the United States. Television advertisements at the time showed the world map being cut into pieces, implying that all countries ought to be involved to deal with a global problem. Equating un-equals isn't a new rhetorical strategy, but it worked effectively to obscure responsibilities in the 1990s well before the full weight of the climate denial movement was felt in American public discourse (Oreskes and Conway 2010).

The 1990s rhetoric of bifurcation, of a world of pacified zones and wild zones, most famously coined by Robert Kaplan's (1994) dystopic warning of "a coming anarchy," has persisted through the war on terror and been updated in such formulations as Thomas Barnett's (2005) "non-integrated gap" in the global polity. Now these ideas of wild zones are linked into Pentagon notions of failed states and forms of political instabilities for which climate change now acts as a "threat multiplier." Climate change is now upgraded to a "catalyst of conflict" in the more recent formulations of the CNA Military Advisory Board (2014).

This threat-multiplier-formulation has become widespread in the international security community. Climate change risks were elevated to the top of the list of global risks in the discussions at the World Economic Forum in Davos in January 2016. The contemporaneous *Munich Security Report* had similar concerns:

> Climate change is a very particular kind of threat. For low-lying countries, it is an existential danger. To most societies, it is a threat multiplier: An increase in extreme meteorological events, droughts, and land degradation as well as the sea-level rise can and do exacerbate political fragility and resource disputes, increase economic hardship and mass migrations, and magnify ethnic tensions and civil strife. (Munich Security Conference 2016: 44)

Subsequent reports from the Munich Security conferences have reiterated these concerns, as have reports on both sides of the Atlantic emphasizing the fragility of many states in the face of climate disruptions (Mobjork, Smith, and Rüttinger 2016; Moran et al. 2018). The dangers in such formulations are, as with the earlier formulations of environmental security after the Cold War (Dalby 2002), that these geographical specifications of dangerous places disconnected from the larger transformations of geopolitics facilitate violent actions in the periphery in ways that perpetuate rather than ameliorate the disruptions set in motion by the interaction of changes in rural political economy in the Global South with climate change. All of this may be aggravated, as shown in chapter 5, by unilateral attempts by some states and corporations to reduce their climate risk and ensure food supplies by purchasing large tracts of land in the South to diversify their holdings, and hence reduce climate vulnerabilities among those in the North regardless of the consequences in the South.

Even more ominous are the warnings from scholars linking historical concerns with Nazi geopolitics to the larger reasoning practices used to shore up its genocidal violence. Welzer's (2012) discussion of how the Nazi regime gradually changed laws and assumptions concerning what was considered 'normal' and how current geographical formulations of wild zones and inevitable war in the South are shaping policy discourse is a cautionary tale that needs to be taken seriously. Likewise Timothy Snyder's (2015) careful reconstruction of the political geography of the holocaust in his *Black Earth* points to the related dangers of geopolitical formulations of lebensraum. Nazi interpretations of "living room" linked geopolitical claims on agricultural land in Eastern Europe to logics of consumerist aspiration and entitlement in Germany, at whatever political and economic cost this may have inflicted elsewhere in the continent. Is this now what is happening at the global scale?

Discourses of consumer entitlement, and fears of numerous environmental threats from external sources, have also been a persistent theme in recent American geopolitical discourses (Szasz 2007). Such formulations simultaneously rely on fantasies of non-porous borders (Kearns 2013) and the implicit assumptions that containment or quarantine are effective security strategies in a world where interconnections are the key to ecological and economic processes. This geographic assumption of separation is powerfully reinforced by claims to territorial jurisdiction, property boundaries, and sovereignty. It is epitomized by the penchant for wall building as a strategy to try to limit migration of various sorts, as well as discourses of invasive species as threats to various forms of farming and economic activity. Territoriality is a key strategy of control in many human affairs, with demarcation, communication, and enforcement being the key interrelated practices in Sack's (1986) classic discussion of the process, but it is much less efficacious when it comes to either economics or ecology than its advocates often assume.

Nonetheless, territorial strategies are being attempted by many states and politicians in an attempt to shore up at least a sense of being in control despite an obviously waning sovereignty (Brown 2010). Donald Trump repeatedly used the issue of building a wall across the American border with Mexico and trying to force Mexicans to pay for it in his 2016 election campaign. Many such walls and fences are being constructed in the world. They reinforce a carceral cartographic imagination, one where political borders often take on cultural significance as though these lines on the map were in some way 'natural' frontiers (Fall 2010).

GEOPOLITICAL VISION

All this is related to the larger questions of geopolitical vision: how the world is represented as an object to be struggled over, divided and dominated by great powers, or shared by an interconnected humanity inhabiting an increasingly artificial world. While Macdonald, Hughes, and Dodds' (2010) series of essays on observant states emphasize the importance of scopic regimes, technologies of seeing, and the constitution of objects to be governed through these practices, the ability to see the globe as a whole, to use satellite imagery to imagine it is now also a key part of the climate discussion. The "zoom in" functions literally contextualize news stories now; mere stationary contextual cartography is now largely passé! In similar mode "The Situation Room" long mimicked military presentations of a central control room monitoring from afar distant events that might have geopolitical repercussions, and used the modern scopic regime to imply a visuality that conveyed a superior panoptical surveillance vantage point on the world's evolving political scene. But in doing so, the connections between places are frequently implied rather than investigated: storms, floods, and disasters are sometimes linked to climate change, but the larger context of a transformed world only sometimes structures these representations.

Frequently, what Donna Harraway (1988) famously called the "god trick" view denies the details of practical struggles related to climate change in particular places, reinforcing a sense of a global problem, a terrifying prospect that 'requires' big science and technocratic planning by great powers (Chaturvedi and Doyle 2015). This is the imperial administrator's view of the world, not the view from the desperate refugee in part of the contemporary carceral archipelago built by metropolitan states on Lampedusa, Lesbos, or Christmas Island. Viewed from there, things are likely to look somewhat different; the fences and guard towers that supposedly provide security for residents of the prosperous suburbs of the Global North are precisely what prevent migrants from gaining access to health services, food, shelter, and employment. Who has human security is very much a matter of geography and how practical matters of bureaucracy play out at international borders in terms of who is admitted and who is not (Mountz 2010).

Failure to understand how geopolitics is shaping the future configuration of the planet, both through processes of globalization directly and indirectly by all the ecological and geophysical transformation the global economy entails, may indeed bring the world to future climate wars (Dyer 2008). But if this kind of geopolitics returns, with all the rhetorical force of the cartographies of enmity that it implies (Dalby 2013a), it will be because of failures of geographical imagination to understand geopolitical forces in motion and the complex causalities of an interconnected global economy that has already caused very considerable geophysical transformations. As chapter 6 shows, it's precisely because of these geophysical transformations that discussions of solar radiation management and other attempted technical fixes to global warming are also being discussed.

Such attempts to artificially manipulate weather patterns in particular regions or the temperature of the planet as a whole have the potential to cause serious political conflicts. If attempts to change rainfall patterns by cloud seeding to enhance agricultural productivity in a particular region have trans-boundary effects, then international politics will be engaged. Given the large uncertainties in weather system behaviour it might be hard to prove that weather modification in one place is related to droughts of storms elsewhere, but the perception that this is the case might be enough for serious political dispute. The potential for conflict is there, even if, given the interconnectedness of the global system, it is probable that careful international cooperation would be essential for any scheme to succeed (Horton 2013).

Once again such discussion emphasizes the importance of the contextualizations structuring geopolitical discussions. While the appearance of nuclear weapons, and subsequently intercontinental ballistic missiles, change the context of super-power rivalries, in the process dramatically heightening both the dangers of great power conflict and the speed with which crises could spiral out of control, this changed context has shaped practices of global security. Restraint is necessary, a matter of 'negarchy' in Daniel Deudney's (2007) terms, where security requires limiting the use of force and constraining the temptations to try to use war as a strategy of statecraft. Now the Anthropocene makes it clear this understanding has to be extended to grapple with the transformation of the biosphere and the potentially destabilizing consequences of climate change in particular if land-use changes, methane leakages and other greenhouse gas emissions aren't dealt with in the immediate future. Restraint on these matters is now key in geopolitics for survival reasons in similar ways to the issue of nuclear weapons in the Cold War period. International leaders have been slow to realize this, and alarmist stories of imminent disaster haven't led to appropriate recontextualization in North American policy making circles despite President Obama's clear designation of these new climate dangers to global security.

The political economy of fossil fuel extraction in North America explains part of this; the enthusiasm for fracking in particular in recent years promised rapid wealth for those in the industry. This, however, has to be understood as related to the larger political campaign from the right wing, in both Canada and the United States, where corporations have lavishly funded political agendas anathema to the steps needed to constrain carbon emissions and move towards a new post-fossil fuel economy (Mayer 2016). The cultural politics of climate change denial involve the construction of various forms of othering in the anthropocentrism that underlies the refusal of environmentalist claims (Jacques 2009). Powerfully reworked in the climate denial movement, assumptions of an autonomous humanity are key to this rhetoric (Black 2018). Once again this is an explicit formulation of spatial separation, one that then invokes hostility and danger from outside, and physical force as the solution to problems that may result. The ecological interconnections that shape humanity's context are once again denied, as modernity in general, and classical geopolitics in particular, has so long done in the powerful dualisms that structure modern thinking (Kearns 2009). These include a separation of culture from nature, civilization from primitive barbarism, urban accomplishment from rural backwardness, industrial acumen from non-western tradition, and consumption 'here' from production and pollution 'there'.

The failure to see the interconnections across these separations has long been the focus of environmentalist thinking, at least since Alexander von Humboldt took Goethe's insights about nature into the rainforests of South America and formulated the ideas of human-induced climate change as he investigated the changing hydrology resulting from deforestation (see Wulf 2015). The struggles over climate change link these long-term political struggles into recast discussions of responsibility and the attribution of blame and geopolitical arguments about peripheral dangers and metropolitan action that once again obscure the motive forces that matter in causing rapid change. Challenging these formulations remains a key task for scholars wishing to make a useful contribution to Anthropocene geopolitics, ones made all the more urgent as Earth System science charts the trajectories of transformation in ever increasing detail. The geographic context for politics in the future is being shaped by current decisions about political economy and energy systems in particular; that point is now unavoidable in any consideration of the future of geopolitics.

SHAPING THE FUTURE

The Anthropocene suggests that while technology is crucial to human changes, it is also part of the overall transformation of the biosphere, the context for humanity that we are actively reassembling, often with disastrous consequences for other species and their habitats. Much more so than in the earlier age of science, we now understand the interconnectedness of life, its various substrates, and its adaptations. We, too, understand that humanity has endangered its own existence in previously unimagined ways, and the political struggles are very much about reshaping the Earth, material transformations designed to enhance particular modes of life and power and prestige among certain groups of humanity (Bonneuil and Fressoz 2016).

These efforts are having cumulative effects that amount to a new geological era, one in which the geophysics of the planet are interlinked in numerous ways with human activities, ones that are causing climate change, acidification of the oceans, and mass extinctions simultaneously. This suggests that we need to add a specifically geophysical understanding to the operations of power, linking physical transformations of context into our understandings of power, prestige and the search for security of various types. We are, as the U.S. military likes to put it, "shaping the future" (Morrissey 2017). But how that future is to be shaped is a matter of geopolitics, a matter in part of collective deliberations, and also the attempts by certain people to control the process and effectively decide on the physical configuration of the future biosphere and its components.

The longstanding suggestion from Earth Systems thinking that our conceptions need a second Copernican revolution where life is now understood as a key part of the planetary system (Schellnhuber 1999), rather than a surficial afterthought, is instructive here. To reiterate the central theme of this book: We are not on Earth. We are Earth. Humanity has reversed the geological processes of carbon sequestration by widespread use of combustion, and as such the key to both human powers and the earthly context in which they play out are tied to these geophysical transformations. Geopolitics is now about how the world is being remade, and how the strategies to do this relate to the types of knowledge, representations, and legitimations invoked in the arguments about who should rule and what kind of a future should be produced to whose advantage. Failure to think about this new understanding of the world and how it is being shaped by geopolitical choices may lead to the kind of future water wars that so worry the climate security analysts, and novelists like Paulo Bacigalupi (2015) in his depiction of violence in his imagined future of the American South West in *The Water Knife,* or Omar El Akkad (2017) in thinking about a future *American War* in which some renegade American states persist in using petroleum despite international agreements to cease as part of climate change mitigation efforts. His future doesn't include Florida, which has by then disappeared under the waves (see Rush 2018).

Such dystopic futures are avoidable if politicians tackle institutional problems appropriately. Making the rapidly changing geographies of the present the key point in geopolitical analyses is essential to both sensible scholarly analysis and appropriate policy advice. It requires directly challenging geographical formulations that inform populist and nationalist invocations of the endangered "here" and threatening the external "there." Not least of all, this is the case because it is the consumption of fossil fuels, historically mostly 'here' in North America and Europe, that is now causing the increasing storms, floods, droughts, and disruptions that set people 'there' in motion. The connections between rural resource sources and their disruption by ever larger demands from the urban centres of the global economy emphasize that in the case of contemporary transformations, globalization is also very much a matter of urbanization.

URBANIZATION AND INNOVATION

Cities are new habitats that effectively extract resources from surrounding landscapes, and transform them in the process. They do this by changing the species mix in terms of deforestation, agriculture, reworking hydrology for water supplies and irrigation, mining minerals and fuels, or somewhat less directly, altering marine environments through fishing and waste disposal. Urbanization is simultaneously a process of colonization (Cronon 1991). Extending the frontier from which resources are extracted, and changing the surrounding landscapes to facilitate the production of commodities for the urban economy, are two sides of the same historical process. This urban driven change is a key part of the human story that has been relatively neglected in modern narratives that have emphasized of the superiority of European civilization and ignored the material transformations involved, often at a distance, as empires exploited colonies for commodities to enrich their metropoles (Davis 2001). These commercial patterns of demand in cities driving rural transformation long predate the rise of European imperialism and its more voracious offshoots in contemporary globalization.

Insofar as artificial climate change is something novel in the Earth system, then understanding it as part, albeit mostly an inadvertent part, of the rise of economic activity, and that economic activity as primarily driven by innovations in cities, suggests a narrative that relegates states, and largely empires too, to relatively minor players in the story. Understanding cities and hinterlands, that may or may not be within the same territorial and state jurisdiction as the city, as the key forces behind economic activity, suggests that the implicit geographies in the discussion of global environmental change need more explicit attention than they usually get in either discussions of political or technical matters of ecological transformation. Crucially it suggests that territorial states, and discourses that link environmental change to matters of climate change and specifically to national security and bordered sovereign states, is a misfit with the processes that matter most in understanding contemporary transformations. At least they are with the notable exception that now these states are the entities that write the rules for the international economy and hence partly shape how innovations play out geographically, not least recently in terms of renewable energy (Lewis 2014).

This argument links to the larger discussion from Jane Jacobs and Peter Taylor, discussed in chapter 2, which suggests the two main modes of social interaction, those of commerce and of "guardian" activities, have very different attributes that will inevitably lead to different modes of conduct. Where guardian functions require assumptions of distrust, potential violence, and competitive social relations, commerce requires degrees of trust, an ability to trade, and having a reasonable expectation that contracts will be honoured. Guardian cultures, with the threats of violence, the ever-present focus on potential threats, the importance of honour in social interactions, and a focus on protecting territory, are not useful settings for thinking about climate specifically or the Anthropocene generally. Confusing the rise of states, civilizations, and cities obscures the key function of city commercial networks in changing the human condition. Trade and commerce, not the activities of the guardians, matter the most in changing the ecological condition of humanity. Competitive state relations, the taken-for-granted premise of much geopolitical thinking, isn't helpful in climate matters, as a generation of climate negotiations focused on relative gains, free riders, and the dangers of defection from collective endeavors has shown repeatedly (Harris 2013).

In many ways cities also compete in economic matters, and attempt to work their way up the hierarchies of the global economy, but their competition isn't as zero sum as that of states in terms of power competition. Innovation is key to attracting new industries and new activities in the global system. In terms of municipal politics, most cities are energy consumers, not producers, and that matters in terms of the possibilities for cities to improve their relative performance in economic terms. And adding climate change, cities can usefully learn from each other in terms of practical innovations in greening their infrastructure as well as the related question of new governance mechanisms; they do so, in part, precisely because they aren't states (Magnusson 2011). As such cities may be much more useful sources of climate change innovation than many states; their institutional context gives them possibilities for innovations, such as supporting power purchases from green electricity suppliers, which makes a difference in energy matters. Reducing coal consumption simultaneously helps with urban air pollution, a lesson that Chinese urban managers have been relearning the hard way. Networks of environmental activists and innovative organizations in cities offer ways of collectively learning that frequently bypass state structures too (Bouteligier 2012; Bernstein and Hoffmann 2018).

All this suggests that, in terms of climate change and what the future of the Anthropocene will look like, it is production decisions that in many ways matter much more than traditional environmental notions of limiting and regulating pollution, resource extraction and preserving traditional land uses (Dauvergne 2016). All these matter, and will continue to matter, but the more important point is that how decisions are taken about what is demanded by urban markets, and hence what gets produced, are now the key to the future of the Anthropocene. Reimagining climate change, in this context, means elevating the role of cities and urban living to a central place in our accounts of the Anthropocene. It requires thinking about security in particular in terms of what is needed to enhance urban life rather than maintain the territorial integrity of competing national states. It is a matter of focusing more on city and commercial activities rather than the traditional preoccupation of state guardian functions.

In the short term this is a matter of making urban infrastructure much more robust to deal with storms, droughts, and other weather disruptions (Graham 2010). In the longer term this requires rebuilding cities as places to live that are much less dependent on fossil fuel systems, regenerating neighbourhoods while also rethinking urban economies, and key things such as the ownership of municipal energy systems (Klein 2014). Now we need to rapidly think about political systems that can produce low throughput affluence, rather than administrative arrangements that further colonize peripheral peoples and places while extending property rights to facilitate further rural extractions. Communal land ownership and leasing arrangements for wind and solar energy generation often provide much more sustainable ways of reconstituting rural ecologies than do distant commercial property markets (Mackenzie 2013).

For city residents concerned with slowing down the pace of climate change, whether because of the dangers of severe weather or, in the case of port cities, their vulnerabilities to rising sea levels, practical innovations in terms of energy supply and more robust infrastructure should allow them simultaneously to mitigate climate change and facilitate adaptation. However, this is not a call for simple market logics; as Peter Taylor (2013) ruefully notes, the provision of relatively cheap air-conditioned housing in the American South has produced energy inefficient sprawl. Cities, if thoughtfully designed, rather than driven only by the dictates of property market logics, ought to be able to buffer their inhabitants from the worst consequences of climate change. Indeed, James Lovelock (2014) has suggested greater urbanization as the appropriate mode of human adaptation to deal with the coming transformation of the climate.

URBAN FUTURES/TERRITORIAL SECURITIES

In the face of climate change, or to be much more precise, rapid climate change, and its potential disruptions to present human arrangements, suggestions for deliberately engineered solutions to climate difficulties, whether by injecting sulfate aerosols into the stratosphere or by other means, are now common. Viewed in Ruddiman's (2010) terms, humanity has actually been doing a version of this for a long time by adding agricultural methane to the atmosphere. Critics are aghast at the apparent hubris in deliberately attempting to try to adjust planetary temperatures, suggesting that the solution may be much worse than the problem to which it is a putative response (Hamilton 2013). But the very fact there is now a serious discussion of the issue emphasizes both the severity of climate disturbances and, more importantly, the failure of efforts to negotiate an international climate regime to constrain greenhouse gas production effectively.

James Lovelock (2014) is among those horrified that humanity should try to geoengineer its way out of climate change by attempting to adjust the whole system through solar radiation management. He suggests that over the long run the Earth is a self-regulating system within which life operates to maintain optimum conditions. As such, letting the planet self-regulate while humanity air conditions greater concentrations of cities (or "hives" in Lovelock's terms), rather than the whole planet, is a better option. What he largely neglects to deal with directly in this account is how the self-regulating system—Gaia, in his famous theory (Lovelock 1979)—will provide food and other ecological necessities for humanity's hives as it deals with the rapid rise in global temperature, which is now inevitable.

Adapt the planet will! How humans will fare is partly a matter of what the rich and powerful decide to try to secure in coming decades. Humanity has already remade many key terrestrial ecosystems. Plants and animals will have to move in order to deal with new climate conditions, many of the decisions about what will move where and when will be artificial decisions as farmers, agricultural corporations, foresters, and land-use planners decide what to plant and build where and when. How the ocean ecosystems will respond to heating, beyond more Arctic and Antarctic ice melting, is far from clear. Increased acidification, unsustainable fish extraction, and pollution from industrial and urban activities will all combine in ways that have yet to be worked out by oceanographers. Lovelock's (2014) argument doesn't provide any guarantees that in the long term the planet will remain conducive to human life. But in the foreseeable future, at least, it is clear humanity will be adapting to circumstances that its actions are continuing to change.

In these circumstances twentieth-century modes of security provision premised on territorial sovereignty and mobility restrictions are likely to be unhelpful. Crucially, adaptation requires the ability of species to move, to colonize more conducive ecological conditions, both higher up mountains and in some cases further towards the poles. In these circumstances, traditional assumptions of preservation of nature in particular places will have to be relaxed to facilitate adaptation and the migration of species. Understanding environmental security as a matter of stability, of new species as a threat because they are "invasive," is not helpful, especially given the wholesale movement of species by gardeners, farmers, and pet owners around the world (Fall 2014). The territorial states that are the major spatial arrangements for administering human affairs may, here too, be an obstacle to securing the flexibilities that adaptive systems require. Thinking of security as a matter of facilitating change, rather than preventing people and species crossing national boundaries, is a key innovation that suggests flows rather than stasis, and connections and networks rather than demarcations, are most important. In Jacobs's (1994) and Taylor's (2013) terms, commercial rather than guardian functions would seem to be much more appropriate in terms of security provision in the next phase of the Anthropocene.

Here the irony of modern modes of administration, the use of stable borders and demarcated geographical spaces as the basis for sovereign authority, when rapid transformation is the essence of modernity, is palpable (Brown 2010). Security understood in terms of stability, rather than adaptability, is more likely to be an obstacle than a help to rapid adaption. If, however, security is reformulated in global and human terms, rather than national terms, it might be a useful political concept in helping facilitate the innovative focus on what humans need in specific places in the face of global changes. The Anthropocene discussion of global politics isn't about states or the themes that usually relate to either peace or war; putting climate security into the traditional terms of national security is misguided although in the short term at least military assistance in dealing with disasters seems likely to be needed.

The fearful prognostications of Malthusian pessimism in the form of fears of nomadic hordes that threaten imperial centres—tropes that animate some of the more rhetorically compelling sections of Malthus's ([1798] 1970) text of two centuries ago—no longer apply in a global system where such nomads are a tiny fraction of the human population, and where high-tech industrial militaries are what matter in terms of combat. However, such imputed environmental causations related to pre-modern territorial arrangements, and in Malthus's case the fall of the Roman Empire, are remarkably persistent in contemporary security narratives, especially those linking environment and conflict in Africa (Hartmann 2014). Now we don't set off in search of greener pastures; nomadic war bands are a thing of the past, or at least they were if most of the currently popular post-apocalyptic fictional genres are ignored! Now, however, migrants forced to move by climate induced disruptions are nonetheless seen as security threats to metropolitan states by xenophobic and populist politicians anxious to build walls and restrict migration. The upshot is more violence at the frontiers and where migrants move (Jones 2016).

While global corporations do seek out new frontiers for production schemes and new lands to incorporate into their global operations, it is important to emphasize that imperial centres disrupt peripheral ecologies, while peripheral peoples do not seriously threaten urban civilization. Portraying peripheral areas as threats to metropolitan security is a pattern powerfully reinforced by the geopolitical formulations of the war on terror, but not an accurate representation of the dramatic disruptions of rural areas that contemporary processes of resource extraction involve (Sassen 2014). Neither is it the appropriate geography for understanding how sustainable practices require simultaneously reducing the urban footprint on rural areas in the Global South while regenerating their ecologies. If innovations driven by cities are to be an important part of the future, they cannot be about ever-larger extractions of energy and resources from rural ecologies (O'Lear 2018).

That interconnectedness has also made it clear that the global economy provides what urban humanity needs to sustain its mode of life, and insofar as global security means anything, making a functional economy work is now key (Stiglitz and Kaldor 2013). The ambiguities and contradictions in such formulations are noteworthy, but now, and this is the key point, unavoidable in any serious effort to engage politics with ecological transformations. It is so because the global economy is what is producing the future configuration of the planet and the conditions of human existence in that future. Decisions about what gets produced and built are key to the future of the increasingly artificial biosphere; this is where crucial decisions are being taken about decarbonizing the global economy (Rockström et al. 2016). Investors and property speculators rarely understand their actions in these terms even if they have to file environmental impact statements as part of their development plans.

No longer is this about economy versus environment. As

the authors of the 2012 *Global Environmental Outlook* put it in subtitle of their report, it is now about "environment for the future we want" (UNEP 2012). This phrasing was used in the United Nations Sustainable Development summit of 2012, the twenty-year follow-on from the 1992 Earth Summit in Brazil. This theme reworks the old environment vs economy discussion. It is now about what kind of environment the economy will produce in future. That key insight is what makes the Anthropocene such a useful concept, one that renders the assumptions of separate environments and economies redundant and, in the process, makes geopolitics a matter of considering such things as the rules and regulations for how the global economy will be remade. The key point here, in terms of how security is rethought in the Anthropocene, is that current geopolitical calculations in trade negotiations are shaping the future climate of the planet, not that climate change may have impacts on the future of geopolitics (Dalby 2014a). Arcane points of international trade negotiations are now the terms of geopolitical competition that matter in terms of building economies less dependent on carbon fuels (Wang, Gu and Li 2012).

If global corporations can invoke local content rules in international trade agreements to effectively prevent some attempts to revive local economies, then clearly geopolitical power, and with it decisions about the future configuration of production systems on the planet, are not located "in" sovereign states, even if those states are technically the agencies that actually write the rules that corporations use. The new geopolitics of renewable energy draw on very different political economies of production (Global Commission on the Geopolitics of Energy Transformation 2019). Not least because of the most obvious point about renewable energy is that it doesn't use fuel. All this suggests a very different set of geographies in future. The next stage of the Anthropocene will be one of dramatic change, either to build sustainable urban habitats or to struggle to deal with increasingly severe climate disruptions should political elites try to reinvent "guardian" modes of security while failing to innovate energy systems and modes of consumption.

CHAPTER 9

ANTHROPOCENE DISCOURSE

> More than a neologism or mere geological label, the Anthropocene is a grand tale about humanity and its place in the world told using a repertoire of tropes. For all its talk of rocks and species and the deep past, it is as much about imagination, futures, and the divine as it is about scientific knowledge, practices, and institutions. (Lauren Rickards 2015: 280)

ORIGINS AND DISPERSALS

The analysis in previous chapters repeatedly suggests the Anthropocene is a key concept for rethinking many things and, in particular, the assumptions underpinning much of the discussion of sustainability. This chapter turns to engage some of the controversies over the use of the term and to think through the political difficulties involved in its invocation. The epistemological difficulties following from the collapse of nature and culture—where the world is increasingly artificial, the consequences of a growing technosphere—need attention if sustainability is to be reworked as a useful way of dealing with rapid and frequently disruptive change (Connolly 2013). Crucially, as this book repeatedly emphasizes, "the Anthropocene" shifts discussions from an environmental register to a geological one, with implications that may yet turn out to be profound for human affairs in general, as well as for numerous scholarly endeavours that can no longer take assumptions of a given natural context for granted in their investigations of humanity.

In popular media, the term spread quickly. In March 2011, *National Geographic* ran a cover story on the Anthropocene written by Elizabeth Kolbert; two months later, in the May 28 issue, *The Economist* ran a cover story simply called "Welcome to the Anthropocene." Its writers did not mince words:

> The Anthropocene is different. It is one of those moments when a scientific realization, like Copernicus grasping that the earth goes round the sun, could fundamentally change people's view of things far beyond science. It means more than rewriting some textbooks. It means thinking afresh about the relationship between people and their world and acting accordingly. (*The Economist* 2011: 80)

Not waiting for a formal scientific decision by the geologists, the journal *Anthropocene* and the *Anthropocene Review* both began publication, to be joined a little later by *Elementa: Science of the Anthropocene*. The rock band Cattle Decapitation's 2015 album is titled "Anthropocene Extinction." Dale Jamieson and Bonnie Nadzam (2015) come at matters differently in their book *Love in the Anthropocene,* using a series of fictions to think about the near future in light of the geological turn in thinking. The Globaia website has multiple imaginative visual representations of the new era. Mark Whitehead's geography textbook using the term appeared in 2014. Adam Trexler's (2015) scholarly study of the novel in a time of climate crisis called *Anthropocene Fictions* appeared soon after. CliFi has now become a new fiction subgenre (Milkoreit 2017). Its themes are also appearing in theatre, poetry, and a growing literature on ecocriticism too (Johns-Putra 2016), all of which suggests a series of cultural innovations that make the Anthropocene discussion, and climate change in particular, part of a larger cultural change.

This change requires rethinking conventional assumptions about how to act as the transformation of the Earth System accelerates, grappling with future possible socio-technical imaginaries, to use Sheila Jasanoff's term (Jasanoff and Kim 2015), in thinking through possible future configurations of the technosphere (Donges et al. 2017). The geoengineering discussion, engaged in chapter 7, is in many ways an important variation on this theme of socio-technical imaginaries on the largest scale (Baskin 2019). The gap between what geological formulations of a rapidly changing biosphere suggest needs to be done and the existing capabilities of human governance suggest an "Anthropocene gap" that needs urgent attention in policy making (Galaz 2014). On this theme, the United Nations Environment Program (2018) has published a series of reports on the emissions gap between what needs to be done to limit climate change and the trajectory of greenhouse gas production. The Anthropocene suggests, in a pithy summation, just how much more is needed in terms of intellectual and political engagement if this gap is to be closed and a sustainable future in a stabilized Earth System is to be constructed. The future of the planet is a matter of power, culture, and politics, not just a matter of climate science (Hulme 2014), and is beginning to be engaged as such.

As the epigraph from Lauren Rickards' (2015) paper suggests, the Anthropocene has become a term loaded with all sorts of cultural meanings; a lightning rod for current deliberations on the human fate. As she suggests, the Anthropocene has clearly become a metaphor for the present, a terminological marker of the turbulent transitory times in which we live as well as a matter of intense discussion within the geological sciences. This has all sorts of implications for many scholarly disciplines, most obviously for the discipline of geography and environmental studies (Castree 2015). This is the case because traditional assumptions of environment—that which surrounds humanity and is the given context for humanity—have to be fundamentally rethought.

Crucially, the Anthropocene suggests that assumptions of an external Earth being controlled by an imperial humanity are no longer tenable; environment, as a given context, has to give way to an understanding of humanity as a key part of a rapidly changing biosphere. The formulation of the technosphere makes clear that the new entities the planetary boundaries framework now includes (Steffen et al. 2015) have to be worked into discussions of the evolving Earth System (Zalasiewicz et al. 2017). The Anthropocene emphasizes the key point that the future for humanity and Earth will be a series of political struggles over how that future is to be shaped, by whom, and for what larger purpose (Harrington and Shearing 2017; Dryzek and Pickering 2019).

Considerable caution is needed in invoking this particular scientific view of present circumstances; science is not unrelated to attempts to govern human affairs, and the political implications of attempting to see the Earth as a whole are not trivial (Lövbrand, Stripple, and Wiman 2009). There is a history to the global environmental change scientific endeavour, one driven by a sensibility that prioritizes "big science," modelling, and its knowledge practices (Uhrqvist 2014). This is frequently in danger of ignoring marginal peoples, gender biases in the research, and the implicit cultural assumptions that drive international collaborations. Nonetheless, insofar as environmental contexts are part of the larger considerations of peace and sustainability in coming decades, the Earth System science perspective provides a contextualization that distances analysis from an undue focus on states and demands an engagement with the specific material contexts of vulnerability in an innovative way that makes it difficult to avoid the key issues of the politics of security (Dalby 2009a).

The larger engagement between humanities, social, and natural sciences that has often been bypassed by disciplinary foci on one or the other is in urgent need of engagement, and Earth sciences provide an especially productive way to link environmental change to history (Hornborg, McNeill, and Martinez-Alier 2007) as well as to a wider range of humanities scholarship (Palsson, Szerszynski, and Sörlin et al. 2013), philosophy (Williston 2015), and political theory (Arias-Maldonado and Trachtenberg 2019). Such intellectual conversations are simply essential in large-scale discussions of sustainability; these frameworks are increasingly being used to discuss innovative development policies as well as climate adaptations (Pisano and Berger 2013; Raworth 2017). Historians and geographers are providing much contextual information to fill in the gaps in the system-driven sciences and, as such, the Anthropocene debate is breaking down disciplinary silos in ways that make the politics of epistemology unavoidable (Castree 2015; Davies 2016). How to use these innovations in pedagogy suitable for the twenty-first century also requires a careful interrogation of the assumptions brought to bear on the Anthropocene discussion (Jagodzinski 2018).

PROLIFERATING TERMS

Not surprisingly, this flurry of activity around the Anthropocene formulation has spun off commentary and additional terminological innovations that nuance and add to the discussion. Alternatives to the Anthropocene have included suggestions that, given how important greenhouse gases are to the current transformation of the planet, and that these gases are the product of combustion processes, we might better name our era the Pyrocene, the age of fire (Pyne 2015). Stephen Pyne's suggestion isn't a serious scientific formulation, at least not yet, but in linking humanity's key innovation in taming and learning to use fire for its own purposes, he provides a key link to the formulation that notes the transformative possibilities of fire and how combustion has unleashed the new Prometheans of our time to remake things on a planetary scale (Dalby 2018). Combustion is key to the processes that humanity lives with, appropriates, uses, and modifies (Clark 2012); fossil fuel combustion links geology to humanity and back to geology very directly.

Perhaps, though, to return to the discussion of a stratigraphic marker as key to the Anthropocene, we might think about the geomorphic processes of deposition to find the key to the new stratigraphy. Numerous plastic wastes are washing up on beaches. The Carboniferous and Devonian deposits or life forms are being reworked into plastics, which in turn are being deposited once again in the geomorphological processes of the planet. These suggest a whole new set of depositional features, a new form of geological material "plastiglomerates." This being the case, Corcoran, Moore, and Jazvac (2014) suggest we might best describe present circumstances in terms of the Plasticene!

Kate Raworth (2014) pointedly noted that most of these discussions about the Anthropocene, and whether we are in it or not, are being held by men. Decisions about it that are likely to emerge from the deliberations of the Anthropocene Working Group are surely influenced by the fact that only five of the thirty-six members are women, and that is only after some women were added to the initial group. If the evils of patriarchy may be more to blame than humanity in general, then perhaps it would indeed be better to term our current age the Manthropocene.

One of the persistent critiques of the Anthropocene argument is that it generalizes the speed and scale of contemporary transformations to humanity in general, whereas only some parts of humanity are primarily responsible for the destruction of many natural phenomena and the huge inequities of the present system (Malm and Hornborg 2014). Or, perhaps, given the obscene injustices involved in the global economy, and the clear dangers of current trajectories to numerous peoples who have done little to generate the increasing hazards to which they are vulnerable, geographers are also starting to consider this theme under the term Anthropo-obscene, as in the title of a September 2015 conference in Stockholm and resulting book (Ernstson and Swyngedouuw 2019).

The suggestion that the Anthropocene is obscene is driven by the concern with the inequalities that the contemporary global economy produces and emphasizes. The dynamics of capitalism are towards the accumulation of wealth in a few hands as the converse of processes that marginalize and dispossess the majority of humanity. Spreading practices of extraction of both resources and labour related to the expansion of the reach of the global economy suggest the driving forces of the current Anthropocene are not humanity in general, but the specific social relations of capitalism with its logics of accumulation. Not surprisingly, 'capitalocene' has thus been added into the discussion to focus more explicit attention on the causes of environmental change as a consequence of particular forms of social organization rather than a matter of humanity undifferentiated (Moore, 2016). Focusing on the extinction crisis and the rapid killing off of numerous species, Justin McBrien (2016) suggests the term necrocene.

Donna Harraway (2016) suggests that we need to think in ontological terms in ways that recognize the interconnectedness of things, a tentacular stringy world about which we are telling very inadequate stories. Surely the hubris of invoking the Anthropocene is misplaced in a world of surprising linkages and transformations? Harraway suggests that chthulucene, a term partly derived from the Greek term khthonios, meaning of the Earth, is more appropriate to capture the multiplicity of entities, evolutions, and remakings of a world imagined as much more complex than the simple assumptions of autonomous interacting entities that populate the modern imagination. Refusing human nature dichotomies is key to this discussion, whichever term is adopted, to tell more efficacious stories of how we got to the current crisis and what can be done by who and where in present circumstances.

Climate scientist James Hansen and colleagues (2016) attempted to emphasize the urgency of dealing with climate change in particular by adding the term Hyper to the discussion of the Anthropocene. In this formulation the authors emphasize that while human actions have long been part of the processes that shape the planetary climate, the recent massive burning of fossil fuels is a novel force that needs to be attended to urgently. Dismissing the claims that the much-discussed limitations of global average temperature to a 2-degree Celsius increase will be adequate to evade dangerous consequences, they suggest that emergency action is needed to curtail the growth of greenhouse gases to prevent rapid and dangerous sea-level rise in coming decades—hence his fee-and-dividend scheme suggestion discussed above in chapter 6.

The dangers of states invoking emergency action and acting in draconian manners has long concerned scholars of contemporary change (Swyngedouw 2010); if elites act on the basis of emergency proclamations, there is no clear indication that they will necessarily act to ameliorate the worst impacts of climate change rather than trying to control the social challenges to the existing social order. In these circumstances, it is all too easy to portray climate activists and their opposition to fossil fuel industries as the security threat that matters most. As the geoengineering discussion makes clear, the potential for attempts at technical fixes which allow political elites to avoid dealing with the consequences of climate change looms over the climate discussion. The politics of who takes what drastic action matter greatly; as the argument throughout this book suggests, the focus has to be on what gets made and who decides.

GOOD OR BAD ANTHROPOCENE

These terminological variations on the theme of the Anthropocene are loosely grouped into what Christophe Bonneuil (2015) terms four narratives. First is the naturalist narrative, one that draws on global environmental data to suggest that humanity has gradually, albeit unwittingly, changed the planet, to a point that has recently become a crisis. As chapter 2 of this volume outlines, this narrative suggests that humanity is on a long-term trajectory of growth in population and economic activity. Man has shifted from hunter-gatherer to telluric force. Sound science will be needed if the human collectivity is to manage the future of planet Earth; in short, this narrative is a retelling of modernity. Second is a grand narrative of a good Anthropocene, one in which science and technology will produce a benign future for humanity in which the unleashed powers of innovation promise the liberation of humanity from nature, an 'ecopragmatist' resolution to the difficulty of the naturalist narrative and the concerns of the Earth System scientists. Third are the eco-catastrophist stories that suggest the Anthropocene is likely to end up being very bad indeed (Wallace-Wells 2019); disaster looms as humanity befouls its own nest beyond its abilities to recoup a functional biosphere, or at least to perpetuate the circumstances of the Holocene where a benign set of circumstances has allowed humanity to flourish. Fourth in Bonneuil's (2015) formulation is the eco-Marxist line of argument that suggests the inequalities of capitalism and the imperial extractions of ecological production from the colonies were a key part of the forces that set the Anthropocene in motion. The failure of capitalism, at least so far, to deal with its major ecological consequences suggests a political crisis is looming, one that, without a resolution that leads to very different modes of economy, will indeed end up as a global ecocatastrophe (Parr 2013). Sustainability is all about preventing this outcome.

All of this suggests the future of the Anthropocene may be very bad if humanity, or at least the decision makers in powerful states and corporations, fail to act to rapidly change matters by thinking about sustainability broadly and in the long term. The imminent destruction of the coastal areas of Bangladesh, China, and the United States in the face of sea-level rise of a few metres—a rise that is an inevitable consequence of warming seas and polar ice cap loss—suggests a very nasty future for substantial parts of humanity and a potential general crisis should governance mechanisms not be put in place to deal with these changes. This would not be, by any standards, a good Anthropocene for much of humanity in the not so distant future. The future of the Anthropocene is unavoidably about political power and whether the current political economy will be retained, with all the implications this has for remaking human inequality (Ciplet, Roberts, and Kahn 2015) or, as climate activists and ecosocialists hope, whether the opportunity is taken to rework human affairs fairly drastically to think seriously about sustainability for all (Wark 2015).

The argument for a good Anthropocene (Revkin 2014) suggests technological innovation, and the ability to learn and adapt to a rapidly changing world, promises prosperity and plenty for humanity (Ackerman 2014). Epitomized by the "Ecomodernist Manifesto" (Asafu-Adjaye et al. 2015), the argument is that the future holds all sorts of promise if ecological innovations and technology are used to reduce the ecological impacts of an increasingly urbanized humanity on the biosphere. To do so has to involve rejecting the implicit and frequently explicit pessimism of traditional environmentalism and recognize that the future will be very different from the past. Protecting a fast-disappearing Holocene world isn't the priority; shaping a benign technological future is where the focus needs to be to ensure a good Anthropocene transpires.

This debate is frequently fraught, and the good Anthropocene advocates are frequently effectively silent on the politics of how this is to be brought about (Dalby 2016). In particular, how the poor and the marginal are to be included in these techno-utopias of the future is far from clear in much of the discussion (Hamilton 2017). What is clear is that there is nothing inevitable about the future; it's a matter of political action. This is especially clear in the case of climate change where, despite a couple of decades of advocacy of market solutions, cap-and-trade schemes, clean development mechanisms, carbon credits, and offset arrangements, the level of carbon dioxide in the atmosphere continues to grow. Thus, the major issues facing anyone postulating a future in the Anthropocene are those of governance and decision-making concerning how the urban humanity of the next few decades will be fuelled and fed. The infrastructure to keep people alive is now largely artificial (Haff 2014); nature, as modernity formulated it, has been transcended—hence the cultural impetus to think in terms of new vocabularies, and to rework the geological categories of the recent past in light of the insights of Earth systems, which is implicit all through the Anthropocene discussion.

But to engage these discussions requires a much larger cultural shift, one well beyond the finer points of debate in the Anthropocene Working Group or the deliberations of stratigraphic commissions. This is starting to happen in numerous venues: from rock bands, to innovative efforts by artists to produce diverse sculptures, to a growing literature on climate fiction, to new ontological speculations in philosophy and media studies. The ecohumanities discussion has been revived around the Anthropocene discussion, too, suggesting disciplines well beyond the ambit of Earth sciences are becoming engaged (Hamilton and Bonneuil 2015). Profound questions for political practice are also generating commentary, not least in suggesting that traditional liberal political invocations of identity in terms of citizenship are now outdated by the urgent necessity to think of ourselves in political terms as Earthlings, not just citizens of particular places (Eckersley 2015).

Such re-imaginings of the human condition, and in particular the growth of fictional representations of the future, are bringing novelists and filmmakers explicitly into debate with Earth Systems thinking, and into the fraught politics of climate change too. While these themes have long been ignored by writers of conventional fiction, the huge silence that Amitav Ghosh (2016) termed the "great derangement," the renewed focus on climate change following the Paris Agreement, and the escalating disasters around the world are all now matters of popular culture and fictional representations. These are also stretching the discussion beyond the focus on collective climate action on adaptation and resilience, and onto conventional assumptions of who acts politically, how, and where. Referring to novels by Kim Stanley Robinson, Paulo Bacigalupi, and Saci Lloyd, Trexler (2015: 236) suggests that they

> begin to describe a world in which politicians must lead massive adaptation efforts while conceding that some problems are irreversible. In addition, such novels begin to assemble new forms of political agency, spanning insurance companies, scientific organizations, governmental groups, international businesses, zoos, spiritual leaders, technology companies, refugees, homeless people, and stay-at-home parents. By necessity these affiliations go well beyond the formal structures of a representative democracy, imagining new kinds of interconnected action in the Anthropocene.

What forms these might take, and how they may yet inform political practice, is a key question for the current generation of social scientists.

The Anthropocene is, thus, a metaphor for more than a scientific debate among geologists. It is also a term raising crucial philosophical questions for the world's social scientists, who ponder the nature of the home that humanity is rapidly remaking—for better or worse. The key point is that the imperial, and metropolitan, assumptions that have long structured the disciplinary perspectives are being undercut by Earth System science in ways that parallel the postmodern and more radical critiques of traditional practice. At least the Anthropocene debate has this potential if its radical implications are fully engaged, rather than if the term is used merely as an addendum to conventional thinking.

THE DANGERS OF ANTHROPOCENOLOGY

Two points in the current discussions of political ecology, resources justice, and environment are especially important when the Anthropocene formulation is brought to bear. First is the clear implication that declensionist fears, ones of humanity degrading a given nature, running down resources, and demolishing ecosystems, have to be countered both by more complicated stories of ecological recovery and reconstruction after damaging events and about discussions of how to design spaces, places, and ecologies that are simultaneously more just and sustainable (Ernstson and Swyngedouw 2019). The discourses of resilience are important here (Grove 2018); ecosystems can rebound from devastation, either directly human induced or otherwise. There are, of course, limits to this as the planetary boundary on biodiversity emphasizes; extinctions of particular species preclude their involvement in ecosystem recoveries. "Sledgehammer transitions," as discussed in chapter 3, may preclude a rebound into something analogous to what went before—hence, inducing a state change. The Anthropocene formulation emphasizes change. It counters former imperial assumptions of a relatively stable nature, partly disrupted by human activities with a much more dynamic understanding of ecology and niche creation, and of humanity as a global scale change agent.

The second, related, point is that terrestrial ecosystems, and increasingly oceanic ones, too, have been dramatically altered by human activity in the Holocene—most obviously by the dramatic changes wrought since the expansion of the European system that has generated the discussion in terms of the orbis hypothesis (Lewis and Maslin 2015). No longer, as Ellis (2011) suggests, can maps of the terrestrial surface accurately show matters in terms of biomes, the traditional colonial mapping practices of the planet in terms of natural ecological assemblages. As Castree (2015) makes very clear, the danger remains that the global view of the Earth as an object for management by a technical elite may well be asserted by scientists unreflective about the social arrangements of the Anthropocene, and who wish for a coordinated technological global response to the crisis of climate change without realizing that much of what we are dealing with now is a consequence of prior attempts at imperial management using such techniques. As chapter 5 suggested, the engineering techniques for climate adaptation projects frequently fail to grapple with either the specific ecological context or the social consequences of their projects. The apotheosis of this mentality is geoengineering proposals for solar radiation management.

The alternatives—more sustainable modes of life not dependent on the financial decisions of the rich and powerful, and financial systems that so frequently continue to dispossess and destroy both modes of life and environments (Sassen 2014)—pose questions of who social science researchers are and from whence they speak, study, and write. They simultaneously challenge the social sciences to re-examine some of their basic pedagogical strategies and to look, once again, at some of the classical debates about possibilism: how future planetary possibilities are conjectured in discussions of urbanism, ecological engineering, conservation, and related matters as well as in the burgeoning genre of climate or eco-fiction and more broadly in the cultural vocabularies of utopian and dystopian fictions (DaSilva 2018; Lipschutz 2018). Crucially in all this, the mode of accumulation and related lifestyles of automobile-based suburban constructions have to be challenged given how unsustainable their resource consumption requirements are (Keil 2019). The Anthropocene requires researchers and activists to clearly focus on the decision-making processes in human affairs, how capital is invested in making the future in ways that are now key to shaping the future configuration of the technosphere, and hence the functioning of the biosphere, and with it the life chances of both urban humanity and other species.

Dipesh Chakrabarty (2017) is especially concerned that social scientists will use the Anthropocene formulation to simply add one more argument to their critiques of the deleterious effects of globalization, and capitalism in general, without appreciating the geological-scale transformations that we are living through, which need to be addressed with appropriately fundamental rethinking of contemporary politics. Despite its obvious applicability to international relations as a discipline, neither are scholars addressing the issues raised by the Anthropocene formulation in anything like the comprehensive way one might expect—hence the need to engage this field with a "Planet Politics" manifesto (Burke et al. 2016). Even when these issues are addressed, the response from some critics has been to suggest that a cosmopolitan sensibility, which is hard to avoid if one is thinking in terms of rapid transformation of the biosphere, is a sleight of hand hiding an imperial agenda to impose global solutions on local situations (Chandler, Cudworth, and Hobden 2018). This problem arises in part because invocations of an undifferentiated humanity on whose behalf social scientists claim to speak slips easily into assumptions of one centralized technological response to contemporary problems. But a more careful reading of what the Anthropocene involves suggests that a highly diverse set of changes in numerous locales is the likely response to climate change in particular, and that a one-size-fits-all solution to global change isn't feasible, certainly not by fiat from some planetary authority (Fishel et al. 2018).

This book is not the place for a detailed engagement with the cosmopolitan tradition, or recent efforts to rethink it and suggest how its flaws might be tackled by imaginative philosophical engagement (see Nussbaum 2019), but at least some aspects of cosmopolitan thinking and a focus on universal notions of the desirability of a dignified life for all humans seems unavoidable when engaging the Anthropocene. Daniel Deudney's (2018) recent rethinking of cosmopolitanism suggests the initial stoic formulations were obviously elitist and the Kantian ones, too, had a top-down view of political change. This seems to be the source of Chandler, Cudworth, and Hobden's (2018) objection to the cosmopolitan formulation in the Planet Politics manifesto (Burke et al. 2016). Deudney (2018: 255) suggests that what he sees as a new third instantiation of cosmopolitanism has "shed their earlier elitist, apolitical, and 'idealistic' (in the sense of utopian) affinities and tendencies, and embraced agendas that are radically democratic, strongly political, and plausibly realizable." This depends on remapping the world as a single place, something that the Anthropocene discussion does, epitomized by Globaia.org images that frequently populate visual representations of the Earth in videos and the ubiquitous PowerPoint presentations used by Earth System scientists.

A serious engagement with the Anthropocene requires a cosmopolitan sensibility, because the growth of the technosphere and, simultaneously, global governance arrangements that are in part shaping its emerging configurations require multiple efforts at regulation in numerous economic sectors. As the Paris Agreement makes clear, state efforts are going to be necessary to tackle climate change; there is no plausible institutional form that can solve climate change in the traditional policy sense (Dimitrov 2019). More pointedly, it's worth emphasizing that non-state actors are frequently taking initiatives where national states fail to act (Bernstein and Hoffman 2018). Insofar as this is consistent with Deudney's formulation of the third phase of cosmopolitanism as a contribution to what he calls a "terrapolitan project," which is about "building a polity suited to the monstrously novel circumstances of the Earth as a place" (Deudney 2018: 257), the multiple centres of authority and the necessity of numerous initiatives are consistent with the geological scale of contemporary transformations.

The point is that globalization renders the world a single place, in stark contrast to the political assumptions of separate polities. The political forms governance now takes are, as chapter 8 suggests, being contested by the rise of nationalism and xenophobia, restrictive trade arrangements, wall-building, and efforts to restrict migration, but global governance as a project has some autonomy and clearly works in agenda-setting mode as a counter to the narrow claims of sovereignty (Zurn 2018). Here, in part, is where the cosmopolitan ethos of living in a "Planetary Earth" (Deudney 2018) engages with the Anthropocene, and in the process requires a rethinking of our place in the cosmos, and a focus on matters of production, on what is made in the global economy, how, and where, and with what consequences along global commodity chains.

A focus on these factors also challenges the framing of climate change as climate terror (Chaturvedi and Doyle 2015), a sense of imminent apocalyptic events, and disaster on the global scale as an inevitable fate. While the urgency to act is clear, what Earth System science is making clear is that a wholesale collapse of the climate system isn't what is coming, but the larger the emissions of greenhouse gases the more disruption will have to be dealt with in the future (Steffen et al. 2018). The planetary boundary for climate change, and irreversible changes to the functioning of the biosphere, is approaching, but even if it is crossed, life will go on. It will just be much more difficult than it need be for much of humanity, and radical social changes are going to follow, either by sensible anticipatory planning, or as a result of conflict set in motion by elites failing to cope with what they perceive as threats to their prosperity and control over social and economic life. Finding the appropriate metaphors and narrative structure to rethink global politics, and the Earth as a single place in which these things play out, is the challenge for social scientists, activists, policy makers, and cultural workers of all kinds in present circumstances.

Collapsing the environment–humanity dichotomy is one of the key consequences of the Anthropocene formulation, one that has been taken up rapidly in the first few years of the second decade of the current millennium. Taking it up suggests the earlier discussions of environmental determinism have been turned on their head (Dalby 2015a); the issue for contemporary investigation is not, as colonial formulations once had it, how environments have shaped human societies. What matters now are questions of the possible futures being constructed by human decisions about what to produce, and how to reshape landscapes that are being both directly remade by agricultural, resource extraction, and urbanization processes, and indirectly remade by climate changes and related ecological disruptions.

Where a philosophy of possibilism was once a response to determinism (Febvre 1996), it is now, it seems, worth revisiting at a larger scale; the future is open in many ways. The human future is an urban one it seems, but what kind of global urbanity matters greatly in coming decades. Urban futures that follow the aspirations of the ecomodernists and integrate ecological processes into urban design while reducing the necessity to extract resources from disturbed rural landscapes, primarily through technological efficiency improvements, may lead to a less severely disruptive Anthropocene. Efforts on the part of elites to build enclaves of affluence that separate the rich from the rest and enforce such divisions with security narratives and the use of fences and violence to keep the poor at bay, may lead to dystopian environmental conflict, as so dramatically suggested by Paulo Bacigalupi in his 2015 novel *The Water Knife*.

The nightmare scenario for latter-day environmentalists is precisely that such violent futures will provide compelling arguments for attempts to artificially manipulate the atmosphere in efforts at solar radiation management. Geoengineering beckons as the ultimate technical fix to human problems, although of course solar radiation management won't deal with the biggest problem of all, which may turn out to be the acidification of the oceans due to their absorption of carbon dioxide (Pierrehumbert 2019). It offers the promise of a global thermostat to adjust the planet's response to human combustion. Exactly who might decide how hot it should get is a key geopolitical question for future decades if more benign modes of planetary management are not adopted soon (Caseldine 2015). These discussions emphasize that environment is over in the sense of any notion of a given context for the human drama.

GAIA AND GEOSTORY

Bruno Latour's (2017) reflections on natural theology highlight the point that traditional notions of nature structuring numerous modes of thinking are also no longer tenable as useful concepts. Nature has frequently acted as a theological concept, a matter of the divine, as a given, beyond human actions. In light of the Anthropocene discussion, such distinctions are no longer useful. While preserving species diversity is a key theme in any discussion of the future, it is important to recognize that maintaining habitat in situ, and anchoring species to particular locales, is no longer necessarily appropriate given changing climatic conditions. Neither is resilience, for all its implicit flexibilities, necessarily useful if it presupposes a return to a prior state after a disturbance; in many cases it's necessary to consider how to transform matters rather than try to return to a status quo ante (Pelling 2011). The point about the Anthropocene is that rapid change is now the norm, and what it is that has to be preserved may now simply be the ability to adapt.

In these terms, where Nature is no longer a given, and change is the norm while the distinction between science and humanities is collapsing, Latour's (2017) suggestion of geostory as a synthesis of geology and history, a dynamic unfolding drama rather than matters written in stone, is apt. With that goes the need to think without nature too, and here Gaia may work better as a category given both its self-regulating adaptive attributes and its ability to accommodate humanity as but the latest of many innovations within its changing configuration. The point about Gaia isn't that any species matters, but that the combinations have in the past worked as a regulatory system regardless of any particular species and in the absence of any design or intention. Indeed, it is that insight that encourages Lovelock (2014) to warn against attempts to geoengineer the planet and to focus instead on protecting the new urban "hives" that are now humanity's most important habitats.

The point about the Anthropocene is that it isn't the end times (Žižek 2011); it's about the next times. It's a time in which humanity is beginning to live, and in which, while there is both a dramatic decline in biodiversity and destruction of many places shaped by the post ice age conditions of the last dozen millennia, new assemblages are being constructed rapidly. The legacy of the carboniferous period in geological history in particular is being reworked very rapidly in geological terms, for that is what is now being done given the current human proclivity for using combustion to turn rocks back into air. Much of the conventional thinking about security perpetuates this problem by posing climate as a risk to the existing social order, and, hence, climate security as a matter of risk governance for NATO and other international security institutions (Lippert 2019).

The cultural politics of this play out in the politics of climate denial, and the petro-masculinist tropes of domination and power-perpetuating automobile culture based on internal combustion engines (Daggett 2018). Premised on the modern assumptions of practically unlimited resources, and the separation of humanity from an external nature, climate denial frequently meshes with concerns that social change is undermining the social order wherein men are dominant and ecological concerns are dismissed as feminine, and hence not a matter for men to take seriously. Focused in 2019 on the intense hostility directed towards some key youthful women activists—Greta Thunberg and Alexandria Ocasio-Cortez in particular—objections to acting on climate raise the key questions of what form of social order is being secured (Gelin 2019). The hostility to climate activists is also tied directly to the politics of white nationalism and the cultural fears of losing control. While much of the discussion might invoke the science, or the rejection of its key findings, much of the political force driving the rejection of climate policy lies in this cultural politics.

The crucial point in Latour's (2017) invocation of geostory is that neither humans nor ecosystems are in control; their mutual constitution in coming decades is something that at least some parts of humanity can actively shape. To be sure, powerful corporate and state actors will certainly be co-authors of the geostory. However, so might social activists. As Naomi Klein (2014) makes clear, social movements, both those resisting the worst excesses of extractive activities and those actively seeking more just and sustainable ways of life, can act to shape key political choices. Making cities more livable while reducing their resource demands from rural hinterlands and the more distant commodity chains of the global economy is key to a more sustainable future. Sustainability now requires thinking in these terms, of rapid adaptations while simultaneously reducing the disruptions to the remaining ecosystems that are struggling to change while building ecologies that minimize the use of carbon fuels and facilitate diversity. These are the key themes for addressing sustainability in a climate-disrupted world (Meadowcroft et al. 2019).

But in all this the necessity of thinking about peaceful transitions to a more sustainable world loom too; the original formulation in *Our Common Future* (World Commission on Environment and Development 1987) emphasized the importance of conflict avoidance for sustainable development. Avoiding conflict both at local levels to facilitate development and at the global scale to avoid the extremely rapid climate onset threatened by potential nuclear winters was seen in the 1980s as a necessary prerequisite for sustainable development. Failure to deal with these matters leaves open the prospect not only of a hothouse Earth trajectory for the future, one that will be profoundly disruptive, but the worse possibilities of these disruptions leading to major nuclear wars in the future. Pondering such a long-term future, and the geological legacy that the plutonium in nuclear weapons would leave in the sedimentary record, Andrew Glickson (2017) has suggested that rather than Anthropocene, the term Plutocene might be more appropriate.

CHAPTER 10

POLITICAL GEOECOLOGY

> The Stabilized Earth trajectory requires deliberate management of humanity's relationship with the rest of the Earth System if the world is to avoid crossing a planetary threshold. We suggest that a deep transformation based on a fundamental reorientation of human values, equity, behavior, institutions, economies, and technologies is required. Even so, the pathway toward Stabilized Earth will involve considerable changes to the structure and functioning of the Earth System, suggesting that resilience-building strategies be given much higher priority than at present in decision making. (Will Steffen et al. 2018: 6)

> To put it baldly: in the face of what is to come, we cannot continue to believe in the old future if we want to have a future at all. (Bruno Latour 2017: 245)

PLANETARY STEWARDSHIP

Implied, but rarely spelled out in the discussion of sustainable development, is the assumption that the planetary conditions inherited from the Holocene are essential for future generations to meet their needs. This discussion of "physical sustainability" has been elaborated in the planetary boundaries framework discussed in chapter 3. It presupposes that the baseline condition of the planet is one given by the

Holocene parameters that facilitated the emergence of human civilization, and that the planetary boundaries are effectively guard-rails beyond which humanity should not venture. At least a complex civilization of billions of humans shouldn't, because relatively stable conditions for growing food, designing and building cities, and the requisite infrastructure to make them work are necessary—not least because it is far from clear that the existing global institutional framework can accommodate major shocks (Homer-Dixon et al. 2015). In terms of climate geopolitics, this point is much more important than the relatively small-scale disruptions that are the focus of much of the scholarly literature that tries (and mostly fails) to directly link climate change and political violence (Mach et al. 2019; Pearson and Newman 2019).

Sustainable development, as formulated in the United Nations Sustainable Development Goals, is implicitly about economic change while effectively maintaining Holocene conditions, ones that are presumably the optimal state for humanity (Dalby et al. 2019). However, the very awkward assumption about this formulation is that it presupposes precisely what current processes of unsustainable development have started to fundamentally change:

> Environmentalist traditions have long called for a halt to human interference in ecology and the Earth system. In the Anthropocene, the anthropogenic biosphere is permanent, the legacy of our ancestors, and our actions as human systems a force of nature, making the call to avoid human interference with the biosphere irrelevant. The implication is clear; the current and future state of the terrestrial biosphere is up to us, and will be determined by human systems of one form or another, whether it is the momentum of our past or new pathways we are able to achieve in the future. (Ellis 2011: 1027)

It is abundantly clear that decisions about human economic activities are not only central to constructing the future of the planet, but are instrumental in determining whether key boundaries will be crossed. Preventing these transgressions, while simultaneously working back to levels within the boundaries in terms of nitrogen and climate change, as well as drastically reducing the rate of loss of biodiversity, is key to any transition to a human condition that lives within the safe operating space. The alternative requires a transition to a very different configuration of the biosphere, one impossible to predict precisely but, given the phase shifts already looming, one very different from the conditions that have given rise to human civilization. The implicit assumption in juxtaposing transitions, and a peace that can be sustained, is that ecological changes will neither be so drastic nor so quick that major powers resort to military force in attempts to control the human consequences of the disruptions. In short, it's about avoiding a Plutocene!

In Steffen et al.'s (2011b) terms, the next phase of the Anthropocene requires planetary stewardship, a complex matter of global governance requiring numerous social innovations if the Earth is to be kept within a safe operating space loosely analogous to Holocene conditions. While production of chlorofluorocarbons and other ozone-depleting substances has largely ceased due to international cooperation, this has occurred despite a remarkable amount of foot-dragging on the part of specific sectors of some economies, notably some very unlikely industries such as the strawberry producers in California, reluctant to give up their particular mode of soil sterilization despite the hazards it presented to the ozone layer (Gareau 2013). The larger lesson of this case emphasizes the necessity of thinking in terms of how humanity produces things; Anthropocene geopolitics is going to be about how these processes are governed. Phasing out the use of ozone-depleting substances emphasizes that merely regulating the use of substances is not enough for at least some of the planetary boundaries; prohibition of certain activities may be required, and that, in turn, is a matter of global governance.

Looking further ahead, it is clear that decisions about such things as the continued production of coal-powered electricity generation stations are matters of industrial policy that have global consequences. If climate boundaries are not further transcended, then thinking in terms of the political economy of energy systems is essential to future planetary governance. But this is more than a matter of governments regulating some detrimental environmental consequences of economic activity; it is about production decisions and, quite literally, *who* decides *what* gets made. In these terms the Anthropocene has also become an investment problem. It all depends on where capital is put to work, another reason to take the term Capitalocene seriously, even if this isn't exactly how its advocates usually use the term (Moore 2016). If money is spent on electric vehicles, smart grids, insulated buildings, and agroecological innovations, the future will be different than if the same funds are devoted to digging more coal mines and building petroleum pipelines—precisely the fuels that have to stay in the ground if the planet is to remain in a safe operating space.

While there are many economic decision-making authorities, the neo-liberal modes of letting markets make decisions seems unlikely to constrain the use of fossil fuels quickly enough to begin reducing carbon dioxide emissions, even if they do focus attention on how markets might work as governance mechanisms. Carbon taxes are one among many instruments that make a difference, but pricing schemes have to be designed to deal with fuel price fluctuations—as happened to the EU emissions trading scheme—and be protected from the vicissitudes of the electoral cycle, as the 2016 election of Donald Trump and of Doug Ford in Ontario eighteen months later indicate clearly. Both set about dismantling climate initiatives once they were in office. All of which suggests that while humanity may accomplish a transition to renewable energy and phase out the use of carbon fuels, the obstructionist policies of Trump and other similarly minded politicians promises a very disorderly transition (Selby 2019)—unless, that is, political mobilization can effectively challenge such retrograde recklessness.

Outright opposition to climate change policy from the fossil fuel industry, epitomized by the large amount of cash spent to defeat referenda in the United States in the 2018 elections in Washington State and Colorado (Crunden 2018), suggests this political struggle will pit citizens against industry in coming years and go beyond the obvious campaigns for divestment and local opposition to pipelines and extraction infrastructure (Routledge 2017). Initiatives in numerous places, most notably on the part of municipalities whose administrators and politicians increasingly see the consequences of climate disruptions, are suggesting climate politics is shifting to new venues as many states seem to remain incapable of breaking the power of fossil fuel corporations and lobbyists (Bernstein and Hoffman 2018).

The implications of such considerations are profound. While arguments for a transition to a sustainable future suggest that rapidly reducing the disruptions to the natural arrangements that humanity has known since the end of the last ice age approximately ten millennia ago are essential, it is no longer the case that this future will occur in the given circumstances implied by the invocation of physical sustainability. The assumption built into environmental concerns through the discussion of the limits to growth in the 1970s, the 1980s discussions of sustainable development, and subsequently through the initial formulations of the UNFCCC in the 1990s is that the planet ought to be kept in more or less the configuration that has so far nurtured civilization. All this is very new in human affairs.

SUSTAINABLE TRANSITIONS IN A CLIMATE DISRUPTED WORLD

The planetary boundaries framework shows that action is needed immediately. Given these novel circumstances, it is hardly surprising that humanity lacks institutions, much less governance structures, to effectively deal with such issues. However, as other chapters in this book suggest, such structures are now urgently necessary, and need to be formulated so that warfare is precluded as an adaptive mechanism, both because it will make other adaptations more difficult and, in the event of major weapon use, add yet further unpredictable perturbations to the Earth System. In the words of the German Advisory Committee on Climate Change, a United Nations 2.0 is needed, a new structure whose purpose

> would be to take the planetary guard rails into account as a guiding principle that governs all UN actions, the pursuit of which would guarantee the protection of climate and environment in order to stabilize the Earth system as much as peace, security and development. (German Advisory Council 2011: 316)

While this remains an aspiration, the speed of current ecological changes make thinking about new habits of cooperation to deal with coming transformations a crucial part of any transition strategy.

Many of the ecological ideas structuring thinking about environmental strategies also presume some form of stability, or at least a notion of homoeostasis, as the desirable state toward which policy should direct human activity. The last generation of ecological management thinking has drawn heavily on notions of resilience, as well as the frameworks of panarchy and non-linear changes (Gunderson and Holling 2001). Earlier assumptions of stable ecosystems and ecological transitions dating back to a climax condition following disruptions have not been entirely abandoned, but ecological thinking is now much more complicated than visions built upon simplistic assumptions of a stable nature disrupted by human economic activity (Kareiva and Fuller 2016). Even in arguments about resilience, however, it is clear that the assumptions of stability are integral to subsequent bounce-back strategies after a major disruption. Policies using such thinking usually postulate a given, relatively stable, situation which, after facing disruption, can return to more or less the situation prior to the disruption.

However, as the growing awareness of the sheer scale of the human transformation of the biosphere becomes clear, and the failure of humanity to curb the use of fossil fuels ensures at least some climate change is inevitable, policy discussions about adaptation are getting more emphasis (Global Commission on Adaptation 2019). In Bangladesh, where poor people are especially vulnerable to flooding and storms moving up from the Bay of Bengal, adaptation is the order of the day. Flood shelters and rebuilding coastal mangrove forests are necessary tools for dealing with rising sea levels and inundations. In such states there is limited choice in terms of policy; they have done little to cause climate change and can do little to change the global energy mix that is accelerating the process. What sustainability, and the transition to it, might mean in such changing circumstances suggests the most important aspect of sustainability is the flexibility to adapt to new circumstances as they arise. How to make social systems that can change quickly without disruptions, social breakdown, or the use of organized coercion is not easy but it is key to any serious attempt to link peace with sustainability.

The clear implication to be drawn from Earth System science is that such questions are in need of immediate attention. "These are admittedly huge tasks, but are vital if the goal of science and society is to steer the biosphere towards conditions we desire, rather than those that are thrust upon us unwittingly" (Barnosky et al. 2012: 57). Sustainable development implies that economic transitions to modes of industrial activity which do not exceed the parameters of the conditions inherited from the Holocene are key to maintaining a relatively stable biosphere, the *sine qua non* for future generations being able to supply their own needs. But if some of those key parameters have already been exceeded, as the discussion of planetary boundaries suggests, then what kind of transition is needed to peacefully move to what kind of future must be much more carefully deliberated. Nature can no longer be taken for granted as some sort of given context for humanity; the Anthropocene discussion makes it clear the future of humanity—and whether that future is peaceful or not—depends on more than traditional discussions of the causes of war. Humanity is shaping its context in novel ways as the technosphere expands, and that, too, has to be a key part of any discussion about transitions to new modes of economy and life and innovations in global governance (McKeon 2017).

Focusing on the insights of Earth System science, and the clear understanding that humanity is shaping the future in ways that are much more profound than has been understood until very recently, requires social scientists and policy makers (those interested in thinking through strategies of sustainable development and peaceful modes of transition to more ecologically benign economic modes of human life) to incorporate at least four key themes in their work: first, a notion of security very different from cold war versions; second, a recognition that geopolitical contexts are changing; third, a perspective on political geoecology; and, finally, a focus on economic production and investment, rather than looking at environmental protection as key to the next phase of the Anthropocene. Transitions to sustainability focusing on the complexity of social change in particular parts of the world are important, but how particular places play a part in shaping the overall configuration of the future matters greatly (Grin, Rotmans, and Schot 2010). Planning for these in advance, rather than relying on force to try to deal with some of the disruptions, is now key; it requires a move towards policies for global human security.

But now, as discussed in chapter 5, adaptations themselves are causing further environmental transformations. States are buying or leasing land in other states to ensure supplies of food in the future; plantations and commercial farming arrangements are leading to the displacement of peoples. These trends add to land use transformations and, in some cases, chemical pollution from agriculture and mariculture that puts stress on ecosystems. Extending the modern agricultural development model has already caused dramatic disruptions to many ecosystems and may accelerate environmental change; these systems need innovations as part of a larger effort to rethink global governance in terms of planetary boundaries (Galaz et al. 2012). As noted in chapter 5, such policies have backdraught effects that need to be considered in terms of unanticipated consequences of trying to deal with climate change while ignoring other aspects of environmental change. Attempts to adapt to climate change have consequences in terms of how landscapes are remade: such changes need to be thought of in those terms if Earth System analysis is to be worked into policy considerations.

This has international repercussions in terms of trade and the international flows of investment that shape how one state impacts another's ecology. All of this emphasizes decisions about what is being made, and how, rather than discussions of protecting an environment that has already been transformed many times over: this is the context for twenty-first-century geopolitics. A further extension of this point is that the geopolitical rivalries of the present are frequently being played out in the arcane details of trade negotiations (Wang, Gu, and Li 2012). Who will write the rules on technological standards related to new generations of energy technologies matters and, here, the mostly neglected dimension of geopolitics in discussions of sustainable transitions needs to be directly engaged. How what gets produced will literally shape the planetary ecology of the future; the technosphere isn't a monolithic entity. It is being shaped and reshaped by production decisions all the time in the global economy, which in turn is primarily driven by urban demands and the cultural politics of consumption.

Understanding that geopolitics is no longer a simple matter of military rivalry or economic power, but a matter of shaping the technological future to the short-term advantage of the rule-writers—with long-term implications for how the biosphere is shaped—is crucial to linking Earth System thinking to matters of geopolitics. Who writes the rules matters—whether it is fossil fuel company lobbyists or ecologists facilitating innovations. This becomes even more important where discussions of possible geoengineering experiments enter the discussion as a contribution to attempts to keep the planet's climate within a safe operating space (Tollefson 2018). But the simplistic invocation of geopolitical conflict remains appealing to political audiences anxious to identify a clear threat against which mobilization provides a moral clarity justifying "security" actions to ensure survival.

DIVESTMENT DISCOURSE

Ironically, this very language has been a galvanizing trope among divestment activists opposed to the expansion of fossil-fuelled economies. The epigraph to chapter 8 of this volume invokes a new geopolitical situation, one of a global chemical war with the weapons being chimney stacks and exhaust pipes. But this invocation suggests these are weapons of war used by only one side in the new conflict. Who are the participants in this new warfare? In his speech to the United Nations, the representative from Tuvalu (Pita 2007) clearly suggested the fossil fuel-burning peoples of the world were now the threat, and the global community would have to deal with this threat of a warming war in the new geopolitics where ecology is crucial. The chimney stacks and exhaust pipes burn mostly fossil fuels; these are now, surely, the enemy that needs to be defeated in a struggle for a sustainable world. In these terms, presumably, peace is what comes after this war is won, a victory that requires the elimination of the forces that use chimney stacks and exhaust pipes. This kind of climate-resilient peace is a very novel formulation (Barnett 2019), one that runs counter to traditional notions of national security, which are designed to sustain a particular national social order into the future. But it is the kind of geopolitical rethinking that is necessary if many of the low-lying island nations are to remain above the waves. Fossil fuels are what needs to be countered as their consumption presents an existential threat to many societies.

As such, one of the most interesting political struggles in recent years has been the divestment campaign trying to switch investment from fossil fuels into sustainable economic options (Mangat, Dalby, and Paterson 2018). More than just a political campaign, the rhetoric in this movement sometimes draws on powerful military metaphors (Mangat and Dalby 2018). At its heart is an insistence that there is a political struggle over climate, one in which there isn't a consensus on the need for sustainability, but one in which fossil fuel companies have been actively working to delay climate policy, explicitly campaigning against democratic actions to curtail the use of fossil fuels. As chapter 6 outlines, what has been secured in much of the struggle over climate in the last few decades is the fossil fuel-powered economy. The divestment movement has clearly suggested a different rhetorical framing of the issue, one in which the fossil fuel industry is (as the representative from Tuvalu implied) an enemy that has to be defeated. It is one threatening not just Tuvalu's continued existence but, if the planet progresses on a hothouse pathway, one endangering much of humanity in a climate-disrupted world. The policy objective here has to be ending the fossil fuel era to prevent moving onto the hothouse trajectory (Princen, Manno, and Martin 2015).

Directly challenging the post-political world of consensus, from markets and technical fixes to ecological problems, the divestment movement argues that fossil fuel companies are the danger, an enemy that must be defeated if a sustainable future is to be secured. Invoking war metaphors and heroic struggle, Rebecca Solnit (2012) wrote in terms of a war for survival, one that pitted activists against the fossil fuel industry.

> But what victory means needs to be imagined on a whole new scale as the news worsens. … Its victories also capture what a lot of our greenest gifts look like: nothing. The regions that weren't fracked, the coal plants that didn't open, the mountaintops that weren't blasted by mining corporations, the children who didn't get asthma or mercury poisoning from coal emissions, the carbon that stayed in the Earth and never made it into the atmosphere.

The damage done by using fossil fuels is huge, and the struggle for a cleaner greener world as an alternative future is hugely evocative. She continues:

> This is, among other things, a war of the imagination: the carbon profiteers and their politicians are hoping you don't connect the dots, or imagine the various futures we could make or they could destroy, or grasp the remarkably beautiful and complex ways the natural world has worked to our benefit and is now being sabotaged, or discover your conscience and voice, or ever picture how different it could all be, how different it will need to be.

The logic here suggests a battlefield, one where long-term security for all depends on defeating the fossil fuel industry.

It's easy to invoke heroic struggles, to see oneself as on the front lines in a struggle for survival. But is this useful and, if so, under what circumstances might it be politically efficacious? Crucial to all this is the importance of thinking through the audience for which such rhetoric is used, how analogies might be interpreted, the cultural vocabulary in which military metaphors are embedded, and the possibilities of misinterpretation leading to politically inappropriate actions. One of the key problems is the invocation of warfare as either a desirable condition or at least one expected as a matter of necessity. Environmentalists frequently understand military actions and warfare as the problem to be countered, rather than as role models or examples of the kind of action needed to protect existing environments or make societies less likely to endanger either themselves or their ecological contexts. Combat, especially that involving industrial systems, is a violent business; battlefields as well as military facilities often suffer substantial ecological damage. At the beginning of the environmental security discussion, Daniel Deudney (1990) warned of the inappropriateness of having the military deal with environmental change.

Historically, warfare has been about extraordinary action, about resource mobilizations to build weapons in emergency circumstances, and there has been little concern about long-term environmental consequences. Immediate pressing necessities to defeat imminent threats take priority over considerations of what comes after war; reconstruction is postponed for consideration after victory. While this view of warfare, of existential struggles between political organizations, heroic combat, and, of course, ecological destruction, is frequently invoked in popular culture, it's noteworthy that American wars following the Cold War mostly don't fit this pattern (Dalby 2009b). While the events of 9/11 were violent assaults on American soil, or at least concrete, they did not involve a mobilization analogous to the Second World War. Instead of diverting production from civilian products to military ones, President Bush told Americans to go shopping to prove their patriotism. War became about violence "over there," not a matter of domestic disruption. The long war in South West Asia has also involved huge quantities of fossil fuel use, gasoline, diesel, and jet fuel; this mode of geopolitics has large climate and ecological consequences too (Belcher et al. 2019). While the long war has involved dramatic disruptions for the families of U.S. military personnel deployed overseas, most of the violence and most of the dead are far from North America, despite the endless security alerts and rhetorical excesses about the dangers of terrorism. It's not clear that cultural analogies from contemporary times work well in linking environmental change and the need for warlike activities; irregular warfare is an altogether different phenomenon (Rogers 2016).

Nonetheless, when warfare is invoked, as it is by Solnit and other activists, it often now draws analogies from historical episodes. Australian activists a decade ago suggested a mobilization on the scale of the British efforts in the face of imminent invasion in 1940 is needed to tackle the dangers of climate change. Although Spratt and Sullivan (2008) mix their metaphors with medical invocations of imminent danger, as in their invocation of *Climate Code Red* as a planetary emergency facing potential death in the near future, the logic of military style mobilization in the face of imminent threat is very clear. It's an open question as to whether current generations can relate to this historical reference or understand the sense of danger motivating British mobilization in 1940 following the Dunkirk evacuation or during the Battle of Britain. Likewise, particularly in 2019, numerous jurisdictions declared climate emergencies; it is far from clear how these rhetorical exercises will trigger fundamental policy changes.

Another similar Second World War analogy also structures Bill McKibben's 2016 *New Republic* article which argued that a rapid roll-out of new factories building wind turbines and solar panels is needed if the United States is to produce a new energy system for a sustainable future. He suggested that if the United States could rapidly expand its production system to provide for the war machine in the aftermath of the Pearl Harbor attack in December 1941, then it was clearly within the capabilities of the United States to once again mobilize its production capabilities to deal with this imminent danger. The article advocated new facilities be rapidly built; accompanying illustrations explicitly invoked an analogy with Second World War events depicting solar panels and wind turbines successfully invading a territory inhabited by smoke-belching facilities. While this was a call for an industrial-scale initiative, and the historical argument suggested it was entirely feasible given the historical experience of the early 1940s, it is important to emphasize the point that emergency measures are invoked here given McKibben's understanding of the need to act quickly on the climate issue, an understanding amply justified by Earth Systems science and the Intergovernmental Panel on Climate Change (2018) report on 1.5 degrees warming.

Solnit (2012) invokes the moral desirability of doing the right thing, and the satisfactions of right conduct, in her appeal to youthful activists to take part in the "fight" for climate change sanity. Her invocation of the need to act appeals on numerous levels not just the satisfactions of struggling for a worthy cause, and indeed one in which failure might have disastrous consequences. Nonetheless, the focus here is on individual actions in support of collective protest. The climate issue, if it is to be imagined effectively however, requires much more than individual moral action. Here the dangers are that once again neoliberal identities are invoked whereby climate struggles are a matter of individual lifestyles, not a matter of larger collective social action (Szasz 2007). Even focusing on the key corporations that have been responsible for greenhouse gas emissions over the last couple of centuries, while focusing on some key actors, is in danger of evading the larger questions of geopolitical culture, and how we are ranged against them. The "we" are the governments of major powers: firstly, the developed nations and, more recently, China and India, and the persistence (despite the Paris Agreement) of numerous incentives and subsidies to fossil fuel companies that distort the operation of energy markets (Coady et al. 2019). The sensible public policy is to move rapidly away from both fossil fuels, and the modes of landscape destruction that frequently bear the label development.

While individual purchasing decisions do matter, and companies are outdoing themselves these days to portray their products as green, the larger disruptions of ecologies and the history of colonial dispossession and destruction matter more in the politics of climate. The environmentalism of the rich—protecting parks and some parts of landscapes while not dealing with the overall throughput of materials, nor the energy systems facilitating the ever-larger movement of products of the current global economy—is simply not up to the task of remaking the Earth System on the scale that Earth System science suggests is necessary (Dauvergne 2016). For Indigenous peoples, dispossessed by the growth of European empires and subsequently the global economy, being the victims of war that is simultaneously environmental change has long been part of their fate (Grove 2019).

STRATEGY FOR SUSTAINABILITY

Insofar as military metaphors are invoked as part of calls to action, or mobilization of resources to fight climate change, it seems appropriate to invoke notions of strategy in discussions of the Earth System and policy innovations. Strategy is about the appropriate matching of means and ends, of arranging what one has to hand in such a way as to best try to attain one's ends despite the worst efforts of an antagonist. In Carl von Clausewitz's (1989) famous formulations terms, war is also about pursuing policy by other than diplomatic means. Crucially, war has usually involved operating in ways to end the enemy's will to fight. In classic discussions of warfare, it is about compelling the antagonist to do your bidding regardless of their desire to do so.

Focusing on the will of the opponent to resist is a key part of a strategy, one that is often obscured in contemporary popular culture renditions that focus on war as obliteration. In Cersei Lannister's famous line in the *Game of Thrones* TV drama, "If you play the game of thrones, you win or you die; there is no middle ground." Much of contemporary peacekeeping operations, and the efforts of the good offices of the United Nations, are precisely about refusing this inevitable fight to the finish logic and attempting to mediate and eventually remove *casus belli.* This will, then, hopefully facilitate peaceful resolution of conflictual dynamics, or even in the event of a victory of one party, attempt to create circumstances in which conflict won't recur as a result of the grievances harboured by the defeated forces (Wallensteen 2015).

In the case of climate change, divestment movement activists see their struggle as something analogous to war: them or us; fossil fuels or human survival. The fossil fuel industries see matters in reverse: either their business model is supported by states or economic calamity will occur; acting on climate is frequently presented in precisely these terms as the political campaigns against climate action in Washington State and Colorado in 2018 exemplify. Bill McKibben (2012) talks of keeping fossil fuels in the ground or else the fossil fuel companies will "crater the planet." There is no obvious mode of peacekeeping and conflict suppression here; in the logic of the divestment movement, fossil fuel companies are a threat to a sustainable future and must be defeated, by denying them funds and legitimacy as responsible social actors and then forcing them to desist from further imperilling humanity.

Chapter 6 suggested it isn't obvious that the state system that has overseen the extraordinary transformations of the period of the great acceleration is able or willing to move quickly to build a new global economy that doesn't rely on combustion to power human activities. As Naomi Klein (2017) argues, the ability of the state system and its leading corporations to take advantage of disasters and shocks to the system that climate change seems increasingly likely to provide, should not be underestimated. All too frequently they have been able to use disasters and disruptions to further their short-term economic interests at the expense of the victims of disasters; this model of governance seems highly unlikely to facilitate sustainability any time soon. This is all the more reason to act to challenge this geopolitical arrangement and tackle its forms of chemical warfare fairly directly.

In terms of strategy, the ends that Earth System science insists on in terms of planetary boundaries and ensuring that climate change doesn't cross tipping points into a new system now have to be matched with the means to accomplish this in terms of an energy system that rapidly removes fossil fuels from the global economy. This has to be an economy focused on more than seven billion humans living well in increasingly urban modes without burning large amounts of material to do so. It will require active strategies to prevent further exploration and exploitation of fossil fuels (Green and Denniss 2018). This requires focusing on much more than traditional economics has done, quite literally on making things that allow life to flourish in something analogous to Holocene conditions. There is no going back to simpler times; nor will moral exhortation be enough to drive the changes in production systems that are needed, as McKibben (2016) suggests, to rapidly make energy systems that arenot reliant on combustion.

Rockström and Klum (2015) have suggested that humanity can live well within planetary boundaries if we rapidly innovate to bring on-stream numerous new technologies. Detailed technical analyses now chart a strategy for reworking the global economy within the boundaries (Stockholm Resilience Centre 2018). But while there may be a demand for these new technologies and modes of economy among new generations of urban dwellers, there remains great inertia in the contemporary political economy, and in the boardrooms of many fossil fuel companies in particular. The assumption that good intentions and the expressed preference for a cleaner greener future will be enough to overcome this opposition to ecological modes of economy is, as the initial actions of the Trump administration and its disavowal of the Paris Agreement show, not anything close to enough by way of an Earth System strategy for a sustainable future.

The divestment movement is but one political innovation struggling for a sustainable future, and it has some promise, not least in that it focuses on a key problem and mobilizes opposition to one of the central causes of climate disruption. The divisions are sharply drawn here between corporations profiting by continuing to make climate change worse and those committed to building a new economy not dependent on burning things (Dalby 2018). The lines of political struggle are sharply drawn here, but not along twentieth-century geopolitical lines; twenty-first-century struggles for sustainability involve very different geographies.

POLITICAL GEOECOLOGY

Thinking about the point that nature is no longer the given context for humanity in terms of international peace and security requires a very different approach from traditional geopolitics, with its attendant focus on territorial states and their rivalries as key to war and peace.

It also requires scaling up the attention in much of political ecology thinking about how power struggles shape particular landscapes, and how more sustainable futures might be constructed in particular places. Thinking of the whole planet as a single place suggests a cosmopolitan sensibility that abandons the urban elitist view of top-down government and thinks about a common future in a single place: Earth (Deudney 2018). Thinking in terms of a "political geoecology," of political ecology at the global scale shaping the future global context, rather than taking it for granted, is now key to any notion of a sustainable peace if serious consideration is to be given to ensuring that climate change (and other ecological disruptions) does not trigger violent policy responses (Brauch, Dalby, and Oswald Spring 2011).

A geopolitical imagination of competing territorial states is simply out of date as the premise for policy prescription or academic analysis. While states may still sign off on many of the rules for international trade, and as such are still a key institution in shaping the future, those rules are often effectively written by leading corporations in particular sectors. But as the rising importance of the renewable energy industry is starting to indicate, who gets to write the rules is starting to change—albeit with as yet unclear geopolitical implications (Global Commission on the Geopolitics of Energy Transformation 2019). Understanding geopolitics in these terms is now much more important than traditional discussions of elite military rivalries and struggles to dominate the planet.

The commodities and resources we extract, often at great distance in rural hinterlands, to supply global manufacturing systems and then urban consumption spaces are now the key connections in geopolitics. Those consumption spaces also function as centres of political innovation in many ways (Magnusson 2011). How cities are rebuilt and governed to reduce their carbon footprint, and to make them less vulnerable to extreme events, will matter in coming decades. Even more important is to think about how suburban sprawl, so dependent on automobiles inefficiently using large amounts of energy, can be reworked with ecological principles. Likewise, informal solutions to the huge challenges of urbanization in the Global South that take ecological issues seriously also present possibilities for adaptation that improve the lot of residents of the new cities there (Robertson, M. 2012). All of this urbanization is dependent on the integration of the global economy, which is, in turn, shaping the life chances of people in the new cities of our time (Graham 2016) and, hence, producing new geopolitical circumstances that make old imperial struggles to gain colonies, or zero sum games to directly control agricultural territories, which are increasingly anachronistic. Struggles over economic activity are now shaping national policies as well as city strategies; the task for political geoecology is to think through these interconnections as they shape the increasingly artificial habitats of the future.

Thinking in these terms makes it clear that production—quite literally *what* humanity is making—is a key consideration in understanding and constructing our future; getting that clearly in focus is integral to a sustainable transition (Harris 2012). The Anthropocene will be shaped by decisions taken both by community planners and executives in boardrooms, who will decide which commodities will be made and how they will be produced. It makes a big difference if new electrical systems are powered by solar panels or coal-burning power stations. If automobile manufacturers stop making gasoline-powered cars in favour of other propulsion systems, this too will have all sorts of ramifications for climate and other ecological changes. Global cooperation on such matters is a key component for transitions to sustainability as the Paris Agreement tentatively recognizes, even if responsibility for acting is delegated to territorial state governments. What the Paris Agreement doesn't recognize, and which policy innovations have to confront, is the continuing disconnect between climate policies and state energy security policies (Nyman 2018). The Anthropocene formulation makes it clear that energy security can no longer be understood simply in terms of reliable supplies of fossil fuels.

Territorial strategies to green some societies by outsourcing the production of energy- and pollution-intensive industries to less regulated societies, an accusation frequently levelled at European states, do not solve problems when viewed in Earth System terms. Authority over ecological processes necessitates deeper action than state territorial strategies of rule, especially when territorial arrangements for such policies as emissions trading quotas and ecological offsets are involved. Outsourcing responsibilities for dealing with pollution may satisfy some limited state-based counting methods (O'Lear 2016), but it is not an ecologically sensible strategy if more than short-term geographically specific spaces are considered.

This new geography of connection in the increasingly globalized economy, and the possibilities of commodity chain governance, suggests traditional assumptions of state-based national security are insufficient frameworks for governance in the next phase of the Anthropocene. Political innovations are coming from places distant from the conventional assumptions of state power and are challenging, among other institutions, the United Nations to do things very differently (Scott and Ku 2018; Conca 2019). Focusing on flourishing ecologies rather than on more concrete constructions, and on the survival of marginal places rather than their incorporation in the circuits of the global economy, are now the priorities that need to inform policy and politics.

Any strategy of transition from present consumption-based extractive modes of economy to ones sustainable in the long run have to recognize that this transition will happen against the backdrop of dramatic ecological change (Brauch et al. 2016). How rapidly change happens is, of course, dependent on current economic production decisions, land use planning, and technological choices . This makes planning more difficult, but also emphasizes the fact that humanity is making the future of the planetary system as well as its own economic and social future. They are two sides of the same coin, a matter requiring a transition to new ways of thinking about economics and politics if peaceful human societies are to be the next phase of the Anthropocene.

Security planners now seem to have a "responsibility to prepare" given that rapid ecological changes, dramatic storms, droughts, and wildfires are increasing in frequency (Center for Climate and Security 2018). The formulation of the Anthropocene provides the contextualization for this thinking at the largest scale, but within it the non-stationarity condition has to be the premise for planning, investment, and politics. Can security be reformulated to emphasize the importance for caring for a rapidly changing world in which ecological flourishing is the priority rather than violent control over supposedly discrete spaces? That remains a difficult proposition in a world where nationalist resentments are used in so many ways to reinforce borders and further the use of firepower to try to dominate a divided planet rather than share an interconnected world.

That said, as the essays for this volume were being assembled and revised for publication in 2019, a number of promising protest movements had emerged to challenge the contemporary neoliberal order and its fossil-fuelled mode of economy. Extinction Rebellion (2019) in the United Kingdom, the climate strike movement started by Greta Thunberg (2019), the Sunrise movement, and the campaigns for a Green New Deal in the United States and elsewhere all understand that action on climate change needs to be understood as a global necessity (Klein 2019). Optimists suggest that, in the transportation sector in particular, the combination of new business models and the possibilities of autonomous electric vehicles are likely to change urban mobility far faster than conventional thinking has yet appreciated, and will do so because of the economics of the new technologies regardless of climate policy initiatives (Arbib and Seba 2017).

Novel international organizations concerned with the rise of renewable energy technologies are emerging which emphasize the implications of innovations leading to the phasing out of fossil fuels and the making of a new geopolitics (Global Commission on the Geopolitics of Energy 2019). How these departures will shape the future remain to be seen, but they all implicitly understand the necessity of making the next phase of the Anthropocene different from the dynamics of the great acceleration period. This volume has suggested that focusing on the interconnections of the Earth System, and the frequently deleterious consequences of using territorial modes of "security" in a rapidly changing world, facilitates effective conceptual challenges to the modes of firepower that have dominated geopolitics for far too long.

It behoves all scholars, academics, and researchers to support innovations that move rapidly towards less resource-consumptive modes of political economy, but to do so requires challenging modern geopolitical formulations based on notions of autonomy, domination, and the inevitability of global state rivalries. There are no guarantees that a "good Anthropocene" will eventuate, but it is clear that our future will be dramatically different from our past; novel technology and rapid ecological change makes that inevitable. How these innovations shape the future is the political question of our times, and the conceptualizations of the planetary context—that is, the representations of Anthropocene geopolitics invoked in these deliberations—remains a key and unavoidable point of critical engagement.

REFERENCES

Abrahamsen, R., and Williams, M. C. 2010. *Security Beyond the State: Private Security in International Politics*. Oxford: Oxford University Press.

Ackerman, D. 2014. *The Human Age: The World Shaped by Us*. Toronto, ON: HarperCollins Publishers.

Agnew, J. A. 2003. *Geopolitics: Re-visioning World Politics*. New York, NY: Routledge.

——. 2005. *Hegemony: The New Shape of Global Power* Philadelphia: Temple University Press.

——. 2009. *Globalization and Sovereignty*. Lanham, MD: Rowman and Littlefield.

——. 2015. "Understanding "Geopolitics" in an Era of Globalization." *Revista Tamoios, 11*(2), 4–22.

Allison, G. 2017. *Destined for War: Can America and China Escape Thucydides's Trap?* New York: Houghton Mifflin.

Amoore, L. 2013. *The Politics of Possibility: Risk and Security Beyond Probability*. Durham, NC: Duke University Press.

Anderson, K. 2015. "Duality in Climate Science." *Nature Geoscience, 8*, 898–900.

Anderson, K., and Bows, A. 2011. "Beyond 'Dangerous' Climate Change: Emission Scenarios for a New World." *Philosophical Transactions of the Royal Society A: Mathematical, Physical and Engineering Sciences,* 369(1934): 20–44.

Andreas, P., and Biersteker, T. J. (eds.). 2003. *The Rebordering of North America: Integration and Exclusion in a New Security Context*. New York, NY: Routledge.

Angus, I. 2016. *Facing the Anthropocene: Fossil Capitalism and the Crisis of the Earth System.* New York: Monthly Review Press.

Archer, K., Martin Bosman, M., Mark Amen, M., and Schmidt, E. 2007. "Hegemony/Counter-Hegemony: Imagining a New, Post-Nation-State Cartography of Culture in an Age of Globalization." *Globalizations*, 4(1), 115–136.

Arias-Maldonado, M., and Trachtenberg, Z. (eds.). 2019. *Rethinking the Environment for the Anthropocene: Political Theory and Socionatural Relations in the New Geological Epoch* London: Routledge.

Arbib, J., and Seba, T. 2017. *Rethinking Transportation 2020–2030*. London: Greener Books.

Asafu-Adjaye, J. et al. (2015). *An Ecomodernist Manifesto*. Retrieved from https://www.ecomodernism.org/.

Bacevich, A. J. 2010. *Washington Rules: America's Path to Permanent War*. New York, NY: Metropolitan Books.

Bacigalupi, P. 2015. *The Water Knife*. New York, NY: Random House.

Baldwin, A., and Bettini, G. (eds.). 2017. *Life Adrift: Climate Change, Migration, Critique*. Lanham, MD: Rowman and Littlefield.

Baldwin, A., Fröhlich, C., and Rothe, D. 2019. "From Climate Migration to Anthropocene Mobilities: Shifting the Debate." *Mobilities*. DOI: 10.1080/17450101.2019.1620510.

Barnett, J. 2019. "Global Environmental Change I: Climate Resilient Peace?" *Progress in Human Geography*, 43(5), 927–936.

Barnett, T. P. M. 2005. *The Pentagon's New Map: War and Peace in the Twenty-First Century*. New York, NY: G. P. Putnam's Sons.

Barnosky, A. D., Hadly, E. A., Bascompte, J., Berlow, E. L., Brown, J. H., Fortelius, M., Getz, W.M., Harte, J., Hastings, A., Marquet, P.A. Martinez, N.D., Mooers, A., Roopnarine, P., Vermeij, G., Williams, J.W., Gillespie, R., Kitzes, J., Marshall, C., Matzke, N., Mindell, D.P., Revilla, E., and Smith, A. B. (2012). "Approaching a State Shift in Earth's Biosphere." *Nature*, 486(7401), 52–58.

Baskin, J. 2019. *Geoengineering, the Anthropocene and the End of Nature*, London and New York: Palgrave Macmillan.

Beck, U. 2008. "Climate Change and Globalisation are Reinforcing Global Inequalities: High Time for a New Social Democratic Era." *Globalizations*, 5(1), 78–80.

——. 2009. *World at Risk*. Cambridge: Polity.

——. 2010. "Climate for Change, or How to Create a Green Modernity?" *Theory, Culture and Society*, 27(2–3), 254–266.

Belcher, O., Bigger, P., Neimark, B., and Kennelly, C. 2019. "Hidden Carbon Costs of the 'Everywhere War:' Logistics, Geopolitical Ecology, and the Carbon Boot-print of the US Military." *Transactions of the Institute of British Geographers*. DOI: 10.1111/tran.12319.

Bell, C. 2011. *The Freedom of Security: Governing Canada in the Age of Counter-Terrorism*. Vancouver, BC: UBC Press.

Bellamy, R. 2016. "A Sociotechnical Framework for Governing Climate Engineering." *Science, Technology and Human Values, 41*(2), 135–162.

Benedick, R. E. 1991. *Ozone Diplomacy: New Directions in Safeguarding the Planet*. Cambridge, MA: Harvard University Press.

Bennett, E. M., Carpenter, S. R., and Cardille, J. A. 2008. "Estimating the Risk of Exceeding Thresholds in Environmental Systems." *Water, Air, and Soil Pollution, 191*(1–4), 131–138.

Benzie, M., Adams, K. M., Persson, Å., and Klein, R. J. T. 2018. *Meeting the Global Challenge of Adaptation by Addressing Transboundary Climate Risk.* Stockholm: Stockholm Environment Institute.

Bernstein, S., and Hoffmann, M. 2018. "The Politics of Decarbonization and the Catalytic Impact of Subnational Climate Experiments. *Policy Sciences, 51*(2), 189–211.

Betts, A. 2010. "Survival Migration: A New Protection Framework." *Global Governance: A Review of Multilateralism and International Organizations, 16*(3), 361–382.

Bieler, A., and Morton, A. D. 2018. *Global Capitalism, Global War, Global Crisis.* Cambridge: Cambridge University Press.

Biermann, F. 2012. "Planetary Boundaries and Earth System Governance: Exploring the Links." *Ecological Economics, 81*, 4–9.

Black, R. 2018. *Denied: The Rise and Fall of Climate Contrarianism*. London: The Real Press.

Blanchot, M. 1995. *The Writing of the Disaster*. Lincoln, NE: University of Nebraska Press.

Blomley, N. 2017. "The Territorialization of Property in Land: Space, Power and Practice." *Territory, Politics, Governance*, 1–17.

Boas, I. 2015. *Climate Migration and Security: Securitisation as a Strategy in Climate Change Politics*. London: Routledge.

Bøås, M., and Jennings, K. M. 2007. "'Failed States' and 'State Failure': Threats or Opportunities?" *Globalizations, 4*(4), 475–485.

Bonneuil, C. 2015. "The Geological Turn: Narratives of the Anthropocene." In C. Bonneuil and C. Hamilton (eds.), *The Anthropocene and the Global Environmental Crisis: Rethinking Modernity in a New Epoch.* 17–31. London: Routledge.

Bonneuil, C., and Fressoz, J.-B. 2016. *The Shock of the Anthropocene: The Earth, History and Us*. London: Verso.

Botkin, D. B. 1990. *Discordant Harmonies: A New Ecology of the Twenty First Century*. Oxford: Oxford University Press.

Bouteligier, S. 2013. *Cities, Networks, and Global Environmental Governance: Spaces of Innovation, Places of Leadership*. London: Routledge.

Braje, T. J. 2015. "Earth Systems, Human Agency, and the Anthropocene:

Planet Earth in the Human Age." *Journal of Archaeological Research, 23*(4), 369–396.

Brauch, H. G., Dalby, S., and Oswald Spring, Ú. 2011. "Political Geoecology for the Anthropocene." In H. G. Brauch, Ú. Oswald Spring, C. Mesjasz, J. Grin, P. Kameri-Mbote, B. Chourou, P. Dunay and J. Birkmann (eds.), *Coping with Global Environmental Change, Disasters and Security: Threats, Challenges, Vulnerabilities and Risks.* 1453–1485. Heidelberg–New York–Dordrecht–London: Springer-Verlag.

Brauch, H. G., Oswald Spring, U., Grin, J., and Scheffran, J. (eds.). 2016. *Sustainability Transition and Sustainable Peace Handbook.* Heidelberg–New York–Dordrecht–London: Springer-Verlag.

Briggs, C. M. 2012. "Climate Security, Risk Assessment and Military Planning." *International Affairs, 88*(5), 1049–1064.

Briggs, C. M., and Matejova, M. 2019. *Disaster Security: Using Intelligence and Military Planning for Energy and Environmental Risks* Cambridge: Cambridge University Press.

Brockington, D. 2002. *Fortress Conservation: The Preservation of the Mkomazi Game Reserve, Tanzania.* Bloomington, IN: Indiana University Press.

Brook, B. W., Ellis, E. C., Perring, M. P., Mackay, A. W., and Blomqvist, L. 2013. "Does the Terrestrial Biosphere Have Planetary Tipping Points?" *Trends in Ecology and Evolution, 28*(7), 396–401.

Brown, W. 2010. *Walled States, Waning Sovereignty*. New York, NY: Zone Books.

Bullough, O. 2019. *Moneyland: The Inside Story of the Crooks and Kleptocrats who Rule the World.* New York: St Martin's.

Burke, A., Fishel, S., Mitchell, A., Dalby, S., and Levine, D. J. 2016. "Planet Politics: A Manifesto from the End of IR." *Millennium: Journal of International Studies, 44*(3), 499–523.

Burns, W. C. G., and Strauss, A. L. (eds.). 2013. *Climate Change Geoengineering: Philosophical Perspectives, Legal Issues and Governance Frameworks.* Cambridge: Cambridge University Press.

Busby, J. 2018. "Taking Stock: The Field of Climate and Security." *Current Climate Change Reports.* https://link.springer.com/epdf/10.1007/s40641-01[\d]–[\d]116-z.

Buxton, N., and Hayes, B. (eds.). 2016. *The Secure and the Dispossessed: How the Military and Corporations Are Shaping a Climate-Changed World.* London: Pluto Press.

Buzan, B., Wæver, O., and de Wilde, J. 1998. *Security: A New Framework for Analysis.* Boulder, CO: Lynne Rienner.

Campbell, K. M., Gulledge, J., McNeill, J. R., Podesta, J., Ogden, P., Fuerth, L., Wollsey, R.J., Lennon, A.T.J., Smith, J,. Weitz, R. and Mix, D. 2007. *The Age of Consequences: The Foreign Policy and National Security Implications of Global Climate Change.* Washington, DC: Center for Strategic and International Studies.

Carius, A. 2017. "Lake Chad Basin: One Long Climate Catastrophe." Retrieved from https://www.aljazeera.com/indepth/opinion/lake-chad-basin-long-climate-catastrophe-170923075220951.html.

Carmody, P. 2011. *The New Scramble for Africa*. Cambridge: Polity.

Caro, T., Darwin, J., Forrester, T., Ledoux-Bloom, C., and Wells, C. 2012. "Conservation in the Anthropocene." *Conservation Biology, 26*(1), 185–188.

Carpenter, S. R., and Bennett, E. M. 2011. "Reconsideration of the Planetary Boundary for Phosphorus." *Environmental Research Letters, 6*(1), 014009.

Carson, R. 1962. *Silent Spring*. Boston, MA: Houghton Mifflin Company.

Caseldine, C. 2015. "So What Sort of Climate Do We Want? Thoughts on How to Decide What is 'Natural' Climate." *The Geographical Journal, 181*(4), 366–374.

Castree, N. 2015. "Geography and Global Change Science: Relationships Necessary, Absent, and Possible." *Geographical Research, 53*(1), 1–15.

Ceballos, G., Ehrlich, P. R., and Dirzo, R. 2017. "Biological Annihilation via the Ongoing Sixth Mass Extinction Signaled by Vertebrate Population Losses and Declines." *Proceedings of the National Academy of Sciences, 114*(30), E6089–E6096.

Center for Climate and Security. 2018. *A Responsibility to Prepare* Washington: Center for Climate and Security. https://climateandsecurity.files.wordpress.com/2018/02/climate-and-security-advisory-group_a-responsibility-to-prepare_2018_02.pdf.

Cerny, P. G. 2010. *Rethinking World Politics: A Theory of Transnational Neopluralism*. Oxford: Oxford University Press.

Chakrabarty, D. 2017. "The Politics of Climate Change Is More Than the Politics of Capitalism." *Theory, Culture and Society, 34*(2–3), 25–37.

Chalecki, E. L. 2013. *Environmental Security: A Guide to the Issues*. Santa Barbara, CA: Praeger.

Chandler, D. 2013. "Resilience and the Autotelic Subject: Toward a Critique of the Societalization of Security." *International Political Sociology, 7*(2), 210–226.

Chandler, D., Cudworth, E., and Hobden, S. 2018. "Anthropocene, Capitalocene and Liberal Cosmopolitan IR: A Response to Burke et al's 'Planet Politics.'" *Millennium, 46*(2): 190–208.

Chaturvedi, S., and Doyle, T. 2015. *Climate Terror: A Critical Geopolitics of Climate Change*. London: Palgrave MacMillan.

Christoff, P. 1996. "Ecological Modernisation, Ecological Modernities." *Environmental Politics, 5*(3), 476–500.

Ciplet, D., Roberts, J. T., and Khan, M. R. 2015. *Power in a Warming World: The New Global Politics of Climate Change and the Remaking of Environmental Inequality*. Cambridge, MA: MIT Press.

Clark, N. 2012. "Rock, Life, Fire: Speculative Geophysics and the Anthropocene." *Oxford Literary Review, 34*(2), 259–276.

——. 2013. "Geoengineering and Geologic Politics." *Environment and Planning A*, *45*(12), 2825–2832.

——. "Geo-Politics and the Disaster of the Anthropocene." *The Sociological Review*, *62*(S1), 19–37.

Clark, N., and Yusoff, K. 2017. "Geosocial Formations and the Anthropocene." *Theory, Culture & Society*, 34(2–3), 3–23.

CNA Corporation. 2007. *National Security and the Threat of Climate Change*. Alexandria, VA: Center for Naval Analysis.

CNA Military Advisory Board. 2014. *National Security and the Accelerating Risks of Climate Change*. Alexandria, VA: CNA Corporation.

Coady, D., Parry, I., Sears, L., and Shang, B. 2017. "How Large Are Global Fossil Fuel Subsidies?" *World Development*, *91*, 11–27.

Coady, D., Parry, I., Nghia-Piotr, L., and Shang, B. 2019. *Global Fossil Fuel Subsidies Remain Large: An Update Based on Country-Level Estimates*. Washington: International Monetary Fund Working Paper.

Committee on Understanding and Monitoring Abrupt Climate Change and its Impacts. 2013. *Abrupt Impacts of Climate Change: Anticipating Surprises*. Washington, DC: The National Academy of Sciences.

Conca, K. 2015. *An Unfinished Foundation: The United Nations and Global Environmental Governance*. Oxford: Oxford University Press.

Conca, Ken 2019. "Is There a Role for the UN Security Council on Climate Change?" *Environment: Science and Policy for Sustainable Development*, *61*(1): 4–15.

Condamine, F. L., Rolland, J., and Morlon, H. 2013. "Macroevolutionary Perspectives to Environmental Change." *Ecology Letters*, *16*(s1), 72–85.

Connolly, W. E. 2013. *The Fragility of Things: Self-Organizing Processes, Neoliberal Fantasies, and Democratic Activism*. Durham, NC: Duke University Press.

Conway, P. H. 2019. *The Historical Ontology of Environment: From the Unity of Nature to the Birth of Geopolitics*. Aberystwyth: University of Aberystwyth, Ph.D. dissertation.

Cooley, H., and Gleick, P. H. 2011. "Climate-proofing Transboundary Water Agreements." *Hydrological Sciences Journal*, *56*(4), 711–718.

Cooper, M. 2006. "Pre-empting Emergence: The Biological Turn in the War on Terror." *Theory, Culture and Society*, 23(4), 113–135.

——. 2010. "Turbulent Worlds: Financial Markets and Environmental Crisis." *Theory, Culture and Society*, *27*(2–3), 167–190.

Corcoran, P. L., Moore, C. J., and Jazvac, K. 2014. "An Anthropogenic Marker Horizon in the Future Rock Record." *GSA Today*, 24(6), 4–8.

Cornell, S. 2012. "On the System Properties of the Planetary Boundaries." *Ecology and Society*, 17(1), 2.

Corry, O. 2017. "The International Politics of Geoengineering: The Feasibility of Plan B for Tackling Climate Change." *Security Dialogue*, *48*(4): 297–315.

Cotula, L. 2012. "The International Political Economy of the Global Land

Rush: A Critical Appraisal of Trends, Scale, Geography and Drivers." *The Journal of Peasant Studies*, 39(3–4), 649–680.

Cowen, D. 2014. *The Deadly Life of Logistics: Mapping Violence in Global Trade*. Minneapolis, MN: University of Minnesota Press.

Cronon, W. 1991. *Nature's Metropolis: Chicago and the Great West*. New York, NY: W. W. Norton and Company.

Crosby, A. 1986. *Ecological Imperialism: The Biological Expansion of Europe 900–1900*. Cambridge: Cambridge University Press.

Crunden, E. A. 2018. "Big Oil Spent Big and Won Big in Washington and Colorado." *Think Progress*. 7 November. Retrieved from https://thinkprogress.org/washington-colorado-big-oil-spending-ballot-initiatives-1b0620a1cc16/.

Crutzen, P. J. 2002. "Geology of Mankind—The Anthropocene." *Nature*, 415(6867), 23.

Crutzen, P. J., and Stoermer, E. F. 2000. "The 'Anthropocene.'" *Global Change Newsletter*, 41, 17–18.

Dabelko, G., Herzer, L., Null, S., Parker, M., and Stiklor, R. 2013. "Backdraft: The Conflict Potential of Climate Change Adaptation and Mitigation." *Environmental Change and Security Program Program Report*, 14(2), 1–60.

Daggett, C. 2018. "Petro-Masculinity: Fossil Fuels and Authoritarian Desire." *Millennium: Journal of International Studies*, 47(1), 25–44.

Dahbour, O. 2017. "On the Ecological Blindspot in the Territorial Rights Debate." *Territory, Politics, Governance*, 1–16. https://doi.org/10.1080/21622671.2017.1360196.

Dalby, S. 2002. *Environmental Security*. Minneapolis, MN: University of Minnesota Press.

——. 2009a. *Security and Environmental Change*. Cambridge: Polity.

——. 2009b. "Geopolitics, the Revolution in Military Affairs and the Bush Doctrine." *International Politics*, 46(2–3), 234–252.

——. 2013a. "Challenging Cartographies of Enmity: Empire, War and Culture in Contemporary Militarisation." In A. Stavrianakis and J. Selby (eds.), *Militarism and International Relations: Political Economy, Security, Theory* (pp. 33–44). London: Routledge.

——. 2013b. "Climate Change: New Dimensions of Environmental Security." *The RUSI Journal*, 158(3), 34–43.

——. 2013c. "The Geopolitics of Climate Change." *Political Geography*, 37, 38–47.

——. 2014a. "Rethinking Geopolitics: Climate Security in the Anthropocene." *Global Policy*, 5(1), 1–9.

——. 2014b. "Environmental Geopolitics in the Twenty-first Century." *Alternatives: Global, Local, Political*, 39(1), 3–16.

——. 2015a. "Environment: From Determinism to the Anthropocene." In *The Wiley Blackwell Companion to Political Geography* (pp. 451–461). Chichester, UK: John Wiley.

——. 2015b. "Geoengineering: The Next Era of Geopolitics?" *Geography Compass*, 9(4), 190–201.

——. 2016. "Framing the Anthropocene: The Good, the Bad and the Ugly." *The Anthropocene Review*, 3(1), 33–51.

——. 2018. "Firepower: Geopolitical Cultures in the Anthropocene." *Geopolitics*, 23(3), 718–742.

Dalby, S., Horton, S., and Mahon, R. (eds.). 2019. *Achieving the Sustainable Development Goals: Global Governance Challenges.* London: Routledge.

Dalby, S., and Moussavi, Z. 2017. "Environmental Security, Geopolitics and the Case of Lake Urmia's Disappearance." *Global Change, Peace and Security*, 29(1), 39–55.

Dalby, S., and Paterson, M. 2009. "Over a Barrel: Cultural Political Economy and Oil Imperialism." In F. Debrix and M. Lacy, (eds.), *The Geopolitics of American Insecurity: Terror, Power and Foreign Policy*. 181–196. London: Routledge.

Dasilva C. 2019. "Imagining Decline or Sustainability: Hope, Fear and Ideological Discourse in Hollywood Speculative Fction." *Elementa*, 7(1): 7.

Dauvergne, P. 2008. *The Shadows of Consumption: Consequences for the Global Environment*. Cambridge, MA: MIT Press.

Dauvergne, P. 2016. *Environmentalism of the Rich*. Cambridge, MA: MIT Press.

Davies, J. 2016. *The Birth of the Anthropocene*. Berkeley, CA: University of California Press.

Davis, M. 2001. *Late Victorian Holocausts: El Nino Famines and the Making of the Third World*. London: Verso.

Davis, R. 2011. "Inventing the Present: Historical Roots of the Anthropocene." *Earth Sciences History*, 30(1), 63–84.

de Vries, W., Kros, J., Kroeze, C., and Seitzinger, S. P. 2013. "Assessing Planetary and Regional Nitrogen Boundaries Related to Food Security and Adverse Environmental Impacts." *Current Opinion in Environmental Sustainability*, 5(3–4), 392–402.

Derber, C., and Magrass, Y. R. 2019. *Moving Beyond Fear: Upending the Security Tales in Capitalism, Fascism and Democracy*. New York: Routledge.

Deudney, D. 1990. "The Case Against Linking Environmental Degradation and National Security." *Millennium: Journal of International Studies*, 19(3), 461–476.

Deudney, D. 1999. "Bringing Nature Back In: Geopolitical Theory from the Greeks to the Global Era." In D. H. Deudney and R. A. Matthew (eds.), *Contested Grounds: Security and Conflict in the New Environmental Politics* (pp. 25–57). Albany, NY: SUNY Press.

Deudney, D. 2007. *Bounding Power: Republican Security Theory from the Polis to the Global Village*. Princeton, NJ: Princeton University Press.

Deudney, D. 2018. "All Together Now: Geography, the Three Cosmopolitanisms, and Planetary Earth." In L. Cabrera (ed.), *Institutional Cosmopolitanism (pp. 253–276)*. Oxford: Oxford University Press.

Diamond, J. 2005. *Collapse: How Societies Choose to Fail or Succeed*. New York, NY: Viking Press.

Dietrich, F., and Wündisch, J. 2015. "Territory Lost – Climate Change and the Violation of Self-determination Rights." *Moral Philosophy and Politics*, 2(1), 83–105.

Diez, T., vonLucke, F., and Wellmann, Z. 2016. *The Securitization of Climate Change: Actors, Processes and Consequences*. London: Routledge.

Dinar, S., and Dinar, A. 2017. *International Water Scarcity and Variability: Managing Resource Use Across Political Boundaries*. Berkeley: University of California Press.

Dillon, M., and Reid. J., 2009. *The Liberal Way of War: Killing to Make Life Live*. Routledge, London.

Dimitrov, R. S. 2019. "Empty Institutions and Global Environmental Politics." *International Studies Review*. doi: 10.1093/isr/viz029.

Dodds, K. 2019. *Geopolitics: A Very Short Introduction*. Oxford: Oxford University Press.

Dodds, K., Kuus M., and Sharp, J. (eds.). 2013. *Ashgate Research Companion to Critical Geopolitics*. Farnham: Ashgate.

Donges, J. F., Lucht, W., Müller-Hansen, F., and Steffen, W. 2017. "The Technosphere in Earth System Analysis: A Coevolutionary Perspective." *The Anthropocene Review*, 4(1), 23–33.

Dryzek, J. S., and Pickering, J. 2019. *The Politics of the Anthropocene*. Oxford: Oxford University Press.

Duffy, R. 2014. "Waging a War to Save Biodiversity: The Rise of Militarized Conservation." *International Affairs*, 90(4), 819–834.

——. 2016. "War, by Conservation." *Geoforum*, 69, 238–248.

Dunlap, A., and Fairhead, J. 2014. "The Militarisation and Marketisation of Nature: An Alternative Lens to 'Climate-Conflict.'" *Geopolitics*, 19(4), 937–961.

Dyer, G. 2008. *Climate Wars*. Toronto, ON: Random House of Canada.

Eckersley, R. 2015. "Anthropocene Raises Risks of Earth Without Democracy and Without Us." Retrieved from http://theconversation.com/anthropocene-raises-risks-of-earth-without-democracy-and-without-us-38911.

Edwards, P. N. 2010. *A Vast Machine: Computer Models, Climate Data, and the Politics of Global Warming*. Cambridge, MA: MIT Press.

El Akkad, O. 2017. *American War*. New York: Knopf.

Elden, S. 2009. *Terror and Territory: The Spatial Extent of Sovereignty*. Minneapolis, MN: University of Minnesota Press.

Elden, S. 2013. *The Birth of Territory*. Chicago, IL: Chicago University Press.

Ellis, E. C. 2011. "Anthropogenic Transformation of the Terrestrial Biosphere." *Philosophical Transactions of the Royal Society A: Mathematical, Physical and Engineering Sciences*, 369(1938), 1010–1035.

——. 2018. *Anthropocene: A Very Short Introduction*. Oxford: Oxford University Press.

Ellis, E. C., Goldewijk, K., Siebert, S., Lightman, D., and Ramankutty, N. 2010. "Anthropogenic Transformation of the Biomes, 1700 to 2000." *Global Ecology and Biogeography*, 19, 589–606.

Elshtain, J. B. 2008. *Sovereignty: God, State, and Self*. New York, NY: Basic Books.

Ernstson, H., and Swyngedouw, E. (eds.). 2019. *Urban Politics Ecology in the Anthropo-Obscene: Interruptions and Possibilities*. London: Routledge.

Essex, J. 2013. *Development, Security and Aid: Geopolitics and Geoeconomics at the U.S. Agency for International Development*. Athens, GA: University of Georgia Press.

Extinction Rebellion. 2019. *This is Not a Drill*. London: Penguin.

Falkner, R. 2016. "The Paris Agreement and the New Logic of International Climate Politics." *International Affairs*, 92(5), 1107–1125.

Fall, J. J. 2010. "Artificial States? On the Enduring Geographical Myth of Natural Borders." *Political Geography*, 29(3), 140–147.

Fall, J. J. 2014. "Governing Mobile Species in a Climate-Changed World." In J. Stripple and H. Bulkeley, (eds.), *Governing the Climate: New Approaches to Rationality, Power and Politics*. 160–174. Cambridge: Cambridge University Press.

Farish, M. 2010. *The Contours of America's Cold War*. Minneapolis, MN: University of Minnesota Press.

Febvre, L. E. G. Mountford and J. H. Paxton, Trans. 1996. *A Geographical Introduction to History*. London: Routledge.

Feldman, S., Geisler, C., and Menon, G. (eds.). 2011. *Accumulating Insecurity: Violence and Dispossession in the Making of Everyday Life*. Athens, GA: University of Georgia Press.

Fierke, K. M. 2007. *Critical Approaches to International Security*. Cambridge: Polity.

Fishel, S., A. Burke, A. Mitchell, S. Dalby and D. Levine. 2018. "Defending Planet Politics." *Millennium*, 46(2): 209–219.

Floyd, R., and Matthew, R. A.(eds.). 2013. *Environmental Security: Approaches and Issues*. London: Routledge.

Foley, J. A., Ramankutty, N., Brauman, K. A., Cassidy, E. S., Gerber, J. S., Johnston, M., Mueller, N.D., O'Connell, C., Ray, D.K., West, P.C., Balzer, C., Bennett, E.M., Carpenter, S.R., Hill, J., Monfreda, C., Polasky, S., Rockstrom, J., Sheehan, J., Siebert, S., Tilman, D., and Zaks, D. P. M. 2011. "Solutions for a Cultivated Planet." *Nature*, 478(7369), 337–342.

Folke, C., Jansson, Å., Rockström, J., Olsson, P., Carpenter, S. R., Chapin, F. S., Crepin, A-S., Daily, G., Danell, K., Sbbesson, J., Elmqvist, T., Galaz, V., Moberg, F., Nilson, M., Osterblom, H., Ostrom, E., Persson, A., Ptereson, G., Polasky, S., Steffen, W., Walker, B., and Westley, F. 2011. "Reconnecting to the Biosphere." *AMBIO*, 40(7), 719–738.

Foresight, 2011. *International Dimensions of Climate Change: Final Project Report*. London: Foresight International.

Foster, J. B. 2009. *The Ecological Revolution: Making Peace with the Planet*. New York, NY: Monthly Review.

——. 2013. "James Hansen and the Climate-Change Exit Strategy." *Monthly Review*, 64(9), 1–19.

Gaffney, O., Crona, B., Dauriach, A., Galaz, V. 2018. *Sleeping Financial Giants: Opportunities in Financial Leadership for Climate Stability*. Stockholm: Stockholm Resilience Centre.

Gaffney, O., and Steffen, W. 2017. "The Anthropocene Equation." *The Anthropocene Review*, 4(1), 53–61.

Galaz, V. 2014. *Global Environmental Governance, Technology and Politics: The Anthropocene Gap*. Cheltenham: Edward Elgar.

Galaz, V., Biermann, F., Crona, B., Loorbach, D., Folke, C., Olsson, P., Nilsson, M., Allouche, J., Persson, A., and Reischl, G. 2012. "'Planetary Boundaries'—Exploring the Challenges for Global Environmental Governance." *Current Opinion in Environmental Sustainability*, 4(1), 80–87.

Gareau, B. J. 2013. *From Precaution to Profit: Contemporary Challenges to Environmental Protection in the Montreal Protocol*. New Haven, CT: Yale University Press.

Gelin, M. 2019. "The Misogyny of Climate Deniers." *The New Republic*. 28 August 2019, Retrieved from https://newrepublic.com/article/154879/misogyny-climate-deniers.

German Advisory Council on Global Change. 2008. *World in Transition: Climate Change as a Security Risk*. London: Earthscan.

——. 2011. *A World in Transition: A Social Contract for Sustainability*. Berlin: German Advisory Council on Global Change.

Gerrard, M. B., and Wannier, G. E. (eds.). 2013. *Threatened Island Nations: Legal Implications of Rising Seas and a Changing Climate*. Cambridge: Cambridge University Press.

Ghosh, A. 2016. *The Great Derangement: Climate Change and the Unthinkable*. Chicago: Chicago University Press.

Gillings, M. R. and Hagan-Lawson, E. L. 2014. "The Cost of Living in the Anthropocene." *Earth Perspectives*, 1(2), 1–11.

Gleditsch, N. P., and Nordås, R. 2014. "Conflicting Messages? The IPCC on Conflict and Human Security." *Political Geography*, 43, 82–90.

Glikson, Andrew. 2017. *Plutocene: Blueprints for a Post-Anthropocene Greenhouse Earth*. Berlin: Springer.

Global Commission on Adaptation. 2019. *Adapt Now: A Global Call for Leadership on Climate Resilience*. Rotterdam and Gronigen: Global Center on Adaptation.

Global Commission on the Geopolitics of Energy Transformation. 2019. *A New World: The Geopolitics of the Energy Transformation*. www.geopoliticsofrenewables.org

Göpel, M. 2016. *The Great Mindshift: How a New Economic Paradigm and Sustainability Transformations go Hand in Hand* Berlin: Springer.

Gough, I. 2017. *Heat, Greed and Human Need: Climate Change, Capitalism and Sustainable Wellbeing*. Cheltenham: Edward Elgar.

Graham, S. (ed.). 2010. *Disrupted Cities: When Infrastructure Fails*. London: Routledge.

——. 2016. *Vertical: The City from Satellites to Bunkers*. London: Verso.

Green, F., and Denniss, R. 2018. "Cutting with Both arms of the Scissors: The Economic and Political Case for Restrictive Supply-side Climate Policies." *Climatic Change, 150*(1–2), 73–87.

Grey, D., Garrick, D., Blackmore, D., Kelman, J., Muller, M., and Sadoff, C. 2013. "Water Security in One Blue Planet: Twenty-first Century Policy Challenges for Science." *Philosophical Transactions of the Royal Society A: Mathematical, Physical and Engineering Sciences, 371*(20120406), 1–10.

Grin, J., Rotmans, J., and Schot, J. 2010. *Transitions to Sustainable Development. New Directions in the Study of Long Term Transformative Change*. London: Routledge.

Grove, J. V. 2019. *Savage Ecology: War and Ecology at the End of the World*. Durham, NC: Duke University Press.

Grove, K. 2018. *Resilience*. London: Routledge.

——. 2012. "Preempting the Next Disaster: Catastrophe Insurance and the Financialization of Disaster Management." *Security Dialogue, 43*(2), 139–155.

Grove, R. H. 1995. *Green Imperialism: Colonial Expansion, Tropical Island Edens, and the Origins of Environmentalism, 1600–1800*. Cambridge: Cambridge University Press.

Gunderson, L., and Holing, C. S. 2001. *Panarchy: Understanding Transformations in Systems of Humans and Nature*. New York, NY: Island Press.

Guzzini, S. (ed.). 2012. *The Return of Geopolitics in Europe? Social Mechanisms and Foreign Policy Identity Crises*. Cambridge: Cambridge University Press.

Haff, P. K. 2014. "Humans and Technology in the Anthropocene: Six Rules." *The Anthropocene Review, 1*(2), 126–136.

Hameiri, S., and Jones, L. 2015. *Governing Borderless Threats*. Cambridge: Cambridge University Press.

Hamilton, C. 2013. *Earthmasters: The Dawn of the Age of Climate Engineering*. New Haven, CT: Yale University Press.

——. 2016. "The Anthropocene as Rupture." *The Anthropocene Review, 3*(2), 93–106.

——. 2017. *Defiant Earth: The Fate of Humans in the Anthropocene*. Cambridge: Polity.

Hamilton, C., and Bonneuil, C. (eds.). 2015. *The Anthropocene and the Global Environmental Crisis: Rethinking Modernity in a New Epoch*. London: Routledge.

Hannigan, J. 2012. *Disasters Without Borders: The International Politics of Natural Disasters*. Cambridge: Polity.

Hansen, J. E. 2009. *Storms of My Grandchildren: The Truth About the Coming Climate Catastrophe and Our Last Chance to Save Humanity*. New York, NY: Bloomsbury.

Hansen, J., Sato, M., Hearty, P., Ruedy, R., Kelley, M., Masson-Delmotte, V., Russel G., Tselioudis, G., Cao, J., Rignot, E., Velicogna, I., Tormey, B., Donovan, B., Kandiano, E., von Schuckmann, K., Kharecha, P., Legrande, A.N., Bauer, M., and Lo, K.-W. 2016. "Ice Melt, Sea Level Rise and Superstorms: Evidence From Paleoclimate Data, Climate Modeling, and Modern Observations that 2°C Global Warming Could be Dangerous." *Atmospheric Chemistry and Physics, 16*(6), 3761–3812.

Hardt, J. N. 2018. *Environmental Security in the Anthropocene: Assessing Theory and Practice*. London: Routledge.

Haraway, D. 1988. "Situated Knowledges: The Science Question in Feminism and the Privilege of Partial Perspective." *Feminist Studies, 14*(3), 575–599.

Harraway, D. 2016. "Staying with the Trouble: Anthropocene, Capitalocene, Chthulucene" in Moore, J. ed. *Anthropocene or Capitalocene? Nature, History and the Crisis of Capitalism*. Oakland, CA: PM Press, 34–76.

Harrington, C., and Shearing, C. 2017. *Security in the Anthropocene: Reflections on Safety and Care*. Bielefeld: Transcript-Verlag.

Harris, P. G. 2013. *What's Wrong with Climate Politics and How to Fix It*. Cambridge: Polity.

Harris, S. R. 2012. "Pushing the Boundaries: The Earth System in the Anthropocene." Retrieved from http://www.schumacherinstitute.org.uk/wp-content/uploads/2015/04/Pushing-the-Boundaries-The-Earth-System-in-the-Anthropocene-Steven-Harris.pdf.

Hartig, J. H. 2014. *Bringing Conservation to Cities: Lessons from Building the Detroit River International Wildlife Refuge*. East Lansing, MI: Michigan State University Press.

Hartmann, B. 2014. "Converging on Disaster: Climate Security and the Malthusian Anticipatory Regime for Africa." *Geopolitics, 19*(4), 757–783.

Ho, B. 2014. "Understanding Chinese Exceptionalism." *Alternatives: Global, Local, Political, 39*(3), 164–176.

Hoffmann, M. J. 2005. *Ozone Depletion and Climate Change: Constructing a Global Response*. Albany, NY: State University of New York Press.

Holden, E., Linnerud, K., Banister, D., Schwanitz, V. J., and Wierling, A. 2018. *The Imperatives of Sustainable Development: Needs, Justice, Limits*. London: Routledge.

Homer-Dixon, T., et al. 2015. "Synchronous Failure: The Emerging Causal Architecture of Global Crisis." *Ecology and Society,* 20(3): 6.

Hommel, D., and Murphy, A. B. 2013. "Rethinking Geopolitics in an Era of Climate Change." *GeoJournal, 78*(3), 507–524.

Hornborg, A., McNeill, J. R., and Martinez-Alier, J. (eds.). 2007. *Rethinking Environmental History: World-System History and Global Environmental Change*. Plymouth: AltaMira Press.

Horton, J. B. 2013. "Geoengineering and the Myth of Unilateralism." In W. C. G. Burns and A. L. Strauss (eds.), *Climate Change Geoengineering* (pp. 168–181). Cambridge: Cambridge University Press.

Hough, P. 2014. *Environmental Security: An Introduction*. London: Routledge.

Huggett, A. J. 2005. "The Concept and Utility of 'Ecological Thresholds' in Biodiversity Conservation." *Biological Conservation, 124*(3), 301–310.

Hughes, T. P., Carpenter, S., Rockström, J., Scheffer, M., and Walker, B. 2013. "Multiscale Regime Shifts and Planetary Boundaries." *Trends in Ecology and Evolution, 28*(7), 389–395.

Hulme, M. 2014. *Can Science Fix Climate Change? The Case Against Climate Engineering Cambridge*. Cambridge: Polity.

Huntington, S. P. 1996. *The Clash of Civilizations and the Remaking of World Order*. New York, NY: Simon and Schuster.

Ikenberry, G. J. 2014. "The Illusion of Geopolitics: The Enduring Power of the Liberal Order." *Foreign Affairs, 93*(3), 80–90.

Intergovernmental Panel on Climate Change. 2018. *Global Warming of 1.5°C* Retrieved from http://www.ipcc.ch/report/sr15/.

International Commission on Intervention and State Sovereignty. 2001. *The Responsibility to Protect*. Ottawa: International Development Research Centre.

International Organization for Migration. 2014. *IOM Outlook on Migration, Environment and Climate Change*. Geneva: International Organization for Migration.

Jackson, R. 2000. *The Global Covenant: Human Conduct in a World of States*. Oxford: Oxford University Press.

Jackson, T. 2009. *Prosperity Without Growth: Economics for a Finite Planet*. London: Earthscan.

Jacobs, J. 1994. *Systems of Survival: A Dialogue on the Moral Foundations of Commerce and Politics*. New York, NY: Vintage Books.

Jacques, P. J. 2009. *Environmental Skepticism: Ecology, Power and Public Life*. Burlington, VT: Ashgate.

Jagodzinski, J. (ed.). 2018. *Interrogating the Anthropocene: Ecology, Aesthetics, Pedagogy, and the Future in Question*. Cham, Switzerland: Palgrave Macmillan.

Jamieson, D., and Nadzam, B. 2015. *Love in the Anthropocene*. New York, NY: OR Books.

Jarvis, B. 2018. "The Insect Apocalypse is Here." *New York Times Magazine*. 27 November. Retrieved from https://www.nytimes.com/2018/11/27/magazine/insect-apocalypse.html.

Jasanoff, S., and Kim, S-H. (eds.). 2015. *Dreamscapes of Modernity: Socio-Technical*

Imaginaries and the Fabrication of Power. Chicago: Chicago University Press.

Johns-Putra, A. 2016. "Climate Change in Literature and Literary Studies: From Cli-fi, Climate Change Theater and Ecopoetry to Ecocriticism and Climate Change Criticism." *WIREs Climate Change*, 7, 266–282.

Jones, N. 2018. "Redrawing the Map: How the World's Climate Zones are Shifting." *Yale Environment, 360*. Retrieved from https://e360.yale.edu/features/redrawing-the-map-how-the-worlds-climate-zones-are-shifting.

Jones, R. 2012. *Border Walls: Security and the War on Terror in the United States, India and Israel*. London: Zed Books.

——. 2016. *Violent Borders: Refugees and the Right to Move*. London: Verso.

Kagan, R. 2015. "The Weight of Geopolitics." *Journal of Democracy*, *26*(1), 21–31.

Kaldor, M. 2007. *Human Security: Reflections on Globalization and Intervention*. Cambridge: Polity.

Kallis, G. 2018. *Degrowth*. New York: Columbia University Press.

Kaplan, R. D. 1994. "The Coming Anarchy." *Atlantic Monthly*. 273(2). 44–76.

——. 2012. *The Revenge of Geography: What the Map Tells Us about the Coming Conflicts and the Battle Against Fate*. New York, NY: Random House.

Kareiva, P., and Fuller, E. 2016. "Beyond Resilience: How to Better Prepare for the Profound Disruption of the Anthropocene." *Global Policy*, *7*(S1), 107–118.

Kearns, G. 2009. *Geopolitics and Empire: The Legacy of Halford Mackinder*. Oxford: Oxford University Press.

——. 2013. "Beyond the Legacy of Mackinder." *Geopolitics*, *18*(4), 917–932.

Keil, R. 2019. "Paved Paradise." In Ernstson, H. and Swyngedouw, E., (eds.), *Urban Politics Ecology in the Anthropo-Obscene: Interruptions and Possibilities*. pp. 165–183. London: Routledge.

Keith, D. 2013. *A Case for Climate Engineering*. Cambridge, MA: MIT Press.

Keucheyan, R. 2016. *Nature is a Battlefield: Towards a Political Ecology*. Cambridge: Polity.

Kitoh, A., Endo, H., Krishna Kumar, K., Cavalcanti, I. F. A., Goswami, P., and Zhou, T. 2013. "Monsoons in a Changing World: A Regional Perspective in a Global Context. *Journal of Geophysical Research: Atmospheres*, *118*(8), 3053–3065.

Klein, N. 2014. *This Changes Everything: Capitalism vs. the Climate*. Toronto: Knopf Canada.

——. 2017. *No is Not Enough: Resisting the New Shock Politics and Winning the World We Need*. Toronto: Knopf.

——. 2019. *On Fire: The Burning Case for a Green New Deal*. Toronto: Knopf.

Klinke, I. 2019. "Vitalist Temptations: Life, Earth and the Nature of War." *Political Geography*, 72: 1–9.

Koch, A., Brierley, C., Maslin, M. M., and Lewis, S. L. (2019). "Earth System

Impacts of the European Arrival and Great Dying in the Americas After 1492." *Quaternary Science Reviews*, 207: 13–36.

Kolbert, E. 2011. "Enter the Anthropocene—Age of Man." *National Geographic*. March. Retrieved from https://www.nationalgeographic.com/magazine/2011/03/age-of-man/.

——. *The Sixth Extinction: An Unnatural History*. New York: Henry Holt.

Koubi, V., Spilker, G., Schaffer, L., and Böhmelt, T. 2016. "The Role of Environmental Perceptions in Migration Decision-making: Evidence from Both Migrants and Non-migrants in Five Developing Countries." *Population and Environment*, *38*(2): 134–163.

Lansing, D. M. 2013. "Understanding Linkages Between Ecosystem Service Payments, Forest Plantations, and Export Agriculture." *Geoforum*, *47*: 103–112.

Latham, R. 1997. *The Liberal Moment: Modernity, Security and the Making of the Post War International Order*. New York, NY: Columbia University Press.

Latour, B. 2017. *Facing Gaia: Eight Lectures on the New Climatic Regime*. Cambridge: Polity.

——. *Down to Earth: Politics in the New Climatic Regime*. Cambridge: Polity.

Laube, J. C., Newland, M. J., Hogan, C., Brenninkmeijer, C. A. M., Fraser, P. J., Martinerie, P., Oram, D.E. Reeves, C.E. Rockman, T., Schwander, J., Witrant, E., and Sturges, W. T. 2014. "Newly Detected Ozone-depleting Substances in the Atmosphere." *Nature Geoscience*, *7*(4): 266–269.

le Billon, P. 2012. *Wars of Plunder: Conflicts, Profits and the Politics of Resources*. New York, NY: Columbia University Press.

Lenton, T. M., Held, H., Kriegler, E., Hall, J. W., Lucht, W., Rahmstorf, S., and Schellnhuber, H. J. 2008. "Tipping Elements in the Earth's Climate System." *Proceedings of the National Academy of Sciences*, *105*(6): 1786–1793.

Lenton, T. M. 2013. "What Early Warning Systems are There for Environmental Shocks?" *Environmental Science and Policy*, *27*(Supplement 1): S60–S75.

Lewis, J. I. 2014. "The Rise of Renewable Energy Protectionism: Emerging Trade Conflicts and Implications for Low Carbon Development." *Global Environmental Politics*. *14*(4). 10–35.

Lewis, S. L., and Maslin, M. A. 2015. "Defining the Anthropocene." *Nature*, *519* (7542): 171–180.

——. 2018. *The Human Planet: How We Created the Anthropocene*. London: Pelican.

Linton, J. 2010. *What is Water? The History of a Modern Abstraction*. Vancouver, BC: UBC Press.

Lippert, T. H. 2019. *NATO, Climate Change, and International Security: A Risk Governance Approach*. London: Palgrave Macmillan.

Lipschutz, R. D. 2018. "Eco-utopia or Eco-catastrophe? Re-imagining California as an Ecological Utopia." *Elementa*, 6: 65.

Lorimer, J. 2015. *Wildlife in the Anthropocene: Conservation after Nature*. Minneapolis, MN: University of Minnesota Press.

Lövbrand, E., Stripple, J., and Wiman, B. 2009. "Earth System Governmentality." *Global Environmental Change*, *19*(1): 7–13.

Lovelock, J. E. 1979. *Gaia: A New Look at Life on Earth*. Oxford: Oxford University Press.

——. 2014. *A Rough Ride to the Future*. London: Allen Lane.

Luke, T. W. 2010. "Geoengineering as Global Climate Change Policy." *Critical Policy Studies*, *4*(2): 111–126.

Lunstrum, E. 2014. "Green Militarization: Anti-Poaching Efforts and the Spatial Contours of Kruger National Park." *Annals of the Association of American Geographers*, *104*(4): 816–832.

Mach, K. J., Kraan, C. M., Adger, W. N., Buhaug, H., Burke, M., Fearon, J. D., Field, C. B., Hendrix, C. S., Maystadt, J-F., O'Loughlin, J., Roessler, P., Scheffran, J., Schultz, K. A., and von Uexkull, N. 2019. "Climate as a Risk Factor for Armed Conflict." *Nature*, 571: 193–197.

MacDonald, F., Hughes, R., and Dodds, K. (eds.). 2010. *Observant States: Geopolitics and Visual Culture*. London: I. B. Tauris.

Mackenzie, A. F. D. 2013. *Places of Possibility: Property, Nature and Community Land Ownership*. Chichester: John Wiley.

MacNeil, R. 2017. *Neoliberalism and Climate Policy in the United States*. London and New York: Routledge.

Magnusson, W. 2011. *Politics of Urbanism: Seeing Like a City*. London: Routledge.

Maisonnave, F. 2017. "Forest Diamonds." Retrieved from http://www.climatechangenews.com/2017/09/26/forest-diamonds/.

Malm, A. 2016. *Fossil Capital: The Rise of Steam Power and the Roots of Global Warming*. London: Verso.

Malm, A., and Hornborg, A. 2014. "The Geology of Mankind? A Critique of the Anthropocene Narrative." *The Anthropocene Review*, *1*(1): 62–69.

Malthus, T. R. 1970. *An Essay on the Principle of Population: and A Summary View of the Principle of Population*. Harmondsworth: Penguin Books.

Mangano, J. J., and Sherman, J. D. 2012. "An Unexpected Mortality Increase in the United States Follows Arrival of the Radioactive Plume from Fukushima: Is There a Correlation?" *International Journal of Health Services*, *42*(1): 47–64.

Mangat, R., and Dalby, S. 2018. "Climate and Wartalk: Metaphors, Imagination, Transformation." *Elementa: Science of the Anthropocene*. *6*. 58.

Mangat, R., Dalby, S., and Paterson, M. 2018. "Divestment Discourse: War, Justice, Morality and Money." *Environmental Politics*, *27*(2): 187–208.

Marzec, R. P. 2015. *Militarizing the Environment: Climate Change and the Security State*. Minneapolis, MN: University of Minnesota Press.

Matejova, M., Parker, S., and Dauvergne, P. 2018. "The Politics of Repressing

Environmentalists as Agents of Foreign Influence." *Australian Journal of International Affairs*, 72(2): 145–162.

Matondi, P. B., Havnevik, K., and Beyene, A. (eds.). 2011. *Biofuels, Land Grabbing and Food Security in Africa*. London: Zed Books.

Mayer, J. 2016. *Dark Money: The Hidden History of the Billionaires Behind the Rise of the Radical Right*. New York, NY: Doubleday.

Mayer, M. 2012. "Chaotic Climate Change and Security." *International Political Sociology*, 6(2): 165–185.

McAfee, K. 2012. "The Contradictory Logic of Global Ecosystem Services Markets." *Development and Change*, 43(1): 105–131.

McBrien, J. 2016. "Accumulating Extinction: Planetary Catastrophism in the Necrocene." In Moore J., ed. *Anthropocene or Capitalocene? Nature, History and the Crisis of Capitalism*. pp. 116–137. Oakland, CA: PM Press.

McCall, M. K. 2016. "Beyond 'Landscape' in REDD+: The Imperative for 'Territory.'" *World Development*, 85: 58–72.

McKeon, N. 2017. "Transforming Global Governance in the Post-2015 Era: Towards an Equitable and Sustainable World." *Globalizations*, 14(4): 487–503.

McKibben, B. 2012. "Global Warming's Terrifying New Math." *Rolling Stone*, 19 July. Available at: http://www.rollingstone.com/politics/news/global-warmings-terrifying-new-math-20120719.

——. "A World at War." *New Republic*. 15 August. Retrieved from https://newrepublic.com/article/135684/declare-war-climate-change-mobilize-wwii.

McNeill, J. R. 2000. *Something New Under the Sun: An Environmental History of the Twentieth-Century World*. New York, NY: W. W. Norton and Company.

McNeill, J. R., and Engelke, P. 2016. *The Great Acceleration: An Environmental History of the Anthropocene since 1945*. Cambridge, MA: Harvard University Press.

Mead, W. R. 2014. "The Return of Geopolitics: The Revenge of the Revisionist Powers." *Foreign Affairs*, 93(3): 69–79.

Meadowcroft, J. 2013. "Exploring Negative Territory: Carbon Dioxide Removal and Climate Policy Initiatives." *Climatic Change*, 118: 137–149.

Meadowcroft, J., Banister, D., Holden, E., Langhelle, O., Linnerud, K., and Gilpin, G. (eds.). 2019. *What Next for Sustainable Development?: Our Common Future at Thirty*. Edward Elgar.

Meadows, D. H., Meadows, D. L., Randers, J., and Behrens III, W. W. 1972. *The Limits to Growth: A Report for the Club of Rome's Project on the Predicament of Mankind*. New York, NY: Universe Books.

Milkoreit, M. 2017. "Imaginary Politics: Climate Change and Making the Future." *Elementa: Science of the Anthropocene*, 5: 62.

Milly, P. C. D., Betancourt, J., Falkenmark, M., Hirsch, R. M., Kundzewicz, Z. W.,

Lettenmaier, D. P., and Stouffer, R. J. 2008. "Stationarity Is Dead: Whither Water Management?" *Science*, 319(5863): 573–574.

Minca, C., and Rowan, R. 2010. *On Schmitt and Space*. London: Routledge.

Mitchell, A. 2014. *International Intervention in a Secular Age: Re-Enchanting Humanity?* London: Routledge.

Mitchell, T. 2011. *Carbon Democracy: Political Power in the Age of Oil*. London: Verso.

Mobjork, M., Smith, D., and Rüttinger, L. 2016. *Towards a Global Resilience Agenda: Action on Climate Fragility Risks.* The Hague: Clingendael–the Netherlands Institute for International Relations.

Mol, A. P. J. 2001. *Globalization and Environmental Reform: The Ecological Modernization of the Global Economy*. Cambridge, MA: MIT Press.

Moore, J. W. 2015. *Capitalism in the Web of Life: Ecology and the Accumulation of Capital*. London: Verso.

——. (ed.). 2016. *Anthropocene or Capitalocene? Nature, History and the Crisis of Capitalism.* Oakland, CA: PM Press.

Moran, A., Busby, J., Raleigh, C., Smith, T. G., Kishi, R., Krishnan, N., Wright, C., and Management Systems International. 2018. *The Intersection of Global Fragility and Climate Risks.* Washington: USAID.

Morrissey, J. 2017. *The Long War: CENTCOM, Grand Strategy, and Global Security*. Athens, GA: University of Georgia Press.

Mountz, A. 2010. *Seeking Asylum: Human Smuggling and Bureaucracy at the Border*. Minneapolis, MN: University of Minnesota Press.

Mumford, L. 1934. *Technics and Civilisation.* New York, NY: Harcourt, Brace and Company.

Munich Security Conference. 2016. *Munich Security Report: Boundless Crises, Reckless Spoilers, Helpless Guardians.* Munich: Munich Security Conference.

National Diet of Japan. 2012. *The Official Report of the Fukushima Nuclear Accident Independent Investigation Commission.* Tokyo.

National Intelligence Council. 2016. *Implications for US National Security of Anticipated Climate Change*. Washington, DC.

National Research Council. 2015a. *Climate Intervention: Reflecting Sunlight to Cool Earth*. Washington, DC: National Academies Press.

——. 2015b. *Climate Intervention: Carbon Dioxide Removal and Reliable Sequestration*. Washington, DC: National Academies Press.

Neocleous, M. 2008. *Critique of Security*. Edinburgh: Edinburgh University Press.

Network for Greening the Financial System. 2019. *A Call for Action: Climate Change as a Source of Financial Risk.* Paris: Banque de France/NGFS Secretariat.

Neukom, R., Steiger, N., Gómez-Navarro, J. J., Wang, J., and Werner, J. P. 2019. "No Evidence for Globally Coherent Warm and Cold Periods Over the Preindustrial Common Era." *Nature*, 571: 550–554.

Newell, P., and Paterson, M. 2010. *Climate Capitalism*. Cambridge: Cambridge University Press.

Nine, C. 2010. "Ecological Refugees, States Borders, and the Lockean Proviso." *Journal of Applied Philosophy*, 27(4): 359–375.

——. 2012. *Global Justice and Territory*. Oxford: Oxford University Press.

Nixon, R. 2011. *Slow Violence and the Environmentalism of the Poor*. Cambridge: Cambridge University Press.

Nordhaus, T., and Shellenberger, M. 2007. *Break Through: From the Death of Environmentalism to the Politics of Possibility*. Boston, MA: Houghton Mifflin Harcourt.

Nussbaum, M. 2019. *The Cosmopolitan Tradition: A Noble but Flawed Ideal*. Cambridge, MA: Harvard University Press.

Nyman, J. 2018. *The Energy Security Paradox: Rethinking Energy (In)Security in the United States and China*. Oxford: Oxford University Press.

O'Lear, S. 2016. Geopolitics and Climate Change: The Case of the Missing Embodied Carbon. In S. O'Lear and Dalby S. (eds.), *Reframing Climate Change: Constructing Ecological Geopolitics*. pp. 100–115. London: Routledge.

——. 2018. *Environmental Geopolitics*. New York: Rowman and Littlefield.

Obama, B. 2013. Remarks by President Obama at the Brandenburg Gate -- Berlin, Germany. Retrieved from https://obamawhitehouse.archives.gov/the-press-office/2013/06/19/remarks-president-obama-brandenburg-gate-berlin-germany.

Oreskes, N., and Conway, E. M. 2010. *Merchants of Doubt: How a Handful of Scientists Obscured the Truth on Issues from Tobacco Smoke to Global Warming*. New York, NY: Bloomsbury.

Palsson, G., Szerszynski, B., Sörlin, S., Marks, J., Avril, B., Crumley, C., Hackmann, H., Holm, P., Ingram, J., Kirman, A. Pardo-Buendia, M., and Weehuizen, R. 2013. "Reconceptualizing the 'Anthropos' in the Anthropocene: Integrating the Social Sciences and Humanities in Global Environmental Change Research." *Environmental Science and Policy*, 28: 3–13.

Panitch, L., and Gindin, S. 2012. *The Making of Global Capitalism: The Political Economy of American Empire*. London: Verso.

Parenti, C. 2011. *Tropic of Chaos: Climate Change and the New Geography of Violence*. New York, NY: Nation Books.

Parker, G. 2013. *Global Crisis: War, Climate Change and Catastrophe in the Seventeenth Century*. New Haven, CT: Yale University Press.

Parr, A. 2013. *The Wrath of Capital: Neoliberalism and Climate Change Politics*. New York, NY: Columbia University Press.

Paterson, M. 2012. "Who and What are Carbon Markets for? Politics and the Development of Climate Policy." *Climate Policy*, 12(1): 82–97.

Paterson, M. 2014. "Commodification." In Death, C. ed. *Critical Environmental Politics*. pp. 53–62. London: Routledge.

Pearce, F. 2017. "How Big Water Projects Helped Trigger Africa's Migrant Crisis." Retrieved October 30, 2017, Retrieved from https://e360.yale.edu/features/how-africas-big-water-projects-helped-trigger-the-migrant-crisis.

Pearson, D., and Newman, P. 2019. "Climate Security and Vulnerability Model for Conflict Prevention: A Systematic Literature Review Focusing on African Agriculture." *Sustainable Earth,* 2(2): 222 pp.

Pelling, M. 2011. *Adaptation to Climate Change: From Resilience to Transformation*. London: Routledge.

Pierrehumbert, R. 2019. "There is no Plan B for Dealing with the Climate Crisis." *Bulletin of the Atomic Scientists,* 75(5): 215–221.

Pisano, U., and Berger, U. 2013. *Planetary Boundaries for Sustainable Development*. Vienna: European Sustainable Development Network.

Pita, A. 2007. "Statement to the United Nations Special Session of the Security Council." 17 April. Retrieved from http://www.tuvaluislands.com/un/2007/un_2007-04-17.html.

Polanyi, K. 1957. *The Great Transformation: The Political and Economic Origins of Our Time*. Boston, MA: Beacon Press.

Pope Francis. 2015. *Encyclical Letter Laudato si' of the Holy Father Francis on the Care for Our Common Home*. Vatican City.

Princen, T., Manno, J. P., and Martin, P. L. (eds.). 2015. *Ending the Fossil Fuel Era*. Cambridge, MA: MIT Press.

Pyne, S. J. 2015. "The Fire Age: How Humans Made Fire, and Fire Made us Human." *Aeon Magazine*. Retrieved from https://aeon.co/essays/how-humans-made-fire-and-fire-made-us-human.

Rasmussen, S. E. 2017. "How Climate Change is a "Death Sentence" in Afghanistan's Highlands." *The Guardian,* 28 August. Retrieved from https://www.theguardian.com/world/2017/aug/28/how-climate-change-is-death-sentence-afghanistan-highlands-global-warming.

Raworth, K. 2014, October 20. "Must the Anthropocene be a Manthropocene?" Retrieved from https://www.theguardian.com/commentisfree/2014/oct/20/anthropocene-working-group-science-gender-bias.

Raworth, K. 2017. *Doughnut Economics: Seven Ways to Think Like a 21st-Century Economist*. London: Random House.

Rayner, S., Heyward, C., Kruger, T., Pidgeon, N., Redgwell, C., and Savulsecu, J. 2013. "The Oxford Principles." *Climatic Change,* 121: 499–512.

Reay, D., Smith, P., and Amstel, A. van. (eds.). 2010. *Methane and Climate Change*. London: Earthscan.

Reeve, R. 2002. *Policing International Trade in Endangered Species: The CITES Treaty and Compliance*. London: Earthscan.

Revkin, A. C. 2014. "Exploring Academia's Role in Charting Paths to a 'Good' Anthropocene." Retrieved from https://dotearth.blogs.nytimes.com/2014/06/16/exploring-academias-role-in-charting-paths-to-a-good-anthropocene/.

Richardson, P. 2015. "'Blue National Soil' and the Unwelcome Return of 'Classical' Geopolitics." *Global Change, Peace and Security*, *27*(2): 229–236.

Rickards, L. A. 2015. "Metaphor and the Anthropocene: Presenting Humans as a Geological Force." *Geographical Research*, *53*(3): 280–287.

Rigaud, K. K., de Sherbinin, A., Jones, B., Bergmann, J., Clement, V., Ober, K., Schese, J., Adamo, S., McCusker, B., Heuser, S., and Midgley, A. 2018. *Groundswell: Preparing for Internal Climate Migration*. Washington, DC: World Bank.

Risi, L. H. 2017. "Backdraft Revisited: The Conflict Potential of Climate Change Adaptation and Mitigation." Retrieved from https://www.newsecuritybeat.org/2017/01/backdraft-revisited-conflict-potential-climate-change-adaptation-mitigation/.

Robertson, M. (ed.). 2012. *Sustainable Cities: Local Solutions in the Global South*. Ottawa, ON: Practical Action Publishing.

Robertson, T. 2012. "Total War and the Total Environment: Fairfield Osborn, William Vogt, and the Birth of Global Ecology." *Environmental History*, *17*(2): 336–364.

Rockström, J., and Klum, M. 2015. *Big World, Small Planet: Abundance within Planetary Boundaries*. New Haven, CT: Yale University Press.

Rockström, J., Schellnhuber, H. J., Hoskins, B., Ramanathan, V., Schlosser, P., Brasseur, G. P., Gaffney, O., Nobre, C. Meinshausen, M., Rogelj, J., and Lucht, W. 2016. "The World's Biggest Gamble." *Earth's Future*, *4*(10): 465–470.

Rockström, J., Steffen, W., Noone, K., Persson, Å., Chapin, F. S., Lambin, E. F., Lenton, T., Scheffer, M., Folke, C., Schellnhuber, H.J., Nykvist, B., deWit, C., Hughes, T., van der Leeuw, S., Rodhe, H., Sorlin, S., Snyder, P.K., Constanza, R., Svedlin, U., Falkenmark, M., Karlberg, L., Corell, R.W., Fabry, V.J., Hansen, J., Walker, B., Liverman, D., Richardson, K., Crutzen, P., and Foley, J. A. 2009a. "A Safe Operating Space for Humanity." *Nature*, *461*(7263): 472–475.

Rockström, J., Steffen, W., Noone, K., Persson, Å., Chapin, F. S., Lambin, E. F., Lenton, T., Scheffer, M., Folke, C., Schellnhuber, H.J., Nykvist, B., deWit, C., Hughes, T., van der Leeuw, S., Rodhe, H., Sorlin, S., Snyder, P.K., Constanza, R., Svedlin, U., Falkenmark, M., Karlberg, L., Corell, R.W., Fabry, V.J., Hansen, J., Walker, B., Liverman, D., Richardson, K., Crutzen, P., and Foley, J. A. 2009b. "Planetary Boundaries: Exploring the Safe Operating Space for Humanity." *Ecology and Society*, *14*(2): Article 32.

Rogers, P. 2016. *Irregular War: ISIS and the New Threat from the Margins*. London: I. B.Tauris.

Rothe, D. 2016. *Securitizing Global Warming: A Climate of Complexity*. London: Routledge.

Rothschild, E. 1995. "What is Security?" *Daedalus*, 124(3): 53–98.

Routledge, P. 2017. *Space Invaders: Radical Geographies of Protest*. London: Pluto Press.

Royal Society. 2009. *Geoengineering the Climate: Science, Governance and Uncertainty*. London: Royal Society.

Ruddiman, W. F. 2010. *Plows, Plagues, and Petroleum: How Humans Took Control of Climate*. 2nd ed. Princeton, NJ: Princeton University Press.

Ruddiman, W. F., Vavrus, S., Kutzbach, J., and He, F. 2014. "Does Pre-industrial Warming Double the Anthropogenic Total?" *The Anthropocene Review*, *1*(2): 147–153.

Rush, E. 2018. "Rising Seas: 'Florida is about to be wiped off the map.'" *The Guardian*. 26 June. Retrieved from https://www.theguardian.com/environment/2018/jun/26/rising-seas-florida-climate-change-elizabeth-rush.

Rushkoff, D. 2018. "How Tech's Richest Plan to Save Themselves After the Apocalypse." *The Guardian*. 24 July. Retrieved from https://www.theguardian.com/technology/2018/jul/23/tech-industry-wealth-futurism-transhumanism-singularity.

Rüttinger, L., Smith, D., Stang, G., Tänzler, D., and Vivekananda, J. 2015. *A New Climate for Peace: Taking Action on Climate and Fragility Risks*. Berlin: Adelphi.

Ruysenaar, S., and Smith, J. 2016. "Biofuels: climate solution or environmental pariah?" In S. O'Lear and Dalby, S. (eds.), *Reframing Climate Change: Constructing Ecological Geopolitics*. 132–149. London: Routledge.

Sack, D. R. 1986. *Human Territoriality: Its Theory and History*. Cambridge: Cambridge University Press.

Sanger, D. E. 2019. *The Perfect Weapon: War, Sabotage and Fear in the Cyber Age*. New York: Broadway.

Sassen, S. 2013. "Land Grabs Today: Feeding the Disassembling of National Territory." *Globalizations*. *10*(1). 25–46.

——. 2014. *Expulsions: Brutality and Complexity in the Global Economy*. Cambridge, MA: Harvard University Press.

——. 2018. "Embedded Borderings: Making New Geographies of Centrality." *Territory, Politics, Governance*, *6*(1): 5–15.

Schapiro, M. 2016. *The End of Stationarity*. White River Junction: Chelsea Green Publishing.

Scheffran, J., Brzoska, M., Brauch, H. G., Link, P. M., and Schilling, J. (eds.). 2012. *Climate Change, Human Security and Violent Conflict: Challenges for Social Stability*. Berlin: Springer-Verlag.

Schellnhuber, H. J. 1999. "'Earth System' Analysis and the Second Copernican Revolution." *Nature*, *402* (Supplement): C19–C23.

Schellnhuber, H. J., Crutzen, P. J., Clark, W. C., Claussen, M., and Held, H. (eds.). 2004. *Earth System Analysis for Sustainability*. Cambridge, MA: MIT Press.

Schmitt, C. 1985. *Political Theology: Four Chapters on the Concept of Sovereignty*. Cambridge, MA: MIT Press (original publication 1932).

——. 2006. *The Nomos of the Earth in the International Law of Jus Publicum Europaeum*. Candor, NY: Telos Press.

Scott, J. C. 1998. *Seeing Like a State: How Certain Schemes to Improve the Human Condition Have Failed*. New Haven, CT: Yale University Press.

Scott, S. V., and C. Ku, (eds.). 2018. *Climate Security and the UN Security Council*. Cheltenham, UK: Edward Elgar.

Seager, R., Lis, N., Feldman, J., Ting, M., Williams, A.P., Nakamura, J., Liu, H., and Henderson, N. 2018. "Whither the 100th Meridian? The Once and Future Physical and Human Geography of America's Arid: Humid Divide. Part II: The Meridian Moves East." *Earth Interactions*, 22(5): 1–22.

Selby, J. 2014. "Positivist Climate Conflict Research: A Critique." *Geopolitics*, *19*(4): 829–856.

——. 2019. "The Trump Presidency, Climate Change, and the Prospect of a Disorderly Energy Transition." *Review of International Studies*, 45(3): 471–490.

Shafer, C. L. 2015. "Land Use Planning: A Potential Force for Retaining Habitat Connectivity in the Greater Yellowstone Ecosystem and Beyond." *Global Ecology and Conservation*, *3*: 256–278.

Sloan, G. 2017. *Geopolitics, Geography and Strategic History*. London: Routledge.

Smith, B. D., and Zeder, M. A. 2013. "The Onset of the Anthropocene." *Anthropocene*, *4*:8–13.

Smith, N. 1984. *Uneven Development: Nature, Capital and the Production of Space*. Oxford: Blackwell.

——. 2005. *The Endgame of Globalization*. New York, NY: Routledge.

Smith, P. J. 2007. "Climate Change, Mass Migration and the Military Response." *Orbis*, *51*(4): 617–633.

Snyder, T. 2015. *Black Earth: The Holocaust as History and Warning*. New York, NY: Tim Duggan Books.

Solnit, R. 2012. "2013 Will Be Year Zero in our Climate Battle." *Mother Jones*. 31 December. https://www.motherjones.com/environment/2012/12/rebecca-solnit-2013-will-be-year-zero-our-climate-battle/.

Sovacool, B., and Linnér, B.-O. 2016. *The Political Economy of Climate Change Adaptation*. London: Palgrave Macmillan.

Spratt, D., and Sutton, P. 2008. *Climate Code Red: The Case for a Sustainability Emergency*. Fitzroy: Friends of the Earth.

Statten, P. W., Lu, J. Grise, K. M., Davis, S. M., and Birner, T. 2018. "Reexamining Tropical Expansion." *Nature Climate Change*, 8: 768–775.

Steffen, W., Crutzen, P. J., and McNeill, J. R. 2007. "The Anthropocene: Are Humans Now Overwhelming the Great Forces of Nature." *AMBIO*, *36*(8): 614–621.

Steffen, W., Grinevald, J., Crutzen, P. J., and McNeill, J. R. 2011. "The

Anthropocene: Conceptual and Historical Perspectives." *Philosophical Transactions of the Royal Society A: Mathematical, Physical and Engineering Sciences*, 369. (1938): 842–867.

Steffen, W., Persson, Å., Deutsch, L., Zalasiewicz, J., Williams, M., Richardson, K., Crumley, C., Crutzen, P., Folke, C., Gordon, L., Molina, M., Ramananthan, V., Rockström, J., Scheffer, M., Schellnhuber, H. J., and Svedin, U. 2011. "The Anthropocene: From Global Change to Planetary Stewardship. *AMBIO*, 40 (7): 739–761.

Steffen, W., Richardson, K., Cornell, S. E., Fetzer, I., Bennett, E. M., Biggs, R., Carpenter, S. R., DeVries, W., deWit, C. A., Folke, C., Gerten, D., Heinke, J., Mace, G. M., Persson, L. M., Ramanathan, V., Reyers, B., and Sörlin, S. 2015. "Planetary Boundaries: Guiding Human Development on a Changing Planet." *Science*, 347 (6223): 1259855.

Steffen, W., Rockström, J., Richardson, K., Lenton, T. M., Folke C., Liverman D., Colin P., Summerhayes, C. P., Barnosky, A. D., Cornel, S. E., Crucifix M., Donges J. F., Fetzer, I., Lade, S. J., Scheffer, M., Winkelmann, R., and Schellnhuber, H. J. 2018. "Trajectories of the Earth System in the Anthropocene." *Proceedings of the National Academy of Sciences*, 115(33): 8252–8259.

Stern, N. 2009. *The Global Deal: Climate Change and the Creation of a New Era of Progress and Prosperity*. New York, NY: Public Affairs.

Stiglitz, J. E., and Kaldor, M. (eds.). 2013. *The Quest for Security: Protection Without Protectionism and the Challenge of Global Governance*. New York, NY: Columbia University Press.

Stockholm Resilience Center. 2018. *Transformation is Feasible* Stockholm: Stockholm Resilience Center.

Stoett, P. J., and Mullligan, S. 2019. *Global Ecopolitics: Crisis, Governance and Justice*. Toronto: University of Toronto Press.

Storlazzi, C. D., Gingerich, S. B., van Dongeren, A., Cheriton, O. M., Swarzenski, P. W., Quataert, E., Voss, C. I., Field, D. W., Hariharasubramanian, A., Piniak, G. S., and McCall, R. 2018. "Most Atolls will be Uninhabitable by the Mid-21st Century Because of Sea-Level Rise Exacerbating Wave-driven Flooding." *Science Advances*, 4(4): 9741.

Swyngedouw, E. 2010. "Apocalypse Forever?" *Theory, Culture and Society*, 27(2–3): 213–232.

Szasz, A. 2007. *Shopping Our Way to Safety: How We Changed from Protecting the Environment to Protecting Ourselves*. Minneapolis, MN: University of Minnesota Press.

Taylor, M. 2014. *The Political Ecology of Climate Change Adaptation: Livelihoods, Agrarian Change and the Conflicts of Development*. London: Earthscan.

Taylor, P. J. 2013. *Extraordinary Cities: Millennia of Moral Syndromes, World-Systems and City/State Relations*. Cheltenham: Edward Elgar.

The Economist. 2011. "Welcome to the Anthropocene." May 28. Cover.

Theisen, O. M., Holtermann, H., and Buhaug, H. 2012. "Climate Wars? Assessing the Claim That Drought Breeds Conflict." *International Security, 36(3):* 79–106.

Thomas, C. 2014. "What Does the Emerging International Law of Migration Mean for Sovereignty." *Melbourne Journal of International Law, 14(2):* 76–104.

Thunberg, G. 2019. *No One is Too Small to Make a Difference*. London: Penguin.

Toal, G. 1996. *Critical Geopolitics: The Politics of Writing Global Space*. Minneapolis, MN: University of Minnesota Press.

——. 2017. *Near Abroad: Putin, The West and the Contest over Ukraine and the Caucasus*. Oxford: Oxford University Press.

Tollefson, J. 2018. "The Sun Dimmers." *Nature*, 563: 613–615.

Trachtenberg, Z. 2019. "The Ecological Circumstances of Politics." in Arias-Maldonado, M., and Trachtenberg, Z. (eds.), *Rethinking the Environment for the Anthropocene: Political Theory and Socionatural Relations in the New Geological Epoch*. pp. 82–93. London: Routledge.

Trexler, A. 2015. *Anthropocene Fictions: The Novel in a Time of Climate Change*. Charlottesville, VA: University of Virginia Press.

Tsigaridis, K., Krol, M., Dentener, F. J., Balkanski, Y., Lathière, J., Metzger, S., Hauglustaine, D. A., and Kanakidou, M. 2006. "Change in Global Aerosol Composition Since Preindustrial Times." *Atmospheric Chemistry and Physics, 6(12):* 5143–5162.

Uhrqvist, O. 2014. *Seeing and Knowing the Earth as a System*. Linkoping: Linkoping University Studies in Arts and Science. 631.

United Nations. 2015. *Transforming our World: The 2030 Agenda for Sustainable Development*. New York, NY.

United Nations Development Program. 1994. *Human Development Report 1994*. New York, NY: Oxford University Press.

——. 2016. *UNDP Support to the Implementation of Sustainable Development Goals*. New York, NY.

United Nations Environment Program. 2012. *Global Environmental Outlook GEO5: Environment for the Future we Want*. New York, NY: UNEP.

——. 2018. *The Emissions Gap 2018 Report*. Nairobi: UNEP.

United States Government. 2017. *The National Security Strategy of the United States of America*. Washington, DC.

Urpelainen, J. 2012. "Geoengineering and Global Warming: A Strategic Perspective." *International Environmental Agreements: Politics, Law and Economics*, 12(4): 375–389.

Vaha, M. E. 2015. "Drowning under: Small island states and the right to exist." *Journal of International Political Theory*. 11(2). 206–223.

Van Munster, R., and Sylvest, C. (eds.). 2016. *The Politics of Globality Since 1945: Assembling the Planet*. London: Routledge.

Vaughan, N. E., and Lenton, T. M. 2011. "A Review of Climate Geoengineering Proposals." *Climatic Change, 109*(3–4): 745–790.

Vidas, D., Zalasiewicz, J., and Williams, M. 2015. "What is the Anthropocene—and Why is it Relevant for International Law?" *Yearbook of International Environmental Law, 25*(1): 3–23.

Vivekananda, J., M. Wall, F. Sylvestre, C. Nagarajan and O. Brown. 2019. *Shoring up Stability: Addressing Climate and Fragility Risks in the Lake Chad Region.* Berlin: Adelphi.

Von Clausewitz, C. 1989. *On War*. M. E. Howard and P. Paret, Trans. Princeton, NJ: Princeton University Press.

Walker, R. B. J. 2010. *After the Globe, Before the World*. London: Routledge.

Wallace-Wells, D. 2019. *The Uninhabitable Earth: Life After Warming*. New York: Duggan.

Wallensteen, P. 2015. *Quality Peace: Peace Building, Victory and World Order*. Oxford: Oxford University Press.

Wang, L., Gu, M., and Li, H. 2012. "Influence Path and Effect of Climate Change on Geopolitical Pattern." *Journal of Geographical Sciences, 22*(6): 1117–1130.

Wapner, P. 2010. *Living Through the End of Nature: The Future of American Environmentalism*. Cambridge, MA: MIT Press.

——. 2014. "The Changing Nature of Nature: Environmental Politics in the Anthropocene." *Global Environmental Politics, 14*(4): 36–54.

Wapner, P., and Elver, H. (eds.). 2016. *Reimagining Climate Change* New York: Routledge.

Wark, M. 2015. *Molecular Red: Theory for the Anthropocene*. London: Verso.

Webersik, C. 2010. *Climate Change and Security: A Gathering Storm of Global Challenges*. Santa Barbara, CA: Praeger.

Welzer, H. 2012. *Climate Wars: Why People will be Killed in the Twenty First Century*. (P. Camiller, Trans.). Cambridge: Polity.

Werrell, C. E., and F. Femia (eds.). 2017. *The Epicenters of Climate and Security: The New Geostrategic Landscape of the Anthropocene*. Washington: Center for Climate and Security.

White, G. 2011. *Climate Change and Migration: Security and Borders in a Warming World*. Oxford: Oxford University Press.

White, R. 2014. "Environmental Insecurity and Fortress Mentality." *International Affairs, 90*(4): 835–851.

Whitehead, M. 2014. *Environmental Transformations: A Geography of the Anthropocene*. London: Routledge.

Williams, M. C. 2003. "Words, Images, Enemies: Securitization and International Politics." *International Studies Quarterly, 47*(4): 511–531.

Williston, B. 2015. *The Anthropocene Project: Virtue in the Age of Climate Change*. Oxford: Oxford University Press.

Wong, D. 2013. "Sovereignty Sunk? The Position of "Sinking States" at International Law." *Melbourne Journal of International Law, 14*(2): 346–391.

World Bank. 2012. *Turn Down the Heat: Why a 4°C Warmer World Must be Avoided*. Washington, DC: World Bank.

World Commission on Environment and Development. 1987. *Our Common Future*. Oxford: Oxford University Press.

World Economic Forum. 2019. *The Global Risks Report 2019*, Geneva: WEF.

Wulf, A. 2015. *The Invention of Nature: Alexander von Humboldt's New World*. New York, NY: Alfred A. Knopf.

Yamamoto, L., and Esteban, M. 2014. *Atoll Island States and International Law: Climate Change Displacement and Sovereignty*. Berlin: Springer-Verlag.

Yergin, D. 1991. *The Prize: The Epic Quest for Oil, Money and Power*. New York: Simon and Schuster.

——. 2011. *The Quest: Energy, Security, and the Remaking of the Modern World*. New York, NY: Penguin Books.

Yusoff, K. 2013. "Geologic Life: Prehistory, Climate, Futures in the Anthropocene." *Environment and Planning D: Society and Space*, *31*(5): 779–795.

Zacher, M. W. 2001. "The Territorial Integrity Norm: International Boundaries and the Use of Force." *International Organization*, 55(2): 215–250.

Zalasiewicz, J., Williams, M., Waters, C. N., Barnosky, A. D., Palmesino, J., Rönnskog, A.-S., Edgeworth, M., Neal, C., Cearreta, A., Ellis, E. C., Grinevald, J., Haff, P., Ivar do Sul, J. A., Jeandel, C., Leinfelder, R., McNeill, J. R., Odada, E., Oreskes, N., Price, S. J., Revkin, A., Steffen, W., Summerhayes, C., Vidas, D., Wing, S., and Wolfe, A. P. 2017. "Scale and Diversity of the Physical Technosphere: A Geological Perspective." *The Anthropocene Review*, 4(1): 9–22.

Zalasiewicz, J., Waters, C. N., Williams, M., and Summerhayes, C. P. (eds.). 2019. *The Anthropocene as a Geological Time Unit: A Guide to the Scientific Evidence and Current Debate*. Cambridge: Cambridge University Press.

Žižek, S. 2011. *Living in the End Times*. London: Verso.

Zografos, C., Goulden, M. C., and Kallis, G. 2014. "Sources of Human Insecurity in the Face of Hydro-climatic Change." *Global Environmental Change*, 29: 327–336.

Zurn, M. 2018. *A Theory of Global Governance: Authority, Legitimacy and Contestation*. Oxford: Oxford University Press.

INDEX

Politics and Public Policy

Series editor: Geneviève Tellier

There has been a resurgence of the study of politics, inspired by debates on globalization, renewed citizen engagement and demands, and transformations of the welfare state. In this context, the study of political regimes, ideas, and processes as well as that of public policy contribute to refreshing our understanding of the evolution of contemporary societies. Public policy is at the heart of political and state actions. It defines the course and the objectives adopted by governments and steering citizen initiatives and collective actions. Political analysis is increasingly complex and dynamic, embracing more diverse political, social, economic, cultural, and identity-related phenomena. The *Politics and Public Policy* series is an ideal forum in which to present titles that promote an exploration of these questions in Canada and around the world.

Previous titles in this collection

Sarah Todd and Sébastien Savard, *Canadian Perspectives on Community Development*, 2020.

Frances Widdowson, *Separate but Unequal: How Parallelist Ideology Conceals Indigenous Dependency*, 2019.

Helaina Gaspard, *Canada's Official Languages: Policy Versus Work Practice in the Federal Public Service*, 2019.

Marie Drolet, Pier Bouchard, and Jacinthe Savard, eds., *Accessibility and Active Offer: Health Care and Social Services in Linguistic Minority Communities*, 2017.

John Hilliker, *Le ministère des Affaires extérieures du Canada. Volume I : Les années de formation, 1909-1946*, 2017.

Monika Jezak, ed., *Language is the Key: The Canadian Language Benchmarks Model*, 2017.

Linda Cardinal and Sébastien Grammond, *Une tradition et un droit : Le Sénat et la représentation de la francophonie canadienne*, 2017.

Hélène Knoerr, Aline Gohard-Radenkovic, and Alysse Weinberg, eds., *L'immersion française à l'université : Politiques et pédagogie*, 2016.

For a complete list of our titles, see:
press.uOttawa.ca

Printed in January 2020
at Imprimerie Gauvin
Gatineau (Quebec), Canada.

CPSIA information can be obtained
at www.ICGtesting.com
Printed in the USA
JSHW041210191220
10431JS00008B/259

9 780776 628899